'Simple in outline; brilliant in conception. This is ᴀ together the thinking of key theorists, activists, lc including a taskforce from Metropolis. We are proud to have been a part of the process.'

Alain Le Saux, Secretary General of World Association of Major Metropolises, Barcelona, Spain

'*Circles of Sustainability* is an extraordinary guide to our way forward. By bringing together the clear insight of political analysts with the citizen-oriented perspective of experienced practitioners, this book changes the paradigm of urban studies. It is a brilliant book that will be used by cities such as Berlin as we seek a better world together.'

Michael Müller, Senator for Urban Development and Major of Berlin, Germany

'An inspirational and practical resource for helping our cities drive a revolution in sustainability. The book expertly shows that cities' toughest issues cannot be solved in isolation. No single actor – government, civil society or the private sector – has the all of the answers, nor can we successfully deal with poverty, climate change, unemployment or rights abuses, for example, if we look at them as separate events. Collaboration and holistic approaches must be driving precepts for achieving a better world.'

Georg Kell, Executive Director, United Nations Global Compact, New York, USA

'Questions of urban sustainable development will be of critical importance around the world. This book presents a profound re-calibration of the once elusive sustainability concept that integrates social and environmental dimensions; an approach that is theoretically informed and practically operational. A must-read for all who are concerned with the urban future.'

Jan Nijman, University of Amsterdam, the Netherlands

'This book, elegantly written, raises one of the most important issues of the 21st century – how to make our cities more liveable. The Chocolatao Project appears, together with many other sustainable practices across the world, as a response to this challenge, by establishing a sound cross-sectoral approach to significantly improve the life of garbage pickers in the city of Porto Alegre.'

José Fortunati, Mayor of Porto Alegre, Brazil

URBAN SUSTAINABILITY IN THEORY AND PRACTICE

Cities are home to the most consequential current attempts at human adaptation and they provide one possible focus for the flourishing of life on this planet. However, for this to be realized in more than an *ad hoc* way, a substantial rethinking of current approaches and practices needs to occur.

Urban Sustainability in Theory and Practice responds to the crises of sustainability in the world today by going back to basics. It makes four major contributions to thinking about and acting upon cities. It provides a means of reflexively learning about urban sustainability in the process of working practically for positive social development and projected change. It challenges the usually taken-for-granted nature of sustainability practices while providing tools for modifying those practices. It emphasizes the necessity of a holistic and integrated understanding of urban life. Finally it rewrites existing dominant understandings of the social whole, such as the Triple Bottom Line approach, that reduce environmental questions to externalities and social questions to background issues. The book is a much-needed practical and conceptual guide for rethinking urban engagement.

Covering the full range of sustainability domains and bridging discourses aimed at academics and practitioners, this is an essential read for all those studying, researching and working in urban geography, sustainability assessment, urban planning, urban sociology and politics, sustainable development and environmental studies.

Paul James is Professor of Globalization and Cultural Diversity in the Institute for Culture and Society, University of Western Sydney, Australia. He was Director of the UN Global Compact Cities Programme from 2007 to 2014.

Advances in Urban Sustainability

Urban Sustainability in Theory and Practice
Circles of sustainability
Paul James

URBAN SUSTAINABILITY IN THEORY AND PRACTICE

Circles of sustainability

Paul James

WITH LIAM MAGEE, ANDY SCERRI, MANFRED STEGER

First published 2015
by Routledge
2 Park Square, Milton Park, Abingdon, Oxon OX14 4RN

and by Routledge
711 Third Avenue, New York, NY 10017

Routledge is an imprint of the Taylor & Francis Group, an informa business

© 2015 Paul James

British Library Cataloguing in Publication Data

A catalogue record for this book is available from the British Library

Library of Congress Cataloging-in-Publication Data

James, Paul (Paul Warren), 1958–
Urban sustainability in theory and practice : circles of sustainability / Paul James ;
    with Liam Magee, Andy Scerri, Manfred Steger.
        pages cm
    Includes bibliographical references and index.
  1. Sustainable urban development.   2. Urban ecology (Sociology)
3. Sociology, Urban.   4. City planning—Environmental aspects.   I. Title.
HT241.J37   2015
307.76—dc23   2014014288

ISBN: 978-1-138-02572-1 (hbk)
ISBN: 978-1-138-02573-8 (pbk)
ISBN: 978-1-315-76574-7 (ebk)

Typeset in Bembo
by Apex CoVantage, LLC

MIX
Paper from
responsible sources
FSC
www.fsc.org   FSC® C013604

Printed and bound by CPI Group (UK) Ltd, Croydon, CR0 4YY

CONTENTS

FIGURES AND TABLES

Figures

Tables

CONTRIBUTORS

Dr Liam Magee is a Research Fellow in the Global Cities Research Institute, RMIT University. He is author of *Towards a Semantic Web: Connecting Knowledge in Academic Research* (with Bill Cope and Mary Kalantzis, 2010).

Dr Andy Scerri is in the Department of Political Science at Virginia. He is the author of *Greening Citizenship: Sustainable Development, the State and Ideology* (2012).

Professor Manfred Steger is Professor of Political Science at the University of Hawai'i. He is author or editor of 16 books including The Rise of the Global Imaginary: Political Ideologies from the French Revolution to the War on Terror (2008).

Urban Profile Process

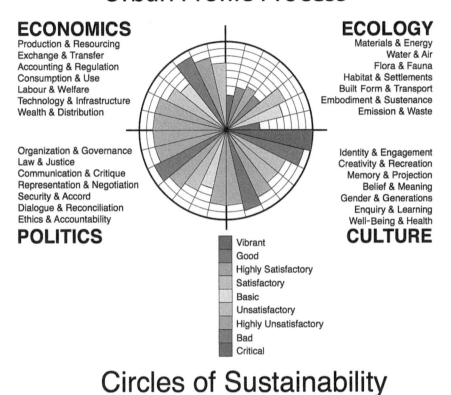

ECONOMICS
Production & Resourcing
Exchange & Transfer
Accounting & Regulation
Consumption & Use
Labour & Welfare
Technology & Infrastructure
Wealth & Distribution

Organization & Governance
Law & Justice
Communication & Critique
Representation & Negotiation
Security & Accord
Dialogue & Reconciliation
Ethics & Accountability

POLITICS

ECOLOGY
Materials & Energy
Water & Air
Flora & Fauna
Habitat & Settlements
Built Form & Transport
Embodiment & Sustenance
Emission & Waste

Identity & Engagement
Creativity & Recreation
Memory & Projection
Belief & Meaning
Gender & Generations
Enquiry & Learning
Well-Being & Health

CULTURE

Vibrant
Good
Highly Satisfactory
Satisfactory
Basic
Unsatisfactory
Highly Unsatisfactory
Bad
Critical

Circles of Sustainability

FIGURE 0.1 *Circles of Sustainability*: Urban Profile Process

The *Circles of Sustainability* figure used throughout this book provides a relatively simple view of the sustainability of a particular city, urban settlement, or region. The circular figure is divided into four domains: ecology, economics, politics and culture. Each of these domains is divided in to seven subdomains, with the names of each of these subdomains read from top to bottom in the lists under each domain name. Assessment is conducted on a nine-point scale. The scale ranges from 'critical sustainability', the first step, to 'vibrant sustainability', the ninth step. When the figure is presented in colour it is based on a traffic-light range with critical sustainability marked in red and vibrant sustainability marked in green. The centre step, basic sustainability, is coloured amber – with other steps ranging in between amber and red or amber and green. The grey-scale used here is intended to simulate the colour range.

PREFACE: TOWARDS A NEW PARADIGM

Cities have become unlikely but crucial zones for the survival of humanity. They are currently spaces for the most consequential attempts at human adaptation and sustainability. They provide a possible focus for the flourishing of future life on this planet. However, for this to take place in more than an *ad hoc* way, we need substantial rethinking, a new paradigm for urban development. Given the depth of the challenges, 'business as usual' or even business-with-a-new-rhetoric will not work. New thinking, including the re-integration of theory and practice, is imperative.

It sounds simple, but the task is considerable. We need a new paradigm that moves beyond the current narrow focus on growth-based productivity and high-technology 'solutions'. We need an alternative paradigm that can respond to the challenge of connecting globally debated principles and new ideas about sustainability with locally engaged practices. This book responds directly to that challenge. It collates concepts and principles into an integrated approach for understanding cities in global and local contexts. It is intended both as a contribution to the theory of urban sustainability and as a practical guide to making better cities.

Criticizing the current emphasis on economic growth, for example, is not to suggest that producing economic prosperity is necessarily the problem. Rather, it is to suggest that we need to interrogate what is meant by 'prosperity'. Similarly, criticizing the current infatuation with high-technology solutions is not to turn away from technologies for living. It is to move the emphasis from technology as 'the answer' to technologies as tools for contributing to a positive way of life.

Why begin such a process now when some suggest that the term 'sustainability' has become problematic? Ironically, there is no better time to develop such a new approach to sustainability than now when, after a period of fashionable overuse (and abuse), the concept of sustainability is being called into question. This questioning suggests that there is now a certain openness to rethinking basic concepts. A time of crisis is precisely the time when a concept might best be given a deeper and redefined life.

The *Circles of Sustainability* method begins that redefinition process as part of a larger project. Here, sustainability intersects with other social conditions, such as resilience, liveability, adaptation, innovation and reconciliation, as basic conditions of positive *social life*. Hence, the encompassing framework is called Circles of Social Life. As will become obvious, treating sustainability in this larger context has the effect of challenging both the classic tendency for sustainability to become treated as an end in itself and the new fashionable search for another holy grail concept such as 'resilience' to replace it.

Fashion produces its own enervation and the concept of 'resilience' will soon find itself out*moded*. Certainly, the concept of 'sustainability' is used without sufficient precision, and it is often abused. But that is not a reason to move on like a travelling circus to another equally problematic concept. All concepts have strengths and limitations. Rather than engaging in the futile search for the perfect concept, we suggest that the interrelated concepts of social capacity such as 'sustainability', 'resilience' and 'adaptation' can be defined and used practically in relation to each other. The concept of 'sustainability' is our central thematic focus here, but in this book, issues of sustainability are always seen in relation to other core conditions of human social life.

Overall, the book breaks with much mainstream thought and ways of acting on cities. First, the approach challenges many of the familiar assumptions of narrow sustainability practices, while providing tools for modifying those practices. Second, it provides a methodology for learning reflexively about sustainability. Third, it emphasizes the necessity of a holistic integrated understanding of urban life, while showing how this can be worked through into a transitional practice. Fourth, it rewrites existing dominant understandings of the social whole, arguing that they tend to reduce environmental questions to externalities and relegate social questions to background issues. It brings back 'the social' into the centre of contention, displacing economics as the focus of all understanding while still taking it seriously. And, finally, it broadens the terms of reference for fields of practice such as urban planning, urban design, geography, corporate responsibility, development studies, environmental studies, sociology and policy development.

Exemplifying this shift, this book challenges the unthinking use of that benign-sounding phrase 'economic, environmental and social sustainability'. How easily that triplet rolls off the tongue. It is a phrase embedded in the present global imaginary, used unreflectively by almost all practitioners and commentators – Left and Right alike. How positive it seems. It is a phrase that has a number of technical names – the Triple Bottom Line, the three pillars of sustainability, and so on – but has become so part of common-sense understanding that it no longer needs to be overtly named. The phrase can be used well despite itself, but it has been largely subsumed as part of a set of ideas called 'market globalism' or 'neo-liberalism'. Market-based sustainability practices continue to proclaim their own practical enlightenment while, in most cases, changing relatively little except the language of development. This false promise does all active institutions a disservice, from municipalities and community-based organizations to ethically motivated corporations seeking to act differently. Unfortunately, the concept of 'resilience' is fast entering the same well-lit narrow space. By contrast, the *Circles of Sustainability* approach takes the positive intention of the 'three pillars' phrase and for the first time locates that well-intentioned spirit in an integrated and generalizing framework that provides more than high-sounding words.

The *Circles of Sustainability* approach is intended to be flexible, modular and systematic. Each part of the approach has been developed so that it operates as part of a toolbox for understanding different urban locales. In fact it is more like a toolshed than a toolbox – more expansive than a toolbox and more open to adding or moving tools around for different tasks. The metaphor of the toolshed also recognizes that the method has more messy corners and places for adding new tools. Each of the tools currently in the shed is developed as part of an integrated whole. The approach is intended to work across time and in different places as practitioners and researchers attempt to understand the complex layering of the local, the regional, the national and the global. This means that the various items in the shed – different concepts, methods, protocols and principles – can be taken out and used singularly. Each tool can be used in relation to any other tools. Or, most comprehensively, the shed can be used as the base from which to build an integrated planning approach useful for your city or urban settlement.

The book is schematic and relatively simple most of the time, although the more thoroughly the method is interrogated the deeper it is capable of going into complex areas of epistemology and theory. At that deeper level, the approach is part of a comprehensive and critical methodology called Engaged Theory. Developing that methodology with all its applied implications is an ongoing task that will become the basis of a series of writings into the future. Engaged Theory thus remains a work in progress.[1] Its aim is to give Critical Theory a new applied focus. Readers who want a guiding outline to whole approach will find it hidden away in Table 4.2 in Chapter 4. That table, along with the process pathway (Figure 6.2), shows how each of the parts relates to whole. The first level of analysis is empirical, focused on understanding patterns of change across the domains of ecology, economics, politics and culture. Deeper levels of analysis are intended to break through current dominant (often neo-liberal) understandings of social change and to point out paradoxes, contradictions, continuities and discontinuities in the contemporary urban condition.

More immediately, the approach is based on the argument that we need useful tools for negotiating what kind of world we want to create and re-create. Over the coming period we will continue to refine and develop various dimensions of the approach. A website is being developed that will support cities in using the approach. Nonetheless, whatever developments of the method occur into the future, considerable care has already been given to making sure that the various definitions, descriptions of method, protocols, propositions and principles, all align and complement each other as part of an integrated approach. The task of writing and arguing about the interconnections has sensitized us to the difficulty of an integrated method and the book represents the outcome of a long struggle to work through these difficulties. Working together across many cities and cultures, we have found it helpful to develop a common language, common definitions of key concepts and crossovers of methods.

The Engaged Theory approach and the *Circles of Sustainability* method presented in this study have been developed for the United Nations Global Compact Cities Programme, Metropolis (the World Association of Major Metropolises) led by Alain le Saux and UCLG (United Cities and Local Governments), led by Josep Roig. This was done in collaboration with UN-Habitat, the Cultural Development Network, World Vision and a large number of researchers and practitioners around the world. Researchers in the Global Cities Institute and the Globalism Research Centre at the Royal Melbourne Institute of Technology, Australia, directly supported the approach. Urban experts including a Metropolis Task Force and members of the World Vision Centre of Expertise for Urban Programming contributed to developing some of its central tools. The context for its writing was partnerships with researchers from the Cities Group, King's College London, led by David Green; the Centre for Urban Studies at the University of Amsterdam directed by Jan Nijman; and the National Institute of Urban Affairs in New Delhi, directed by Jagan Shah. Most recently, the institutional home for organizing this work has become the Institute for Culture and Society at the University of Western Sydney led by Ien Ang.

There are many people that we need to thank. Much more than most books, this volume emerged slowly out a deeply collaborative process with considerable consultation over its various methods, principles and processes. Some authors will say modestly that they stand on the shoulders of others or that their writing is socially dependent. With *Urban Sustainability* this is more acutely the case than usual. The appropriate metaphor for our authorship is the medieval concept of *compilators* – writers slowly drawing the words and thoughts of others into a broadly agreed framework, representing the method in various stages for further responses, and writing those responses into the developing approach. The names of the principle authors are therefore points of reference for those compilers who took responsibility for the writing over a seven-year period. Authority for the ideas rests broadly and consequentially on a cooperative team, but with all the weaknesses of the book attributable to the limits of the main author and the constraints of time. Concurrently, it should be said that any political views present in the book cannot necessarily be attributed to various partners or advisors to this project.

The writing of the present volume goes beyond the named authors on the book's cover. Numerous other people contributed directly to writing this book. Lin Padgham, James Thom, Hepu Deng, Sarah Hickmott and Felicity Cahill contributed to writing Chapter 6. Sunil Dubey is co-author of Chapter 7. Hans-Uve Schwelder, Michael Abraham and Barbara Berninger were co-authors of Chapter 9. Darryn McEvoy and Hartmut Fünfgeld were co-authors of Chapter 10. George Cairns and George Wright were co-authors of Chapter 11. Dominic Mendonca and Simon Vardy contributed fundamentally to Chapter 12. Malcolm Borg was co-author of the profile of Valetta and Paolo in Malta. Research on various parts of the method was supported by the expert work of interns and associates, including Cynthia Lam, Adriana Partal and Ailish Ryan. Tim Strom was an astute editorial assistant. Lida Ghahremanlou wrote her PhD evaluating the software and testing the methodology. We learned a lot from seminal writers in the field such Simon Bell, Mike Davis, Robert Gibson, Brendan Gleeson, Peter Hall, Stephen Morse, Lewis Mumford, Peter Newman, Richard Sennett and Deborah Stevenson, *et alia*.[2]

Secondly, beneath that extended process of collaborative writing was an extended global consultation process. The basic four-domain model was first developed across the period 2007 to 2009 through a consultation process hosted by the Cities Programme. Paul James and Andy Scerri convened the research team with advice from a Critical Reference Group comprising Caroline Bayliss (then with United Nations Global Compact Cities Programme), Sally Capp (then Director of the Committee for Melbourne), Alex Fearnside (City of Melbourne), Meg Holden (Simon Fraser University), Liz Johnstone (Municipal Association of Victoria, Melbourne), Mary Lewin (Metropolis), Stephanie McCarthy (UN Global Compact Cities Programme), Liam Magee (RMIT), Heikki Patomäki (University of Helsinki), Mike Salvaris (RMIT), Martin Mulligan (RMIT), Dom Tassone (State Government of Victoria), Wayne Wescott (then with the International Council for Local Environments Initiative, ICLEI), Andrew Wisdom (ARUP) and John Wiseman (University of Melbourne).

Refining and testing the approach in the field occurred across the second period of 2009 to 2012. In Australia, the working group which developed the sustainability matrix was comprised of Paul James, Liam Magee, Andy Scerri, John Smithies and Manfred Steger. Martin Mulligan was a crucial collaborator in developing the social mapping approach. With Yaso Nadarajah, he applied and tested the approach in their work on communities in Sri Lanka and India after the South-East Asian tsunami (Mulligan & Nadarajah 2012). Anni Rowland Campbell, Bill Cope, Amanda Keogh, Greg Stone and others at Fuji Xerox, Microsoft, Cambridge College and Common Ground collaborated with us on an Australian Research Council grant that was used to test the method.

A Metropolis Taskforce guided the process through a third global consultation period in 2012 through 2014. The Taskforce included Barbara Berninger (Berlin) and Paul James (Melbourne) as co-convenors, with Michael Abraham (Berlin), Tim Campbell (San Francisco), Emile Daho (Abidjan), Sunil Dubey (Sydney), Jan Erasmus (Johannesburg), Jane McCrae (Vancouver) and Om Prakesh Mathur and Usha Raghupathi (New Delhi). Relevant meetings were held in Barcelona, Guangzhou, Johannesburg and Berlin. Sunil Dubey was a constant inspiration for this engagement. We are beholden to Agnés Bickart, Alain Le Saux and Christine Piquemal for auspicing this process. We also thank the people of the New York Office of the Global Compact for their collegial support and initiation of the Process Pathway, in particular Carrie Hall, Georg Kell, Gavan Power and Kristina Wilson.

Across the second and third periods, pilot studies were conducted in a number of cities across the world using the various parts of the method in draft form. An early version of the method was the basis for a major project in Papua New Guinea (James, Nadarajah, Haive, & Stead 2012). In Porto Alegre, Vania Goncalves de Souva,

Cezar Busatto and their colleagues remade their city while using the approach in a way that allowed basic rethinking. In Milwaukee, Dean Amhaus and his colleagues were inspirational across a project of sustained engagement beginning in 2009. In India our work began with an invitation in 2011 by Mary Lewin and Metropolis to work on one of their major initiatives. The *Circles of Sustainability* methodology became central to the approach used by the 'Integrated Strategic Planning Initiative' organized by Metropolis, in 2012–13, for Indian, Brazilian and Iranian cities. Workshops were held in New Delhi in July 2012 and July 2013. In each of these cases, and in a dozen other meetings in the Middle East and South Asia, Sunil Dubey was the key figure presenting and getting feedback on the approach. Senior planners from New Delhi, Hyderabad and Kolkata used assessment tools from the *Circles of Sustainability* approach to map the sustainability of their cities as part of developing their urban-regional plans. Representatives from Sao Paulo – Sania Baprista, Catarina Mastellaro and Ravena Negreiros – used the approach in relation to their city. In India we particularly acknowledge the contribution of Om Prakash Mathur, Jagan Shah and Chetan Vaidya. In Melbourne, we thank Halvard Dalheim, Neil Houghton, Mary Lewin and Christine Oakley from the Department of Transport, Planning and Local Infrastructure in the Victorian government, who made important contributions to the project. Neil Houghton read the manuscript chapter by chapter and made many astute suggestions for its refinement.

Most recently, in Malta, Malcolm Borg and his colleagues have been using the method to develop a cultural heritage sustainability assessment process for twelve cities. Other cities to use the same tools have been Tehran (in relation to their mega-projects plan) and São Paulo (in relation to their macro-metropolitan plan). Our team in Curitiba, Brazil, led by Eduardo Manoel Araujo and Rosane de Souza, has done considerable work, and we are conducting studies of cities across the state of Parana and elsewhere as they roll out the *Circles of Sustainability* method across the state. In Dubai, Mahmood El Burai is central to a series of projects in the Middle East. In Melbourne, Nick Rose, Kathy McConell and their colleagues from the Food Alliance innovatively took the work into the area of food sustainability.

Circles of Sustainability was presented in joint sessions with UN-Habitat at the Rio+20 Summit in 2012 and the World Urban Forum in Napoli in the same year. It was presented at the Caribbean Urban Forum in Port of Spain in March 2013 and was then used as the basis for an assessment for the Government of Trinidad and Tobago's national spatial plan. There we worked in particular with Hebe Verrest from the University of Amsterdam and Steve Kemp and his team from Open Plan in the United Kingdom. In June 2013, UN-Habitat and Urbego hosted a training event in London led by Claudio Acioly and Giulia Maci integrating the *Circles of Sustainability* method. We followed up with a joint session at the International Federation of Housing and Planning Centenary Congress, also in London. In July 2013, Johannesburg hosted a major Metropolis forum through which the method was further developed. Hans-Uve Schwedler and Barbara Berninger were central to this process. Michael Abraham was the lead author on the Rea Vaya report that followed the forum. In October 2013, at another forum called 'No Regrets' hosted by the City of Berlin, the method was used to frame the principles for climate change adaptation. In 2014, the Cities Programme joined with the International Real Estate Federation and the Dubai Real Estate Institute at forums in Dubai and Luxembourg to take the method forward in relation to property development.

There were numerous other consultants and critics involved in setting up this method. In Australia, apart from those already mentioned, we particularly need to thank Tony Fry and Eleni Kalantidou for introducing us to the concept of onto-logical design. Their inspiration, along with insightful responses by John Smithies and Kim Dunphy helped in taking the work to a new stage. In Brazil, particularly helpful responses came from Eduardo Araujo, Luiz Berlim, Marcia Maina, Luci-ano Planco and Paulo Cesar Rink. In the United States important suggestions for reworking the approach came from Jyoti Hosagrahar (Columbia University, New York) and Giovanni Circella (University of California, Davis). In Canada, Cor-rine Cash, Michel Fromovic and Meg Holden were important correspondents. In Spain, Jordi Pascual and Adrianna Partal provided inspiration for our work on the cultural dimension of sustainability. We also want to thank Frank Zhang, Shanghai Academy of Social Sciences, who supported our work on urban futures in China, and Chris Hudson who was central to running the Cities Programme urban forum in Shanghai in 2011.

Overseeing all of this, the working group, which worked to develop the matrix of tools, comprised Paul James, Liam Magee, Andy Scerri and Manfred Steger with others including Felicity Cahill, Hepu Deng, Sarah Hickmott, Cynthia Lam, Lin Padgham and James Thom. Individuals who provided strong impetus for the devel-opment of the approach included, particularly, Sam Carroll-Bell, Damian Grenfell, Chris Hudson, Supriya Singh and Frank Yardley. The editors and core writers of *Arena Journal* – particularly Alison Caddick, Simon Cooper, Lindsay Fitzclarence, John Hinkson, Geoff Sharp and Nonie Sharp – provided inspiration through their devel-opment of the constitutive abstraction method. We acknowledge their importance in providing an intellectual base for the Engaged Theory method presented here. Lindsay Fitzclarence read the manuscript and helped to clarify a number of issues.

Closer to home, Peter Christoff and Robyn Eckersley were wonderfully sup-portive. Stephanie Trigg was an amazing interlocutor and always a superb sounding board for ideas.

Finally, deep appreciation is extended all the people – interns, researchers, global advisors, administrators, in-country convenors, local secretariats and urban activists who trialled this method. Many of those individuals, only some of whom we have had the space to name in this Preface, have been inspirational to the *Circles of Sus-tainability* approach through the ways they have worked to change their local worlds.

Paul James
Institute for Culture and Society
University of Western Sydney
July 2014

Notes

1 If, as a reader of this essay, you want to get a sense of the depth of work behind the discussion then articles and books written by the present authors and others are available in the public domain that take the discussion much further. The website www.citiesprogramme. org is a key source. See also for example Scerri (2013), Steger (2008) and James (2006).
2 For example see Bell and Morse (2003) and Gibson (2005).

References

Bell, Simon & Morse, Stephen 2003, *Measuring Sustainability: Learning from Doing*, Earthscan, London

Gibson, Robert, with Hassan, Selma, Holtz, Susan, Tansey, James & Whitelaw, Graham 2005, *Sustainability Assessment: Criteria and Processes*, Earthscan, London.

James, Paul 2006, *Globalism, Nationalism, Tribalism: Bringing Theory Back In*, Sage, London.

James, Paul, Nadarajah, Yaso, Haive, Karen & Stead, Victoria 2012, *Sustainable Communities, Sustainable Development: Other Paths for Papua New Guinea*, University of Hawaii Press, Honolulu.

Mulligan, Martin & Nadarajah, Yaso 2012, *Building Local Communities in the Wake of Disaster: Social Recovery in Sri Lanka and India*, Routledge, New Delhi.

Scerri, Andy 2013, *Greening Citizenship: Sustainable Development, the State and Ideology*, Palgrave McMillan, Basingstoke

Steger, Manfred B. 2008, *The Rise of the Global Imaginary: Political Ideologies from the French Revolution to the Global War on Terror*, Oxford University Press, Oxford

PART I
Setting the global–local scene

1

CONFRONTING A WORLD IN CRISIS

The city, now the dominant form of human settlement, exemplifies and displays the fundamental concerns of the human condition. In a period of intensifying globalization, urban life draws people into zones of intense interconnectivity. Cities are places of passion, hopes and dreams. However, they are entering an epoch of protracted crisis. All urban settlements face a practical crisis of sustainability, just as human beings face a comprehensive crisis of social life on this planet.

At the same time, there is an unacknowledged theoretical crisis. Mid-range writing tends to be characterized by disconnected contentions, and false hopes abound. Even as urban living concentrates us in close proximity, the city engenders clichés and slogans, stereotypes and self-serving assurances. Seemingly self-evident claims come thick and fast. The world's most liveable cities are prosperous. It's the economy, stupid. Cities are the engine house of economic growth. Slums are places of wretched squalor. Slums are productive places too. Electric vehicles are the answer. Planning for density is good. Inclusion is an essential good.

These shibboleths all need to be substantially qualified as the basis for comprehensive understanding. Planning for density is good only when it is based on good planning *and* when the conditions for increased density are well designed. Electric vehicles are useful only when renewable resources are used and when the vehicles do not become part of a fetish of green consumption. Although slums are often places of wretched housing, they can also be places of vibrant life and livelihoods. However, defending them as being 'productive too' – just like 'normal cities' – is to concede that economic productivity is the pre-eminent quantifier of what is good. Inclusion is good only when the terms of positive exclusion are negotiated with care, transparency and so on.

Recognizing this complexity leads us to two fundamental questions that need to be addressed across the course of this book. First, what makes something good or positively sustainable? Second, why, if planners and sustainability experts seem able to identify the core problems and have many real answers to these problems, do many of our cities continue to slide into this series of interconnected crises? The first question is rarely even asked. What is *good* sustainability? That is, what is *positive* and strong sustainability, as opposed to that which will enable urban life to endure in a minimal sense through weak sustainability? This question is at its core a question about the human condition. It has its roots the ancient dialogues of Socrates and the question of what makes for a good polis. Without actively returning to such central considerations, we will continue to be confounded by the perplexing ideological tensions of the present.

One of the simple tensions carried by the usual arguments about the future of the world is that people advocate 'social change for sustainability'. It almost sounds pedantic to point this out, but those who use this phrase never point to the tension involved in such a conjunction of terms. Changing the world is said to be an aspiration. Sustaining the world is said to be a necessity. Yet, without specifying what is good, what is to be changed and what is to be sustained, holding to both aspirations at the same time is completely contradictory. That is, sustainability means conditions of enduring continuity whereas social change generates discontinuities. They are not necessarily comfortable travelling companions. Despite this analytical discomfort, and without most practitioners and activists thinking about the tension, using both concepts concurrently has slipped into the dominant way of speaking. This simple exercise of showcasing the contradictions between common mantras suggests that our habitual ways of describing these issues need serious attention. Rhetoric needs to be connected to practice.

This book is thus directed towards understanding how practitioners can best go about changing urban centres for the better in the context of rushing global change and intensifying crises of sustainability. Here the concept of 'practitioners' is important – they are people who act. The book is addressed to that broad coalition of people across three fields of action – civil society (including universities and non-government organizations), governance organizations (including municipalities) and business – who want to get beyond 'business as usual' and think that more can be done than just mouthing platitudes.

Cities are at the centre of these crises

Across the world we are facing crises of sustainability, resilience, security, stability and adaptation. Many of our cities have become sprawling and bloated zones of unsustainability. In the meantime, too many politicians and commentators squabble over schedules, timetables, and buck-stops. From problems associated with climate change or sustainable water supply to those concerning increasing economic inequality or the break-up of communities, processes such as escalating resource use or increasing cultural anomie, problems that we once responded to as singular concerns are now bearing back on us in a swirl of compounding pressures. Cities are at the centre of this human-made maelstrom. For all their vibrancy and liveliness, cities face a growing challenge to provide secure and sustainable places to live. Even the world's most 'liveable cities' – Melbourne, Munich, Vancouver and Vienna – are utterly unsustainable in global ecological terms. If all city residents across the globe consumed at the rate of the world's most liveable cities the planet would be in catastrophic trouble. Despite their inconsequential geographical footprint, cities are responsible for around 80 per cent of global energy consumption, and some of the world's most wonderful exciting cities contribute at a proportionally much higher rate.

Melbourne – the city where many of the people who worked on this book now live – is currently listed on *The Economist*'s index as the world's most liveable city (2013).[1] The indicators are commercial-in-confidence, but we know that they are grouped around five domains: stability, health care, culture and environment, education and infrastructure. All are important considerations. However, the report accompanying the survey reveals that the highest-scoring cities tend to be mid-sized, wealthier cities with a relatively low population density. Seven of the top-ten scoring cities are located in Australia and Canada, with population densities between 2.88 and 3.40 people per square kilometre, respectively. This is telling. At a time when sustainability is increasingly associated with positive high density, it is glaringly apparent that liveability, as so measured, is parting company with sustainability. It is also clear that issues of how we are to live are difficult to research.

Shockingly, Melbourne has *per capita* an ecological footprint of twenty-eight times its direct physical footprint, one of the highest in the world. If everybody lived as the good people of Melbourne do, the planet would be doomed. For all the wonderful public sensitivity in Melbourne to ecological sustainability issues, the city continues to use more and more resources, to emit more and more carbon, and to bury more and more of its fertile hinterlands under asphalt and bricks. One of the few clear successes in the sustainability stakes in Melbourne has been a widely supported political campaign to place legal and cultural limits on water use. Nevertheless, an energy-intensive desalination plant, the largest in the Southern Hemisphere, has been built to supply fresh water to the city, and the entrance to the bay on which the city sits has been dredged to allow 'supersized' freight ships to import global commodities through Australia's largest container port. The initiating government defended both projects in terms of environmental and economic sustainability.

This brings us to the first of a set of urban paradoxes.

Paradox 1. *The more the language of sustainability is used, the more it seems to be directed at rationalizing unsustainable development.*

Almost everybody is now attuned to sustainability talk, but despite this subjective awareness the world becomes objectively less and less sustainable. This makes the first question, 'What then makes for *positive* sustainability?' even more important. And it makes the second question, 'Why are we not acting effectively to achieve that sustainability?' increasingly perplexing.

The new urban paradoxes

As many writers now tell us, our cities face a manifold crisis of sustainability: economic, ecological, political and cultural. For example in Mike Davis's words (2006), slums are increasingly part of our cities. Every day, 180,000 people join the global urban population; each year, the equivalent of two cities the size of Tokyo are built; one in six urban dwellers lives in slums; and we are heading towards that black figure of 2 degrees Celsius global warming. UN-Habitat research suggests that over the next decades virtually all of the world's population growth will occur in cities with massive consequences for infrastructure stress (2010, 2012). Why, under these circumstances, do we focus on symptomatic solutions – on white paint on roofs to increase the albedo of the city, on bulldozers to clear away unwanted and irregular urban dwellers and on cranes to build new high-rise apartments in the hinterland cities of the new world? Why do we vacillate between easy short-term solutions and complex deferral, when it is so obvious that something much more fundamental needs to be done?

Slum clearance appears to work for a while in specific locales, but displaced people, especially those who are shifted to the periphery, tend to move back to more central urban sites of continuing desperation, seeking to maintain livelihoods. White roofs deflect heat in the cities of the Global North, while in the Global South, intensifying weather shifts and rising sea levels bring the chaos of floods.[2] Thousands were killed in the Philippines in 2013. Typhoon Haiyan had wind speeds faster than Hurricane Katrina. Bangladesh has had a disastrous few years with a series of floods. Bangkok was under water for months in 2011 because of the flooding of the Chao Phraya River and its urban canals. A little earlier in the 2011 season, floods in Pakistan killed 270 people. And lest we forget, in the media-induced haze of recent extreme events, it is worth recalling that these were in addition to the floods of 2010 that inundated a fifth of Pakistan, leaving 11 million people homeless.

The urban planning focus on symptomatic solutions relates to a second urban paradox.

> Paradox 2. *Cities are at the heart of the problems facing this planet, but developing a positive and sustainable mode of urban living is the only way that we will be able to sustain social life as we know it past the end of this century.*

In fact, given the world's current population growth, sustainably increasing the density of our urban settlements along with increasing energy efficiency and decreasing resource use is the only alternative. It is simply no longer the case that building rural idylls on small, self-contained plots of land can save the planet. If, without changing other considerations, we started dividing the non-urban world into rural allotments to cope with a bourgeoning global population, we would only speed up the crisis. According to the World Bank (2014), the United States has only 0.5 hectares of arable land per citizen, while China has 0.08 hectares. Unless there was a revolution in the way we live, neither would allow for allotment self-sufficiency.

Like the first paradox, this presents a new quandary. The newness relates to our current standing upon this planet. We live in what is now being called the Anthropocene Period, an era in which humans have had a recognizable impact on the earth's ecological systems. Although the concept goes back to the late nineteenth century when Antonio Stoppani coined the term the *anthropozoic*, and although those who argue for the anthropocene hypothesis contest the dating of the period (with its origins ranging from the industrial revolution to the beginning of systematic agriculture 8,000 years ago), something new is happening.

To comprehend this newness we need to use the term more precisely. We are now in the fourth phase of the anthropocene period. If Tribalia, Agraria, and Industria were earlier dominant and continuing ways of living, the most recent phase, still unnamed, began with our capacity to make our own lives on this planet unsustainable. From the possibility of nuclear winter ushered in by the words of J. Robert Oppenheimer – 'I am become Death, the shatterer of worlds', quoting the Bhagavad Gita – to the disruption of climate change, we now have the capacity to destroy ourselves (as well as the choice not to do so). Through the intersection of techno-science and capitalism, from bioengineering to hypercommodification, we are now reconstituting the basic building blocks of nature, including our own bodies. We are the first human civilization with the technological and social capacity to override prior senses of planetary boundaries and limits – and we know it. If we continue on current trajectories, the phase could well be called Exterminia. It could become the phase during which humanity drives in hybrid vehicles towards its own extermination, talking all the way about sustainability and resilience.

This brings us to a third paradox.

> Paradox 3. *The more we recognize that we face contradictory pressures, the more we give ourselves an excuse for not responding decisively or comprehensively.*

When Charles Dickens wrote the *Tale of Two Cities*, seventy years after the French Revolution, his words were telling:

> it was the season of Darkness, it was the spring of hope, it was the winter of despair, we had everything before us, we had nothing before us, we were all going direct to Heaven, we were all going direct the other way – in short, the period was so far like the present period, that some of its noisiest authorities insisted on its being received, for good or for evil, in the superlative degree of comparison only.
>
> (1902, p. 3)

These words spoke of a new world of ambivalence in which the people of Paris and London, or at least their less-than-democratic planners and politicians, were confronted with choices to make about their future. However, over the next century neither of those cities changed course in the fundamental ways needed. These days, instead of debating and acting upon the complexities of urban life in a concerted collective way, we are all going in different directions. Some deny the challenges to the present 'growth economy'. Some throw up their hands in despair. Others seize on singular technical solutions, deferring the consequences of a comprehensive politics. Many try in our localized ways to respond as best they can. Many good people are doing good things, but we have reached the stage where individuated good works are not enough. As evidenced by the issue of climate change, humanity has entered a phase in which the manifold crisis cannot be turned around by even the accumulating weight of individual actions or a single pieces of legislation. Responding to structures of power through collective engagement has become more important than ever.

Why do our responses remain short term?

In this context why our responses to the manifold urban crisis remain piecemeal, isolated, and short term starts to become clear. It is not just vested interests, short-term thinking, global capitalism, global financial tumult, greed or the fetishism of growth that explains the crisis – although they are key ingredients of the mix.

Part of the problem is that too many people have convinced themselves that, given the complex challenges of the current circumstances, we are already doing the best that we can given the circumstances. In relation to the vexed issue of slums, the approach taken by the UN-Habitat report *State of the World's Cities* is indicative of the third urban paradox. Under the heading 'Good news on slum target', it frames its report thus: 'Since the year 2000, when the international community committed to the Millennium Development Goals (MDGs) and associated targets, the global effort to narrow the starkest, slum-related form of urban divide has yielded some positive results' (2012, p. 30). The target of improving the lives of 100 million, the report says, has been achieved ten years earlier than scheduled. In Southern and Eastern Asia, it documents an estimated 172 million slum dwellers moving out of the 'slum-dweller' category (UN-Habitat 2012, p. 30).

On the surface, these figures seem to give us reason to be optimistic, but the fine print tells another story. China and India may have shown the greatest improvement, but both tend to use the bulldozer method of slum clearance, and China has an authoritarian disregard for people's lives when the party decides to level a slum area. Most disconcertingly, despite the improvement when the figures are read against MDG targets, the number of slum dwellers overall in the Global South has actually gone up from 767 million in 2000 to 828 million in 2010. That is, although some of the statistics can be interpreted optimistically, overall, things are actually getting worse for more people.

For a large wealthy minority in some parts of the world, life in the city is materially good. The well-to-do, urban Global North continues to export an increasing number of the urban problems associated with crude industrialism to the Global South or to the peripheral zones of their own countries. The hardware supporting urban lifestyles is being manufactured under Dickensian conditions in places such as Shenzen, China, and Dhaka, Bangladesh. This occurs while 'post-industrial' cities are dressed in the cosmetic glamour of urban renewal. Once dreary central business districts have been turned into entertainment zones. Any sense of face-to-face discomfort or community isolation is recoloured by the relentless imperatives of Facebook and media connectivity.

The world's poster cities appear cleaner, brighter, and more vibrant than ever before. Put that together with critique fatigue exacerbated by melodramatic depictions of satanic mills, and it has become harder and harder to criticize urban conglomerations. *Don't Call it Sprawl* says the title of a book by William Bogart. 'How Our Greatest Invention Makes Us Richer, Smarter, Greener, Healthier and Happier' says the front cover of Edward Glaeser's book *Triumph of the City*. If you do not have time to read the fine print, the life of the city seems hunky dory (Gleeson, 2012). Since W. H. Auden wrote the devastating 'City Without Walls' in 1967, novelists no longer write of our world as being stuck in 'real structures of steel and glass'. Instead of Auden's 'Hermits . . . With numbered caves in enormous jails . . . Hobbesian Man is mass-produced' (1991, p. 748), the dominant tendency is to celebrate autonomy and just-in-time production while expressing concern about carbon emissions. In the 2000s, Auden's mass-produced Hobbesian Man has given way to the self-projecting urbanite who can choose amongst the amazing array of consumption opportunities on offer.

In many cities across the world, ongoing community relations have become secondary or residual, confined to discrete periods of people's lives or to moments of celebratory focus. Urban dwellers increasingly come together in moments of screen time or as passing strangers in the street, moving in parallel and consuming parallel lifestyle possibilities. One lineage of academic and popular writers celebrates this development. Richard Florida's book *Who's Your City?* turns the important life-forming question of 'Where do you want to live?' into a commodity choice. Why have others missed the 'where factor,' he asks disingenuously: 'Perhaps it's because so few of us have the understanding or mental framework necessary to make informed decisions about location' (Florida 2009, p. 5). He could not be more wrong – location, location, location is the constant refrain of every housing-advice program on television today. Consuming the street and buying into a prime urban locale are now globally prevalent as a way of understanding property.

> Paradox 4. *As social life is mediated by technologies of communication and is reduced to consumption choices, the more the immediacy of face-to-face community life is romanticized.*

By contrast, writing a couple of generations ago, Lewis Mumford in an essay called 'The Natural History of Urbanization' argued more soberly that '[t]he blind forces of urbanization, flowing along the lines of least resistance, show no aptitude for creating an urban and industrial pattern that will be stable, self-sustaining, and self-renewing' (cited in Brugman 2009, p. 16). This remains true today. But in the popular consciousness (and for Richard Florida) the individual's freedom to choose sets the conditions for the greatest creativity and most exciting urban frisson. Serendipity, helped by genius or celebrity architects, is said to give us the most beautiful cities. And such a sensibility becomes self-confirming once iconic buildings are attributed the power to revivify decaying city precincts. Frank Geary's Guggenheim Museum is an example of a single building being credited with bringing the whole city of Bilbao back to life.

There are many partial answers to the question of why we have become like frogs in inexorably warming water (James & Scerri 2012). As citizens, we might be a little worried, but in the words of one advertiser 'life's good' for those who can choose – even despite the increasing heat. One more point of partial explanation can be added. Across the late twentieth century, generalized utopian alternatives have faded away. Not only have the projection of blueprints for change become unfashionable and the genre of utopian novel writing died; we have also come to distrust deeply the residual utopianism of our urban planners. The authoritarian tradition of Corbusian radiant cities, the liberal-socialist tradition of Ebenezer Howard's beauteous garden-city concept and the architectural tradition of Frank Lloyd Wright's broadacre city have all been lumped together as complete failures.[3] Apart from the command planning of China and the discipline-based planning of Singapore, all-of-city planning has tended to be reduced either to legislated building restrictions and zoning or to good ideas for possible implementation by the market. It is true that there are good developers and imaginative planners, but this tends to be restricted to innovative urban precincts.

During the same period that utopianism went into near-mortal decline, the concept of the future became linked to the techno-sciences. The word *future* now seems to conjure up either post-human scenarios of techno-science or greenfields 'new cities' that have given us the disasters of the technopolis, the multifunction polis and the less-than-satisfactory outcomes of zones that look best from the air. For a greenfield site, Canberra was beautifully designed as a garden city, but it largely failed to consider transport other than cars or to achieve cultural vibrancy. Brasília was designed to look like a butterfly from above but has been criticized as a futuristic fantasy. In Robert Hughes's (1980) words, it is a 'jerry-built platonic nowhere infested with Volkswagens'. In the global imagination Dubai is perhaps the ultimate futurist fantasy, with high-end residential zones that reach into the ocean, designed from the air to look like a palm tree or planet Earth. For a period, Dubai hovered on the edge of ecological and economic disaster. Futurism is not turning it around now but, rather, the careful planners of the Land Department and those solid developers who are now trying to make an extraordinary city in which ordinary people live sustainably.

The dominant way in which we currently imagine the future can perhaps best be seen in corporate advertising of the many companies that project the idea of a good city as a high-tech 'Smart City'. It can be seen in the global mega events in which a global imaginary of capitalism, techno-science and planetary romance come together. One recent example, 'Expo Shanghai' in 2011, was conceived through envisaging the city as the world on display. Its overarching theme was sustainability. At the same time, the nature of the display itself was temporary, energy intensive, status oriented and destined for the dump heap (the first urban paradox). The British pavilion, for instance, presented a Seed Cathedral with 60,000 transparent plastic rods swaying in the wind, containing seeds of different plants collected in the Millennium Seed Bank project. The message was clear. Instead of saying, 'Let us stop the unsustainable development that is increasing species extinction', it suggests that protecting biodiversity can be comfortably underwritten by scientific collection and storage.

Overall, behind the perfectly rendered correct-line presentations of sustainability, romantic projections of individual freedom and environmental sustainability prevail. Techno-scientific projections of connectivity and efficiency are brought together with global projections of material wealth and local projections of lifestyle choice. The 'Smart City' future is thus imagined as a contradictory mixture of controlled, regulated, inside, and as far from the messiness of uncultivated nature and organic chance as possible while contradictorily also being serendipitously exciting for all the individuals who inhabit that world.

Paradox 5. *Inappropriate and badly conceived planning has often produced worse outcomes than has leaving the process to serendipity, but in the context of global crisis we now need long-term planning more than ever before.*

Towards flourishing sustainable cities

If our cities are to flourish, we need to go back to basics. Answering the animating question of this book is part of the process, although the overall answer that the book offers is not an easy one. Why are our cities in crisis? Because our cities *are us*. We have yet to come to terms with our place on this planet. We take for granted older conceptions of community, but the changing nature of social relations now requires engaged work to sustain community in a meaningful and practical way. We compartmentalize the parts of the manifold crisis and seek technical solutions to each problem severally.

Cities express our aspirations and hopes. They are local citadels of the evolving global urban system, built to protect us from our fears and insecurities. Family by family, person by person, the world's population is gravitating towards the bright lights of urban intensity and high mass consumption. Across the globe, unevenly but inexorably, people have been entering the process that Raymond Williams (1974) calls 'mobile privatization' – making our lives increasingly private and linking to the public more than to each other by the mediation of television, the Internet and social media than by public engagement in the street or in community settings. Individual by individual, the denizens of cities turn on air conditioners to cope with the higher temperatures we all have produced and to meet our private 'needs' for increasing levels of comfort – thus paradoxically increasing the production of greenhouse gases which lead to higher temperatures. In other words, cities represent the best and worst of us. They are the home to the most crass and the very grandest things that we can achieve. Conversely, to improve them, we need to attend to our own weaknesses.

If part of the problem is that each of us thinks that we, individually, are doing something for the planet while we continue collectively to slide towards unsustainability, then, even though the idea might provoke unease, we need to return comprehensive *public* dialogue over urban futures. Auden's words from 'Memorial for the City' (1947) still haunt such a proposition:

> . . . the packed galleries roared
> And history marched to the drums of a clear idea,
> The aim of the Rational City, quick to admire,
> Quick to tire.

In other words, badly conceived utopian planning has in the past produced outcomes that are unsustainable, objectively and emotionally. But this does not mean that communities and municipalities, together with planning and architectural experts, should not get together to confer and argue over the future directions of the whole city, its priorities and directions – even if this means revisiting first principles.

Positive sustainable urban development needs alternative visions that take seriously the integral importance of economic, ecological, political and cultural factors. In particular, questions of culture need to be taken more seriously and directly. This is not to succumb to the culturalist view that the aesthetic visions of high-end architects should drive the remaking of cities. Rather, it is to argue for a city where cultural friction is returned to the streets and where cars give way to people, public spaces, basketball courts and urban food gardens.

It sounds simple, but current practices remain caught in inappropriate dominant understandings. Language is part of the problem, but it goes deeper to the relationship between knowledge, power and practice. As a way of going in a different direction we begin with the four social domains that we earlier posited as useful for understanding the human condition: the economic, ecological, political and cultural. The *Circles of Sustainability* metaphor cuts straight across the Triple Bottom Line approach. John Elkington extols the Triple Bottom Line 'revolution' as the act of giving cannibals forks (1997). It supposedly works to civilize capitalism. However, when put in terms of 'cannibals with forks', the inherently rapacious nature of the process starts to be exposed. And once exposed, the critique comes quickly. Tempering self-eating cannot be a sustainable approach to economics, let alone to the human flourishing as a whole.

Whereas the Triple Bottom Line approach, even it is latest variations of Integrated Reporting and One Reporting, treats financial accounting as *the* core discipline of economics, the Circles of Social Life approach treats each social domain as part of an integrated social whole. In contrast to the usual conception put forward in the triplet of economic, social, and environmental activities, economics is not considered a strangely independent master domain outside social relations. Economics is important, but when treated as primary it threatens to rip the heart out of prior cultural and ecological ways of life.

Whereas the Triple Bottom Line approach practically prioritizes economics – although rhetorically appearing to qualify it – the holistic view of social domains firmly put economics in its place as one of four equal social domains. Whereas 'business as usual' is predicated on treating nature as a residual zone to be saved, the Circles approach acknowledges that all social relations, including economics, is always already beholden to – built on – a fragile but irreducible natural world (see Figure 1.1). Whereas the usual approach treats the environment as a series of metrics, such as in carbon accounting, this alternative approach recognizes that as humans we are part of nature. Human activity is treated as located *in* the ecological domain, concerned with basic questions of needs and limits, which in turn now finds itself 'scientifically' fading at its edges into nature beyond the human. To be sure, over the last half century, human impact on the planet has been expanding into basic environmental systems that were once much bigger than us, but this does not involve the end of nature. It presents us with the final paradox: the more humans seek *instrumentally* to control the implications of nature and its fragility, the more we risk our own future. These paradoxes have become damaging contradictions that we need to confront directly.

The Circles of Social Life approach shown in Figure 1.1 is foundational to the method used in the book. It shows, as best one can figuratively, that all of social life is grounded in natural life while simultaneously being lifted out of this ground through social practice and meaning formation. This remains a basic tension for all practice and meaning. Over the course of the anthropocene period, the circle of social life has been expanding to fill more and more of the ground of being. By being named Circles of Social Life, the figure also indicates that the *Circles of Sustainability* emphasis is only one way of approaching social life assessments and profiles. Other circles that we have been developing include the Circles of Resilience, the Circles of Climate Change Adaptation, the Circles of Property Development and then a series of cohort-specific profiles beginning with Circles of Social Life: Children.

CIRCLES of SOCIAL LIFE
and beyond

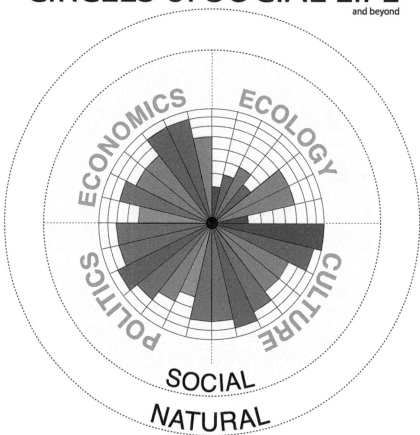

DOMAINS OF THE SOCIAL

ECONOMICS
Production & Resourcing
Exchange & Transfer
Accounting & Regulation
Consumption & Use
Labour & Welfare
Technology & Infrastructure
Wealth & Distribution

ECOLOGY
Materials & Energy
Water & Air
Flora & Fauna
Habitat & Settlements
Built Form & Transport
Embodiment & Sustenance
Emission & Waste

POLITICS
Organization & Governance
Law & Justice
Communication & Critique
Representation & Negotiation
Security & Accord
Dialogue & Reconciliation
Ethics & Accountability

CULTURE
Identity & Engagement
Creativity & Recreation
Memory & Projection
Belief & Meaning
Gender & Generations
Enquiry & Learning
Well-Being & Health

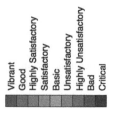

Vibrant
Good
Highly Satisfactory
Satisfactory
Basic
Unsatisfactory
Highly Unsatisfactory
Bad
Critical

FIGURE 1.1   Circles of Social Life

CASE STUDY: MELBOURNE, AUSTRALIA

Melbourne is a profoundly paradoxical city. It has a strikingly diverse multicultural population of about 4 million people,[4] but is founded on an Anglo-European heritage that, until the late 1960s, fiercely attacked multiculturalism as anathema to its cultural–political harmony. It is a densely urbanized and vibrant city of high-rise buildings, restaurants, parks and bluestone footpaths. But its metropolitan footprint radiates outwards into a region of ever-stretching car-dependent suburbs, mixed-use peri-urban zones and a hinterland of temperate dry-land farming, where most of the trees have been cut down. It is a trading city with a global port, though its manufacturing base for export has steadily declined since the 1970s. It is the administrative and service centre for the south-east corner of Australia, and yet 90 per cent of traded imports stay in the metropolitan area. It is a global city with a well-educated population who have a growing and sophisticated public consciousness about climate change, recycling, and water-consumption issues. However, Melbourne is becoming less sustainable, even as it maintains good liveability in certain dimensions of social life (see Figure 1.2).[5]

In summary, in the metropolis of Melbourne issues of liveability and sustainability cut across each other in complex ways. For example, for all the public sensitivity to ecological sustainability issues in the city, resource use and carbon emissions continue to grow, including land and energy consumption on a *per capita* basis. As mentioned earlier, one of the few clear successes in this area has been a widely supported political campaign to place legal restrictions on water use.

The Melbourne 2030 plan of 2002 designated twelve 'Green Wedges' for protection from inappropriate development. However, this was much less impressive than it sounded. The Green Wedges of the 1970s were set-aside green spaces that cut into the expansion of the greater urban boundary; now they merely designate non-urban areas beyond the existing built-up metropolitan zone. Seven years on, from the Melbourne 2030 plan, this became both rhetorically more elaborate and substantively even less impressive. In 2009, rethinking Melbourne 2030, the Brumby Labor government announced in a new document, *Melbourne@5Million*, that it would establish a 15,000-hectare grassland reservation to protect some of the world's largest concentrations of volcanic-plains grasslands, as well as a range of other habitat types including wetlands, riparian habitats, and open grassy woodlands. While, on the face of it, this sounded good, the announcement was made in the context of a decision to significantly extend the urban-growth boundary previously reset in the first Melbourne 2030 plan. The urban expansion of Melbourne would now encompass the open areas that had earlier been designated part of the rural hinterland. It is estimated that less than one-third of native vegetation remains within the current boundaries of the metropolis, with approximately one-third of the balance situated on private property. More than eighty introduced plant species cause significant damage to waterways.

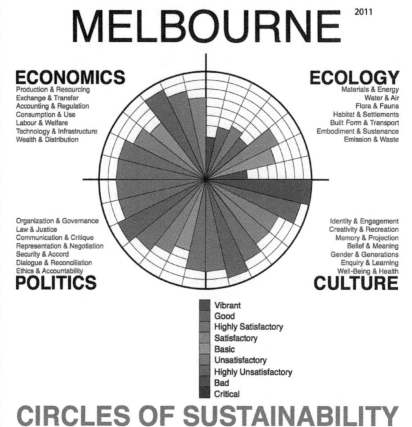

MELBOURNE ²⁰¹¹

ECONOMICS
Production & Resourcing
Exchange & Transfer
Accounting & Regulation
Consumption & Use
Labour & Welfare
Technology & Infrastructure
Wealth & Distribution

ECOLOGY
Materials & Energy
Water & Air
Flora & Fauna
Habitat & Settlements
Built Form & Transport
Embodiment & Sustenance
Emission & Waste

Organization & Governance
Law & Justice
Communication & Critique
Representation & Negotiation
Security & Accord
Dialogue & Reconciliation
Ethics & Accountability
POLITICS

Identity & Engagement
Creativity & Recreation
Memory & Projection
Belief & Meaning
Gender & Generations
Enquiry & Learning
Well-Being & Health
CULTURE

Vibrant
Good
Highly Satisfactory
Satisfactory
Basic
Unsatisfactory
Highly Unsatisfactory
Bad
Critical

CIRCLES OF SUSTAINABILITY

FIGURE 1.2 Urban Sustainability Profile of Melbourne, 2011

In response to these ecological challenges the state of Victoria has developed and implemented a range of programs to help Victorian communities, yet the substantive effects of these programs continue to be unproved. Even more problematic is the fact that there are larger structural issues linked to the strength of the economy that cut across whatever these programs do achieve. The electricity utilities in Melbourne, which were privatized in the mid-1990s, are reliant for energy generation on *critically* unsustainable brown coal-fired power plants in the nearby La Trobe Valley. These plants primarily serve Melbourne and form major contributions to Australia's status as one of the highest *per capita* greenhouse-gas emitters in the world.

The controversial Port Phillip Bay Channel Deepening Project, recently completed to enable entry of larger shipping vessels to Australia's largest working port, has further challenged the environmental sustainability of the city. As have two other major and equally controversial water-infrastructure projects: the Wonthaggi desalination plant and the Sugarloaf Pipeline, a seventy-kilometre pipeline linking the Goulburn River near Yea to the Sugarloaf Reservoir in Melbourne's north-east at a cost of AU$750 million. As with other Australian cities and towns, a key environmental constraint on the development of the city is the availability of fresh water. The experience of a long-term drought affecting south-eastern Australia over the last decade had prompted stringent water restrictions on commercial and residential water use, but this was not seen as sufficient for dealing with the long-term problem. The pipeline will transfer water from the Goulburn River to Melbourne Water's Sugarloaf Reservoir, thereby reducing natural flows to watercourses, while the desalination plant is intended to supply potable water to the city. These initiatives will generate an exorbitant cost in terms of the greenhouse emissions generated by the plant's demands on the electricity grid.

Major development projects with degrading environmental consequences, from the desalination plant to a new tollway tunnel for cars, paradoxically, are defended by the government in terms of environmental and, of course, economic sustainability.[6] At the same time as allowing these projects to go ahead with a minimal if heated critical response, Melbournians have become increasingly concerned to nurture lifestyle amenities, urban aesthetics, place-making activities, tourist-oriented events and cafés. Although such aspects of liveability are important, this complex mix of civic concern and complacency is symbolized by the way in which the city's politicians and media respond to being consistently listed as one of the world's most liveable cities.[7]

The city thrives on its reputation and, indeed, the reality of being extraordinarily liveable and prosperous. Meanwhile, the liveability standing of the city is being slowly but noticeably eroded. The social wealth of the city is being increasingly privatized or 'developed' through public–private partnerships that are wrapped in commercial-in-confidence contracts, while the unevenness of income distribution and the access to amenities are overlooked and allowed to increase.

Notes

1 See the Economist Intelligence Unit (2013). As part of the new world of commodified knowledge thirty-day full-access subscription costs US$5,250.

2 Here the distinction between how the Global North and Global South is treated as a socio-economic distinction based on a geographical tendency for poorer countries to be located in the Southern Hemisphere.

3 For a sympathetic history of the various approaches to planning, see Peter Hall's classic *Cities of Tomorrow* (1988).

4 There were 3,995,000 in the Melbourne metropolitan area according to 2009 Australian Bureau of Statistics figures. Of those persons, 31 per cent were born outside of Australia,

and 27.9 per cent speak a language other than English at home (2006 Census). Accessed 25 July 2014, <www.abs.gov.au/websitedbs/censushome.nsf/home>.
5 Here we are using broad criteria of social sustainability drawing on works such as Peter Newman, Timothy Beatley and Heather Boyer (2009); Phil Wood and Charles Landry (2008); and Matthew E. Kahn (2006).
6 PricewaterhouseCoopers is primarily a study of economic benefits, it notes 'a reduction in local air pollution and greenhouse gas emissions which would result from fewer total ships calls to the Port of Melbourne because larger ships could call at the port' (2007, p. 9).
7 On the two main indices, the Economist Intelligence Unit, Melbourne was ranked first in 2003 and 2004, 2011, 2012, and 2013. On the Mercer Quality of Living Survey, Melbourne was eighteenth-ranked city globally in 2010, down from ranked twelfth in 2005. On the way in which this is interpreted instrumentally see, for example, the commissioned report by Gerrard Bown (2006).

References

Auden, W. H. 1991, *Collected Poems*, Vintage Books, New York, 1991.
Gerrard Bown 2006, *Liveability Report: Capitalizing on Melbourne's Status as One of the World's Most Liveable Cities*, Committee for Melbourne, Melbourne.
Brugman, Jeb 2009, *Welcome to the Urban Revolution*, University of Queensland Press, St Lucia.
Davis, Mike 2006, *The Planet of Slums*, Verso, London.
Dickens, Charles 1902, *The Tale of Two Cities*, James Nisbet, London.
The Economist Intelligence Unit 2013, viewed 5 February 2013, <http://store.eiu.com/product.aspx?pid=455217630>.
Elkington, John 1997, *Cannibals with Forks: The Triple Bottom Line of Twenty-First Century Business*, Capstone, Oxford.
Florida, Richard 2009, *Who's Your City? How the Creative Economy Is Making Where to Live the Most Important Decision in Your Life*, Basic Books, New York.
Gleeson, Brendan 2012, 'The Urban Age: Paradox and Prospect', *Urban Studies*, vol. 49, no. 5, pp. 931–43.
Hall, Peter 1988, *Cities of Tomorrow*, Basil Blackwell, Oxford.
Hughes, Robert 1980, *The Shock of the New*, 'Episode 4: Trouble in Utopia', television series, produced by the BBC in association with Time-Life Films.
James, Paul & Scerri, Andy 2012, 'Globalizing Consumption: Jouissance, Lassitude, and the Deferral of a Politics of Consequence', *Globalizations*, vol. 9, no. 2, pp. 225–40.
Kahn, Matthew E. 2006, *Green Cities: Urban Growth and the Environment*, Brookings Institute Press, Washington, DC.
Newman, Peter, Beatley, Timothy & Boyer, Heather 2009, *Resilient Cities: Responding to Peak Oil and Climate Change*, Island Press, Washington, DC.
PricewaterhouseCoopers 2007, *Economic Analysis of the Port of Melbourne*, Department of Treasury and Finance and the Department of Infrastructure, Melbourne.
UN-Habitat 2010, *State of the World's Cities 2010/2011: Cities for All: Bridging the Urban Divide*, Earthscan, London.
UN-Habitat 2012, *State of the Cities Report 2012/2013: Prosperity of Cities*, Earthscan, London.
Williams, Raymond 1974, *Television: Technology and Cultural Form*, Fontana, Glasgow.
Wood, Phil & Landry, Charles (2008) *The Intercultural City: Planning for Diversity Advantage*, Earthscan, London.
The World Bank (2014) Data Indicators, viewed 1 July 2014, <http://data.worldbank.org/indicator/AG.LND.ARBL.HA.PC>.

2

DEFINING THE WORLD AROUND US

The world is in crisis and yet the argument here is that we need to slow down and go back to basics. Are we being overcautious? Doesn't this mean fiddling while Rome burns? Doesn't redefining terms and processes mean further deferring crucial action even further? There is that danger, of course, but there are so many issues that need challenging, from definitions to protocols and from principles to processes, that returning to basics has unfortunately become absolutely necessary. Rethinking why and how – in theory and in practice – we can make and remake cities does not need to be incompatible with continuing to do things in the world and adjusting our theories and principles accordingly. In fact, this is what we are proposing: a transitional practice for learning from experience, remaking theory and attempting to construct now what we want for our futures. Reflexive learning is crucial.

The approach presented in this book is intended to be both critical and useful. Simple as that sounds, it is horribly difficult to achieve. It requires a different way of working. All the concepts and methods, protocols and principles are given a place within the *Circles of Sustainability* approach only insofar as they are developed within a number of analytical principles. Are they heuristically useful? Do they enable us to map the complexity of social life without those maps becoming too arcane or too complicated to use? Can they offer us the possibility of moving between analysing dominant patterns of practice and meaning (structures) and recognizing the contingency of any particular practice or idea? Can they contribute to a broader analysis that can move between empirical description and understanding the grounding of a particular pattern of practice and meaning?

One of the intentions of the book is to destabilize current dominant ways of understanding urban development, and to set up an alternative framework of analysis that allows globally supported local work to occur that actually makes a difference in improving social and natural life. The Circles approach brings the local and global together, just as it draws heavily on Engaged Theory to bring theory down to earth. The first part of that double process of destabilizing dominant understandings and engaging theory in guiding practical outcomes entails redefining some basic concepts.

In this chapter, some definitions that are fundamental to making sense of the world of urbanization in global context are outlined. It redefines terms such as *development*, *sustainability*, *globalization* and *community*, paving the way for Chapter 3, which elaborates on the importance of the apparently simple recognition of different domains of social life. Despite the basic orientation of the discussion, beginning in this way has fundamental consequences for practice. Defining concepts is highly contested and foundational to making better cities and better lives. Defining the world around us, the title of this chapter, has a double inflection that suggests that just as we define the world, the world makes us through both our own definitions of it and its social force on us.

Sustainable and good development

Sustainable urban development in many parts of the world continues to be a struggle. The lives of the people that such development is meant to enrich are often being made more difficult by these same developmental processes. Despite well-intentioned attempts to the contrary, the managers of most development projects do not know how to engage with the complexity of community life. Although a paradigm shift from 'things' to 'people' has been discussed and encouraged rhetorically in some local government and corporate settings, mostly this has been translated into practice badly. Something of a consensus has emerged amongst commentators in the fields of education, anthropology, community development, geography and political ecology that sustainable development is something that comes from within communities rather than something that can be imposed from the outside. This nevertheless leaves us with many questions about how to actually do it.

Let us first go back to the big picture. How is good development to be understood? Both history and current driving forces complicate the possibilities of non-exploitative development of any kind, let alone good development. In the past local landscapes have often been changed by colonial or imperial experiences, and they are now beset by intensifying forces of globalization – most pressingly by the rolling global fiscal pressures, the competing demands for natural resources and the intensifying movement of people including rural–urban migration. In this context, the term *development* itself is complex and difficult.

How are issues of social equity and communality, ecological sustainability, grass-roots economic viability and respect for different ways of life to be negotiated in the practice of sustainable development? Some writers have suggested that the term *development* should be dropped or that the concept of 'sustainable development' is an oxymoron. However, as is often the case, the problem is not the term but its dominant definition and the practices that build on its definition. In the business sphere, development is usually equated with generating physical infrastructure, political stability and workforce training – all of which are directed towards enhancing corporate profit-taking. In the state-led model of development, this commonly means building layers of civil administration and providing the legislative, infrastructural and educational framework for economic-based development – all understood in terms of a nation-building programme. In the area of community and civil-society studies, ideas of development often simply mean getting more goods and services to the people or building 'social capital'. None of these emphases provides our starting point. Without diminishing the need for large-scale infrastructure planning, for example we begin with alternative notions that advocate the enhancement of social sustainability, resilience, security and adaptability, involving local people who make decisions about how this translates into practice for them.

How then can we define development so that there is no presumption in this definition that development entails either modernization or modern progress? How can we define development so that there is no presumption that all development is good? To answer this question we begin by recognizing that any value orientations automatically attached to the concept need to be stripped away. Development is a process – not an intrinsically good or bad thing. Deciding what is good or bad comes after the definition has been settled. Development needs to be defined in terms of social change and what is changing.

> *Development is defined as social change – with all its intended or unintended outcomes, good and bad – that brings about a significant and patterned shift in the technologies, techniques, infrastructure, and/or associated life-forms of a place or people.*

This definition does not assure that all development, even 'good development', is necessarily sustainable. There are too many possibilities of unintended consequences, reversals and counterproductive outcomes. Nor, it should be added, is all 'sustainable development' good. This last point is one rarely made in the mainstream Global North. The classic report *Our Common Future*, more commonly known as the Brundtland Report, defined sustainable development as 'development that meets the needs of the present without compromising the ability of future generations to meet their own needs' (World Commission on Environment and Development 1987, p. 8). This definition still works for many purposes. However, its meaning turns on the undefined implications of the word *needs*. It leaves unspecified the assumed importance of specifying cultural, political and ecological needs as well as economic material needs. (This is developed later in Chapter 4 in relation to a series of social themes in tension, including the dialectic of needs and limits.) These are issues to be debated publicly rather than just glossed over.

Negative and positive sustainability

Sustainability, for all the emotion and debate that the concept evokes, is a relatively flat term. Again whereas some writers have suggested that the concept is too empty to carry the current weight given to it, we would prefer to redefine and reinvigorate it rather than pass it over for some 'new' concept such as 'resilience'. Resilience is itself fast collecting a massive baggage of problems. Indeed, 'sustainability' remains a very important new concept, which initially became part of the discourse of the global justice movement and then was quickly appropriated by the dominant market globalist discourse of neoliberalism (Steger, Goodman & Wilson 2013, pp. 42–3). Both of these concepts, and a number of related concepts such as 'liveability', can be reclaimed and used in relation to each other. (See Table 2.1) This is the key – using different concepts that convey different core conditions of being human and that bring those 'ways of engaging' into productive relation to each other.

Each of these conditions of human engagement in the world bear back on the core concern in this book. Sustainability is usually defined in terms of being able to carry on, endure, or have a future. This is what, in our terms, can be called 'negative sustainability' – not negative in the sense of being bad but negative in the sense of *just* keeping a system or process going through acts of negation: reducing pollution, mitigating the excesses of development and keeping law and order.

Negative sustainability keeps things going through reducing the bad effects of previous rounds of development. This can be understood across the four domains

TABLE 2.1 Core Conditions for Engaging in Social Life

Core conditions	Definitions of the positive side of these core conditions
1. Adaptability	The ability to adapt to change, including adapting to changes brought about by external forces that threaten the sustainability of conditions of liveability and security.
2. Learning	The capacity to seek knowledge, learn and use that understanding for enhancing social life. When learning becomes reflexive understanding, the highest form of learning, it includes the possibility of acknowledging the profound limits of one's knowledge.
3. Liveability	The life skills and milieu that allow for living in ways that enhance well-being. Liveability includes having the resources to secure social life for all across the various aspects of human security, both in an embodied sense and an existential sense. One of the capacities here is the possibility of debating and planning possible alternative ways of living.
4. Reconciliation	The capability to reconcile destructive or *negative* differences across the boundaries of continuing and flourishing *positive* social differences.
5. Relationality	The capacity to relate to others and to nature in a meaningful way. This includes the capacity to love, to feel compassion, to reconcile.
6. Resilience	The flexibility to recover and flourish in the face of social forces that threaten basic conditions of social life.
7. Sustainability	The capacity to endure over time, through enhancing the conditions of social and natural flourishing.

of social life. Negative ecological sustainability currently centres on reducing carbon emissions. For example, negative cultural sustainability is achieved by reducing the number of suicides or attempting to integrate youth back into community life. Negative political sustainability turns on processes such as reducing corruption, reducing excesses of power by checks and balances and reducing violence through reconciliation commissions. Under contemporary globalizing capitalism, processes of negation and risk management dominate economic sustainability. By contrast, positive sustainability requires defining the terms and conditions of what are positively good. It entails projecting practices for achieving the enduring future of those conditions.

This shift in the definition means, for example, that it is possible to argue for 'positive' *sustainable conservation*. That is, in a world in crisis, conservation requires active engagement about what from the past and the present is being projected into the future. Such a conception is distinct from that of *sustainable preservation*. In the sense that preservation seeks to reduce the impact of change, sustainable preservation becomes predominantly a negative ideal and practice – namely protecting heritage. Sustainable conservation by comparison projects a vibrant and living future for the natural and social heritage of the past. Rather than fixing a time segment or a physical representation of the past, sustainable preservation requires development, adaptation and reintegration of the past into the present and active planning for projection into the future.

The distinction between positive and negative sustainability recalls and modifies the well-known distinction between positive and negative liberty.[1] As with positive liberty, aiming for positive sustainability appears to be either utopian or dangerous. By contrast having the capacity to endure through reducing what is bad appears to be more comfortable. It has been normalized. However, because neither positive nor negative sustainability are end states, and because the dominant focus of the last three decades on mutually assured negative sustainability has not saved us from the current manifold crisis, then something more radical is needed. Positive sustainability in these terms is a negotiated process projected beyond the present about how we want to live.

> *Positive sustainability can be defined as practices and meanings of human engagement that make for lifeworlds that project the ongoing probability of natural and social flourishing, vibrancy, resilience and adaptation.*

The term *lifeworld* is used to encompass both the social/natural and global/local bases for human living. It emphasizes local settings with global relations. Hence, our focus here is on local urban settlements and community sustainability, always in global context. Second, the relationship between the social and the natural remains crucial, even if natural spaces beyond the social are being increasingly colonized. From the realms of nano-nature to the steppes of arctic wilderness and the depths of the ocean, 'the natural' beyond a human-intersecting ecology are being diminished. Nevertheless, for the purposes of this discussion we are concerned with ecology as the enmeshment of the social and the natural (see Figure 0.1).

The emphasis on lifeworlds brings in the concept of 'community sustainability'. It is a recent concept that is still undergoing development in the literature. Depending on how it is defined, it can be both a more specific and a more expansive concept than that of 'sustainable development'. It is more specific in that it looks at the practices and actions that are needed in relation to existing communities to achieve sustainable development, yet it is more expansive in that it has the potential to move beyond schematic or instrumental accounts of sustainable development to encompass the various domains of the social, including cultural aspects of how communities cohere through time. Beyond such general accounts, however, there is little agreement on what it means or entails, particularly in integrated social terms. Although much research has been carried out on community sustainability from an economic or even an ecological standpoint, little work exists on the potential of cultural or political practices in strengthening communities. Some writers point to the vagueness of the concept, but it is possible to be quite clear about its meaning.

> *Community sustainability is defined as the long-term durability of a community as it negotiates changing practices and meanings across all the domains of culture, politics, economics and ecology.*

Again it should be clear that communities could be (negatively) sustainable without necessarily being good places to live. Part of the significance of the present work, then, lies in its attempt to address the gaps in the current literature on community sustainability and to extend theoretical observations about a new qualitative conception of community sustainability informed by substantial and innovative empirical research in urban settings. In this context, sustainability is conceived in terms that include not just practices tied to development but also forms of well-being and social bonds, community building, social support and urban infrastructure renewal. Processes such as urbanization and globalization have been changing the nature of community

In summary thus far, the concern with sustainability here entails undertaking an analysis of how communities are sustained through time, how they cohere and change, rather than being constrained within discourses and models of development. From another angle, the present project presents an account of community sustainability somewhat detached from instrumental concerns with narrow economic development while recognizing how powerful such concerns continue to be. Although concerns about production and exchange continue to be imperative for community sustainability, this project will suggest that an approach driven by economistic concerns will be reductive and will fail to account for the real complexity of interactions and effects produced by the matrix of ecological, economic, political and cultural practices – the *Circles of Sustainability*. We need now to define what is meant by an urban settlement and to link this to processes of globalization and localization, but we will return to the question of forms of community relations before the end of the chapter.

Cities and urban settlements

The challenge of conducting research or initiating social change in the contemporary world is complicated by what is often a rapid and radical reconfiguration of social space. Only in simple geographical or municipal political terms do urban settlements have singular boundaries. This has major consequences for acting sustainably. Among the many issues this raises are problems of definition. In relation to defining a phenomenon as apparently simple as an urban settlement, debates and practices in the fields of anthropology, sociology and ethnography confront us with one set of issues, while debates in the fields of human geography and demography present others.

One concern is that mainstream analyses of human settlements – whether they are by governments, intergovernmental organizations, economists or non-government organizations (NGOs) – tend overwhelmingly to use the urban–rural dichotomy as the dominant modality of categorizing locales and land use. The urban–rural distinction was first proposed in the early 1950s, and a few writers criticized it at the time for being overly simplistic. Nevertheless, it quickly entered into popular usage. It has persisted as the dominant classification system for studying human settlements and is used by virtually all countries. Beyond that there are a number of significant problems with the widespread usage of the various settlement categories. First, there is no uniform approach to defining rural and urban settlements. The United Nations Statistics Division (1998) concedes this difficulty: 'Because of national differences in the characteristics which distinguish urban from rural areas, the distinction between urban and rural population is not yet amenable to a single definition that would be applicable in all countries'. Thus, it is said to be best for countries to decide for themselves whether particular settlements are urban or rural. The Organisation for Economic Co-operation and Development (OECD) has adopted the same approach. However, while recognizing that it is a difficult task to create categories which are applicable to a diverse range of landscapes, contexts and regional settings, failing to define the terms being used simply means that there is an overabundance of opportunities for confusion and inconsistent use.

The usual urban–rural distinction also fails to account for the changing nature of human settlement across the globe. Cities have come to dominate landscapes far beyond the official metropolitan zone. Significant changes include the changing forms of urbanization such as urban sprawl and the decentralization of non-residential functions, for example retail parks close to intercity highway junctions, massively increased levels of commuting between urban and rural areas, the development of communication and transport technologies and the emergence of polycentric urban configurations.

Although the urban–rural dichotomy was always over-simplistic, it is arguably more misleading today than it was half a century ago. In countries from Timor Leste and Papua New Guinea to Senegal and Tanzania, the relationship between the urban and the rural needs to be treated very carefully. Networks of customary exchange relations are entangled with modern market relations, intensively connecting different locales, including through marriage and retirement relations. Third, the generality of the terms overwhelms the significant variation in settlement forms that exist between the extremes of the most urban and the most rural. *Rural* is, in general use, a catch-all category for 'not urban'.

This reductive binary has led to a number of intermediate categories being proposed, including suburban, peri-urban, ex-urban and peri-metropolitan. These new forms of categorization are intended to respond to the increasing complexity of settlement patterns and they partly do so. The difficulty is that marking the differences is sometimes reduced to a set of arbitrary metrics. One approach uses two criteria – population density and accessibility – to distinguish between three categories of rural areas: peri-urban rural; intermediate rural; and remote rural. In that approach rural areas are considered to be those with a population density lower than 150 inhabitants per square kilometre, while the three subcategories are defined according to the level of access to major services. This certainly marks actual differences. However, the technical precision is pseudoscientific rather than in keeping with the present social mapping approach that takes objective and subjective dimensions of social life equally seriously. Another approach identifies three dimensions through which human settlements can be addressed. As opposed to the one-dimensional nature of the urban-rural distinction it posits a set of settlement sizes, from hamlet to metropolitan centre; it measures concentration, from dense to sparse; and it evaluates accessibility, from central to remote.

Integrating material from different sources, however, helps us to build a basic framework for a general set of definitions that we will use as part of our toolshed. Although not fixed in stone, these definitions nonetheless form a steady part of the overall conceptual framework of this study.[2]

A city or urban area can be defined as a human settlement characterized – 'ecologically,' economically, politically and culturally – by a significant infrastructural base; a high density of population, whether it be as denizens, working people, or transitory visitors; and what is perceived to be a large proportion of constructed surface area relative to the rest of the region. Within that area there may also be smaller zones of non-built-up, green or brown sites used for agriculture, recreational, storage, waste disposal or other purposes.

A suburban area can be defined as a relatively densely inhabited urban district characterized by predominance of housing land-use – as a residential zone in an urban area contiguous with a city centre, as a zone outside the politically defined limits of a city centre, or as a zone on the outer rim of an urban region (sometimes called a peri-urban area). For example suburban areas in cities of the Global South can be made up of village communities or squatter settlements, sometimes edged by bushland. This also includes 'settlements' or 'squatter areas'. Thus, our definition of *suburb* does not made the usual distinction between formal suburbs and informal or squatter settlements – they are in our terms different forms of suburbanization.

A peri-urban area is a zone of transition from the rural to urban. These areas often form the immediate urban-rural interface and may eventually evolve into being fully urban. Peri-urban areas are lived-in environments. The majority of peri-urban areas are on the fringe of established urban areas, but they may also be clusters of residential development within rural landscapes and along transport routes. Peri-urban areas in the Global North are most frequently an outcome of the continuing process of suburbanization or urban sprawl, although this is different in places where customary land relations continue to prevail.

A hinterland area is a rural area that is located close enough to a major urban centre for its inhabitants to orient a significant proportion of their activities to the dominant urban area in their region.

A rural area is an area that is either sparsely settled or has a relatively dispersed population with no cities or major towns. Although agriculture still plays an important part in numerous rural areas, other sources of income have developed such as rural tourism, small-scale manufacturing activities, residential economy (location of retirees) and energy production. A rural area can be characterized either by its constructed (though non-industrial) ecology or its relatively indigenous ecology.

All these zones bear on the formation and reproduction of cities or urban settlements. They are spatial domains. However, there is another way of understanding spatial domains that complements what has just been outlined. It concerns processes rather than zones – in particular, processes of globalization and localization

Globalization and localization

Cities in the current world are faced with intensifying global interconnections: therefore, understanding processes of globalization and localization is crucial. Globalization is always enacted at the concrete local level. Even the global financial crisis was manifest in patterns of local practice, including how poor people bought houses in depressed urban neighbourhoods such in New York and Miami. At the same time, the viability of the local now largely depends on the global. In the lead up to the financial crisis, the act of buying a house on easy credit in the United States was swept up in a global system of credit swaps and derivatives as sets of subprime mortgages swirled through the financial world. Foreclosures followed. People lost their homes. The crisis compounded.

Notions of 'glocalization' or the 'glocal' have long been part of the vocabulary of the growing transdisciplinary field of global studies (e.g., see Robertson 1992; Steger 2013). Although they are ugly terms, this book explicitly acknowledges the crucial importance of this global–local nexus for urban development. Fortunately, there has been a growing awareness of the close interrelation between the local and global. Indeed, recent studies have used such insights to reconfigure democratic global governance around the urban by advocating a global association of cities or a global parliament of mayors (e.g., see Barber 2013).

To be sure, the challenges the world's mayors face are nothing short of immense. Talk of global climate change or a global financial crisis gives a sense of the range of globalizing pressures on cities. These are very real pressures. However, despite this obviousness, the process of globalization is still badly understood and poorly defined. Economic definitions still dominate people's imaginations. For example the claim that only those cities that channel the global movement of finance can be called 'global cities' depends on an economically reductive understanding of globalization. Similarly, the claim that globalization *causes* resource depletion and environmental destruction, depends on the one-sided assumption that globalization equals the rapacious consumption of the planet. There is no doubt, across the world, that cities are consuming their hinterlands, and it is not just relevant for metropolitan New York or the double city of Tokyo/ Yokohama, considered to be the largest conurbations in the world. Globalization contributes to that process of urban spread without being its overdetermining cause.

Peter Christoff and Robyn Eckersley's book *Globalization and the Environment* manages to respond precisely to the second of these misunderstandings. Contemporary globalization, they argue, is 'not the primary or only cause of global environmental change, although it has certainly intensified such change to the point where we are moving towards an environmental crisis of planetary proportions' (2013, pp. 29–30).

One of the problems with much analysis is that globalization has been badly defined. Defining globalization in terms of extension and intensification of social relations across world-space provides a good way out of most of the definitional issues. The definition is intended to stop any presumptions about the inevitable effects of globalization, including on cities.

> *Globalization is defined as a process of extension and intensification of social relations across world-space, where the nature of world-space is understood in terms of the temporal frame or of the social imaginary in which that space is lived – ecologically, economically, politically and culturally.*

The definition also has critical implications for sustainability analysis. By being clear that we are talking about a process – not an end point – and, in particular, a process that extends social relations, the definition is intended to get away from the mainstream emphasis on economics as the raison d'être of global change. Globalization occurs across ecological, economic, political and cultural domains. This means for example that, despite eminent historians claiming the opposite, globalization did not go into decline during the Second World War. By the same definition, it is not the constant increase in financial engagement that defines globalization. If a city is feeling the pressure of a downturn in foreign direct investment this is not necessarily because globalization is decreasing.

The qualifying phrases need further elaboration. They turn on two concepts – world-space and social imaginary. In this sense, the changing global space, the space of the world, needs to be defined in terms of the historically variable ways in which it has been practised and socially understood. To give one illustration, the world as understood by Claudius Ptolemaeus 2,000 years ago was based on a Roman revival of the Hellenic belief in the Pythagorean theory of a spherical globe. This understanding was a substantially different globe from that understood by George W. Bush when he initiated the Global War on Terror. Both conceptions take the world to be a spherical globe – hence globalization. However, the nature of that sphere and how a particular empire or a state reaches across that world-space is understood and practised in fundamentally different ways. By analytically defining globalization in this variable way, we can say that the phenomenon of globalization has been occurring across the world for centuries, but in changing ways, and massively intensifying across the mid-twentieth century to the present. Across history, globalization has involved the extension of uneven connections between people in far-distant places through such processes as the movement of people, the exchange of goods and the communication of ideas. (For an extended discussion of the concept of the social imaginary, see Chapter 5.)

There are a number of dimensions to an understanding of globalization as the extension of social relations across world-space. First, as many commentators now agree, the phenomenon of globalization is a relational process. That is, globalization is not a state of being or a given condition. The notion of a 'global condition' is addressed by the concept of globality, but even this concept does not imply that everything has or will become global. In these terms, globalization is not a totalizing condition, nor is it an end point that will be achieved when everything that is local becomes global. Rather, a series of relations continue to be uneven and contingent, even as we can see dominant patterns emerging. *Globalisms*, in this sense, are the ideologies of globalization (again, see Chapter 5).

Second, globalization is a spatial process. It involves social connections across space – organized and unorganized, intended and unintended, patterned and messy. More than that, the spatiality of this phenomenon needs to be specified as global in some way. Those interrelated points might seem an unnecessary thing to say given their obviousness. However, for the concept to have any meaning, globalization needs to carry global spatial implications of some kind. Despite this, there has been a tendency for some writers to define globalization in terms of transcontinental or inter-regional relations, or in terms of the demise or end of the nation state. There is no good reason to make such relations or effects part of the definition.

Ironically, intensifying globalization has brought about a significant self-consciousness about local places. In this sense, although, *at one level*, we have always lived locally and continue to do so, contemporary forms of globalization have been changing what this means. This requires a different way of understanding spatiality and spatial layering. Old twentieth-century conceptions of vertical spatial scales running from the local to the global must give way to more complex understandings of overlapping spatial scales that can no longer be neatly separated and treated in isolation from each other.

Third, globalization is a variable, often uneven, process. Cities are crossed by different kinds of globalization processes. One possible way of refining our analytical understanding of different kinds of globalization to help with this overlaying spatial change involves the following set of distinctions:

- *Embodied globalization* – the movements of peoples across the world
- *Object-extended globalization* – the movements of objects across the world, in particular, traded commodities

- *Agency-extended globalization* – the movements of agents of institutions such as corporations, NGOs and states
- *Symbolically extended globalization* – the movements of symbols across the world, often carried as objects, but also now overwhelmingly projected as electronic images
- *Disembodied globalization* – the movements of immaterial things and processes, electronic texts and encoded capital

Cities have choices – constrained choices – about how they deal with these different forms of globalization. Embodied globalization extends across the globe in networks of the movement of people, but it is also the most palpably localized in the way in which it is lived. Migrants usually come to particular places, increasingly urban places, through chains of connection that link localities, families and ethnic diasporas. Alternatively, at the most materially abstract end of the spectrum, disembodied globalization, although always localizing in some way or other, and with profound consequences for how people live locally, is the least embedded in local places. (To see how this fits into the larger schema see Table 4.2 in Chapter 4; note how the objects of analysis relate to the ways of relating.) It bears back on cities in profound ways that make all cities increasingly global whether they like it or not.

All of this means that the current approach to global cities, to the extent that it emphasizes global financial connectivity, is reductive and skewed. Here we confront a shibboleth in scholarly writing – not only has the urbanization of the world been a long term if massively accelerating process, but it should also be said that cities have long been the locus of globalization processes. Against those writers who, by emphasizing the importance of financial exchange systems, distinguish a few special cities as global cities – commonly London, Paris, New York and Tokyo – we recognize the uneven global dimensions of all the cities that we study. Los Angeles, the home of Hollywood, is a globalizing city, although perhaps more significantly in cultural than economic terms. And so is Dili globalizing, the small and 'insignificant' capital of Timor Leste – except this time it is predominantly in political terms. Dili was established as an administrative town by the Portuguese in October 1769, a year before the English explorer Captain Cook 'discovered' Australia, seven years before the American Revolution and two decades before the French Revolution. It has been the subject of globalizing political intersections for all of its existence, from the intersection of the Portuguese, Dutch, English and, later, Indonesian empires to the recent United Nations experiment in ruling a national territory with a multi-national force.

Community and sustainability

Ever since Ferdinand Tönnies (1963) introduced the terms *Gemeinschaft* and *Gesellschaft* to describe a shift from a society dominated by relatively stable, mainly non-urban, communities that emphasized mutual obligation and trust (*Gemeinschaften*) to more mobile, highly urbanized societies in which individual self-interest comes to the fore (*Gesellschaften*), commentators have been interested in the ever-changing nature of community. Until recently, belonging to a community was usually seen as unqualifiedly positive. Although community is now seen in more circumspect terms, the erosion of community is still predominantly interpreted as being the cause of social problems.

In the West, the term *community* is often used interchangeably with *neighbour-hood* to refer to the bonds that come with living alongside others in a shared space. Alternatively, it is used to refer to people bound by a particular identity defined by nation, language group, ethnicity, clan, race, religion or sexual orientation. Or, again, it refers to groupings of mutual self-interest such as a profession or association. Cutting across all of these, community can also be defined by a particular mode of interaction, such as virtual or online communities. Community often seems to be whatever people say it is, potentially incorporating every conceivable form of human grouping, even those that might otherwise strike one as contradictory.

In the context of the supposed new 'fluidity' of global interchange, community has come in for sustained critique in relation to its effects on social well-being. For example Zygmunt Bauman has argued that communitarianism creates an ideal of community that is like the 'home writ large' in which there is no room for the homeless and which can also turn into an unexpected 'prison' for many of the residents. Bauman believes that a new kind of unity is possible – 'a unity put together through negotiation and reconciliation, not the denial, stifling or smothering out of difference' (2000, pp. 171–2). However, under conditions of what he problematically calls globalizing 'liquid modernity', he sees community as entirely a matter of individual choice – a desire to redress the growing imbalance between individual freedom and security. This is clearly not the case in many of the cities across the world or all the spaces within them. It is our contention that the theorists of this supposedly 'postmodern fluid world' fail to understand the enduring, if changing and variable, possibilities of existing communities as they exist in a complex matrix of relations from the local to the global.

In the contemporary world – whether it is Port Moresby or Paris – an emerging sense that one's sense of community is changing and that it is no longer lived as given is in tension with powerful subjective continuities. That is community is no longer a relationship that a person might be drawn into, or even born into, without being forced at some time to think about its meaning, but for the most part we take such social relations for granted. Given all the variations, continuities, and transformations, the distinction made by Tönnies between 'the social' cast in the predominance of stable, traditional *Gemeinschaften* and the more fluid and displaced *Gesellschaften* is too dichotomous to be useful. However, the metaphor of flows just reverses the previous misplaced emphasis on customary and traditional societies as fixed. What is becoming more obviously necessary is to look at the ways in which forms of community identity are being created and re-created in relation to continuities under changing circumstances, both objectively and subjectively. The definition of community thus needs to be generalized across quite different settings but without simply being a matter of subjective and changing self-definition and without including all forms of association or sociality that happen to be important such as the family.

> *Community is defined very broadly as a group or network of persons who are connected (objectively) to each other by relatively durable social relations that extend beyond immediate genealogical ties and who mutually define that relationship (subjectively) as important to their social identity and social practice.*

A definition that recognizes variable objective and subjective dimensions allows us to recognize that communities do not have natural or singular boundaries. The nature of all locales is that they are crossed by different and overlapping social relations. The following discussion offers four ways of characterizing community relations defined in terms of how they relate to categories such as time, space and embodiment: (1) *grounded community relations*, in which the salient feature of community life is taken to be people coming together in particular tangible localized settings based on face-to-face engagement; (2) *cosmological community relations*, binding people together through a universalizing connection such as that to God or to gods; (3) *lifestyle community relations*, in which the key feature bringing together a community is adherence to particular attitudes and practices; and (4) *projected community relations*, in which neither particularistic relations nor adherence to a particular way of life are pre-eminent but, rather, the active establishment of a social space in which individuals engage in an open-ended processes of constructing, deconstructing and reconstructing identities and ethics for living (see Table 2.2).

Before elaborating these categories further, we should sound a couple of notes of caution about how these different accounts of community relate to each other.

TABLE 2.2 Community Formations

Forms of community relations	*Dominant ontological formations*
• Grounded community relations	Customary
• Cosmological community relations	Traditional
• Lifestyle community relations	Traditional to modern
1. Community life as interest based	
2. Community life as proximately related	
• Projected community relations	Modern to postmodern
1. Community life as thin projection	
2. Community life as reflexively but uncritically projected	
3. Community life as reflexively and critically projected	

First, we are in the first instance distinguishing between forms of community relations, not types of communities. In other words, the distinctions between the community relations as embodied, as a lifestyle, or as projected are intended as analytical distinctions *and* shorthand designations.

Second, in these terms, it is not being claimed that the bundle of relations in a given community exists in practice as one or other of those pure variations. Rather, the terms are intended as offering a way into an analytical framework across which the dominant, coexistent and/or subordinate manifestations of different community relations (and therefore different communities) can be mapped. Cities are full of overlapping forms of communities and community relations. Though one dimension of community relations can certainly predominate in a given community – and a community can thus be designated as such – the temptation to pigeonhole this or that community into a single way of constituting community should be resisted.

Third, in proposing this framework, the terms *grounded community, cosmological community, lifestyle community* and *projected community* are used here not as normatively charged descriptions but as shorthand terms to refer to the dominant forms of social relations that constitute a given community. They refer to the way in which social relations are framed and enacted without making any implicit judgement about whether they are good or bad. The purpose here is to offer a way of thinking about how communities are constituted across different ways of living and relating to others and to see how communities are constituted through the intersection of different forms of social integration.

Why is all of this important? It has profound practical considerations. Without understanding the kinds of community relations that characterize social relations in the locale or urban region in which a project or process is to be enacted it is impossible to managed good community relations or to conduct meaningful community consultations. Engendering positive sustainability depends upon knowing what kinds of community relations are important to the people who live in a particular locale.

Grounded community relations

Attachment to *particular* places and *particular* people are the salient features of what we are calling 'grounded community relations'. In other words, relations of mutual presence and placement are central to structuring the connections between people. Except for periods of stress or political intensification – usually in response to unwanted interventions from the outside – questions about active social projection are subordinate in accounts and practices of grounded community. Such projection is usually seen in terms of what is already given and in place. In such a setting, questions about the nature of one's lifestyle are assumed to take care of themselves so long as a given social and physical environment is in place with appropriate infrastructure such as community-defined dwellings and amenities.

Grounded community relations can sometimes be extended over spatial distances, stretched for example between the city and the country. Urban–rural diasporas often continue to be connected by abiding embodied relations, such as through regular powerful ceremonies of birth, marriage and death. For example during the working week for people living in the City of Rhodes in Greece, modern open-community relations are important at one level, but customary and traditional relations form the web of social life at another. These underlying relations are carried to the city from the rural villages, to where many people return 'home' on the weekends.

Thus, adherence to particular ways of life tends to spring from a sense of commonality and continuity. It arises from face-to-face bonds with other persons in one's locale rather than from thinking about the lifestyle itself. People do not have to read from community-development tomes, self-help books or religious tracts to learn how to act with one another. Norms of behaviour emerge from people in meaningful relations as the *habitus* of their being. Here the term *habitus* is used in the sense of an immediate and present lifeworld. Even when the religious observances of such communities break out of the confines of mythical time – in the sense that it transcendentally looks forward to a world to come and goes back to the beginning of time – the sense of community is strongly conditioned by local settings and is carried on through rituals and ways of living that are rooted in categories of embodiment and presence.

Cosmological community relations

The basis of cosmologically framed community relations is something held as existing beyond the community: God, Being, Nature. Such relations can be localized or stretched across a globalizing space, as in Christendom or the Ummah. At a local level such relations tend to reinforce relationships of trust and mutual obligation between people who agree to abide by certain morally charged ways of life. Local communities are formed around a specified normative boundary – certain norms of right and wrong, appropriate and inappropriate behaviour. This is the form taken by many *traditional* religious communities. Community here is essentially a regulative space, a means of binding people into particular ways of living. In the contemporary world, grounded community relations tend to be drawn into cosmological community relations. Village and church or mosque become wedded, if uneasy, partners.

Lifestyle community relations

In contrast with grounded community relations where the emphasis is on the particularities of people and place as the salient features of community, there are accounts and practices of community that give primacy to particular ways of living. In practice, this tends to take one of two major forms: interest-based and proximity-based relations. *Interest-based* community relations form around an interest or aesthetic inclination, where lifestyle or activity, however superficial, is evoked as the basis of the relationship. In Papua New Guinea this includes sporting and leisure-based communities that come together for regular moments of engagement, and expatriate or diaspora communities who share commonalities of lifestyle or interest. *Proximate* community relations come together where neighbourhood or commonality of association forms a community of convenience. This is not the same as a grounded community, even though both are based in spatial proximity. As distinct from conceptions of grounded community, the cultural embeddedness of persons in this or that place does not define the coherence of community, nor does the continual embodied involvement of its members with each other. This is the predominate form of community in Australian and North American suburbs or of communities lifted into the media-sphere.

Because the salience of lifestyle community relations lies in their morally framed, interest-based or proximate coherence, such communities can be de-linked from particular groups of people and particular places. In other words, they can be deterritorialized and globalized. A sense of place can be made and remade in ways that communities formed in grounded communities find anathema. Face-to-face embodied relations may be subjectively important to such communities, but they might equally be constituted through virtual or technologically mediated relations where people agree to abide by certain conventions and bonds. In this regard, it is a *potentially* more open and mobile form of community. This is its strength but also its weakness. It tends to generate culturally thinner communities than grounded relations. On the other hand, lifestyle relations tend to allow for more adaptability to change.

Projected community relations

Unlike the two other conceptions of community relations, this notion is not defined by attachment to a particular place or to a particular group of people. Neither is it primarily defined by adherence to a shared set of moral norms, traditions or mutual interests. The salient feature of projected community relations is that a community is self-consciously treated as a created entity. Because of this primacy accorded to the created, creative, active and projected dimension of community, the word *projected* is used. This is perhaps the most difficult idea of community to grasp, partly because it is so apparently nebulous. For the advocates of projected community, such relations are less about the particularities of place and bonds with particular others or adherence to a particular normative frame, and more an ongoing process of self-formation and transformation. It is a means by which people create and re-create their lives with others.

Communities characterized by the dominance of projected relations can be conservative or radical, modern or postmodern. And they can be hybrid and uneven in their forms of projection. At one end of the spectrum this process can be deeply political and grass-roots – based projected communities, at least in their more self-reflexive political form, can take the form of ongoing associations of people who seek politically expressed integration, communities of practice based on professional projects and associative communities which seek to enhance and support individual creativity, autonomy and mutuality.

At the other end of the spectrum, projected communities can also be trivial or transitory, manipulative or misleading. They can be overgeneralized and more akin to advertising collations. They can live off the modern search for meaning rather than respond adequately to it. Realized in this way, notions of 'community' might be projected by a corporate advertiser or state spin doctor around a succession of engagements in the so-called third place of a Starbucks café or a self-named 'creative city' or 'creative community'. Here older forms of community relations dissolve into postmodern fluidity in which notions of settled, stable and abiding bonds between people recede into the background.

Setting up definitions of these kinds enables a different approach to research and practical action. Communities cease to be understood as fixed entities with singular characteristics and clear spatial edges. For example, engaged research intends to restore the distinctive roles of insiders and outsiders, providing perhaps a more open and fruitful dialogue between the research partners as well. Of course, such dialogue needs time, and it requires considerable negotiation, skill and goodwill from both sides to move across cultural and epistemological boundaries. This whole process of building relationships involves a process of dealing with 'the cultural other', whether from another ontological setting or even just another region or place. This occurs most productively in face-to-face dialogue. This dialogue is about acquiring deeper understanding and new perspectives through listening *and* talking – not just listening and gathering data.

To come into conversation with a diverse group of people with different cultural and epistemological backgrounds and locations can be a disturbing thing, exposing and altering, but it is also imaginatively charging and positively transforming. In *Decolonizing Methodologies*, Linda Tuhiwai Smith (1999), talks of the importance of the 'seen face', turning up at cultural events, returning again and again to the community and being aware of the indigenous and local protocols for being present. Smith's notion of the 'seen face' has inspired us with one important layer of our engaged social theory, and relates strongly to our distinction between modes of social integration ranging from face-to-face relations to the disembodied relations at a distance. While as researchers or practitioners it is often a mistake to aspire to be *integrated* into communities at the level of the face-to-face – for example as fictive kin or through ritual rites of passage – it is important to seek meaningful face-to-face interaction such that a researcher or practitioner always returns as a *significant* outsider. In this context, all else is empty pseudo-consultation.

Taking all of this together, sustainability thus relates not only to questions of environmental crisis or to the nexus between economy and ecology. It also concerns the human condition from the local to the global, including both the nature of urban settlements and the forms that community life takes. It concerns the basis question of how we are to live.

CASE STUDY: NEW DELHI, INDIA

Located in the north-west of India, the metropolis of Delhi is part of the National Capital Territory of Delhi, adjacent to the Punjab region. The greater sprawl of metropolitan Delhi consumes an area of 1,438 square kilometres, an expanse flanked by the rocky hills of the Aravalli Range and the Yamuna River. Neighboured by the territories of Uttar Pradesh and Haryana, Delhi is a largely dry zone, with significantly hot summers, transitioning into a monsoon season with the most of the city's annual rainfall recorded before winter begins. With climate change, seasonal change seems to be becoming more variable. For example in 2013, the monsoon rains came early, causing flooding problems in the city and agricultural crises in rural India (see Figure 2.1).

Delhi was ranked the tenth-largest city in the world in 2011 with about 17 million residents. A spike in population growth occurred during the 1940s because

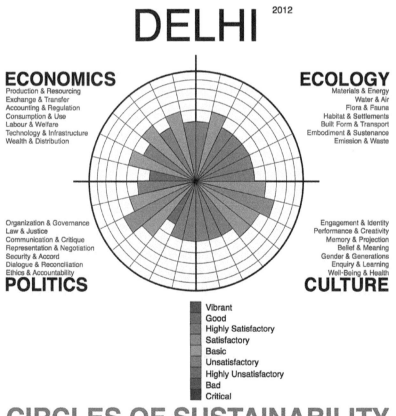

FIGURE 2.1 Urban Sustainability Profile of Delhi, 2012

of the migration of displaced Sikhs, Hindu Punjabis and Sindhis. It was one of the largest forced resettlements in human history, and the movement continued into the following decades. The intensification of Delhi's population has continued to be notably high in the last few decades with a decadal rate in population growth across the 1990s of 47 per cent. Most recent figures show that population growth from 2001 and 2011 was 21 per cent. Whilst this was a significant drop from the decade before, population growth is still unsustainably on the rise.

The number of people projected to be living in Delhi by 2026 is around 30 million. Rapid urbanization has in conjunction with the intensified challenges of environmental degradation, placed pressure on infrastructure, housing availability and the spread of slums. Another major impact of rapid population increase is change in the way that land is used. Once fertile grounds and water bodies, along with agricultural lands now have been covered over by built-up urban sprawl. Statistics show that in 1951, the total area of agricultural land in the Delhi region was 97,067 hectares. Today, it is less than 25,000 hectares.

Replacing agriculture as the primary economic driver has been a mixed capitalist economy. The establishment of high-tech industries in the late twentieth century, particularly information technology and telecommunications, has overlaid older commodities trading in such goods as spices, and made Delhi an important commercial capital. In turn this process of globalizing economically, has generated an increasing division of rich and poor, and put tremendous pressure on the access of the poor to land and housing.

Currently, Delhi has a carbon footprint of 0.70 metric tons per person. In comparison to other megacities around the world including Mexico City and London, Delhi's carbon footprint is notably lower. Although this may seem positive, it is the uneven development of Delhi that underlies such data and therefore its carbon footprint still remains a critical issue, particularly because it is well above the national average of India. One only has to look as far as census data on housing to see that although the majority of houses in Delhi have either stone, slate or concrete as their roofs, 86 per cent of households in Delhi are constructed with burnt-brick walls. The processes involved with burnt-brick production are not environmentally friendly. And so the conundrum is highlighted: How can today's populations achieve better health and overall life-quality outcomes whilst ensuring environmental prosperity in the future?

Ecological issues of Delhi are widespread, covering many different facets of daily life. In relation to air quality, transport regulations remain inadequate to the task of limiting pollution. Between 2000 and 2010, the number of motor vehicles in Delhi almost doubled and it remains the major factor contributing to Delhi's increasingly poor air quality. Whilst in 1998, the Supreme Court of India passed orders to attempt to control pollution due to vehicles throughout

Delhi, this has not initiated any greater capacity to respond to air-pollution problems. Delhi accounts for 2 per cent of the national population, contributes 5 per cent of the total national emissions. Of this figure, transportation accounts for two-thirds of the city's total emissions.

The Central Pollution Control Board has established stations to monitor the levels of pollutants in the air. It is through numerous studies that links between air pollutants and morbidity due to respiratory issues have been established. The World Bank estimates that a 10 per cent reduction in particulate matter levels (PM10) would reduce mortality by 1,000 deaths each year. This further highlights the seriousness of Delhi's air quality. Although rulings by the Supreme Court have aided this and the presence of monitoring stations have initiated improvements since 2002, air pollution still remains a critical topic.

Half a kilogram of waste is created per capita in Delhi, with 70 per cent of this being collected and disposed of through formal means. This therefore implies that 30 per cent of waste is disposed of through the streets or in illegal dumping places. This has lead to piles of garbage and other litter across the city being increasingly common. This creates not only environmental and health issues, but dramatically affects the city's aesthetic value. Although receptacles are put in place to collect community wastes, no formal policy dictates the areas that these should be in and their accessibility. Furthermore, it is well known that not all of the waste is collected, and because of a combination of lack of political attention and general education, many households dispose of their rubbish unsustainably, such as in waterways. Disposal of waste collected by the government is largely unsystematic and outdated, being dumped at low-lying areas which poses further risks of contamination. Presently there are three major sanitary sites for the city of Delhi: Ghazipur, Bhalswa and Okhla. The use of these sites as landfill locations is rapidly moving towards operational completion, which means there is an increased demand for the government to initiate new and safe alternatives. There is also a growing demand for better operational practices in waste management, with acts such as street sweeping being rarely conducted on roads other than those used commercially as well as an evident lack in appropriate supervision of staff responsible for the waste disposal.

Why then, given all of this, does *ecological* sustainability for New Delhi look better than for Melbourne with all its aesthetic beauty; green, leafy suburbs; and efficient recycling? When Figure 2.1 for New Delhi is compared with Figure 1.1 for Melbourne, discussed in the previous chapter, the reason that New Delhi is still more ecologically sustainable turns predominantly on the massive *per capita* consumption, car dependency, waste and emissions of Melbourne. If New Delhi continues to develop in a conventional sense, this will change for the worse.

Notes

1 Negative liberty is freedom from external constraint or 'freedom from' (see Berlin 1969), whereas positive liberty turns to 'freedom to' – namely what persons or communities aspire to through freedom. It should be noted that our definition of positive liberty is thus different from Berlin's and his emphasis on the autonomy of the individual.
2 Here we have drawn on the European Conference of Ministers Responsible for Spatial/ Regional Planning (2006).

References

Barber, Benjamin R. 2013, *If Mayors Ruled the World: Dysfunctional Nations, Rising Cities*, Yale University Press, New Haven.
Bauman, Zygmunt 2000, *Liquid Modernity*, Polity Press, Cambridge.
Berlin, Isaiah 1969, *Four Essays on Liberty*, Oxford University Press, Oxford.
Christoff, Peter & Eckersley, Robyn 2013, *Globalization and the Environment*, Rowman and Littlefield, Lanham.
European Conference of Ministers Responsible for Spatial/Regional Planning (CEMAT) 2006, *Glossary of Key Expression Used in Spatial Development Policies in Europe*, CEMAT, Lisborne.
Robertson, Roland 1992, *Globalization: Social Theory and Global Culture*, Sage, London.
Smith, Linda Tuhiwai, 1999, *Decolonizing Methodologies: Research and Indigenous Peoples*, Zed Books, London.
Steger, Manfred B. 2013, 'It's about Globalization, after All: Four Framings of Global Studies', *Globalizations*, vol. 10, no. 6, pp. 771–7.
Steger, Manfred B., Goodman, James, & Wilson, Erin K. 2013, *Justice Globalism: Ideology, Crises, Policy*, Sage, London.
Tönnies, Ferdinand 1963, *Community and Society*, Harper and Row, New York.
United Nations Statistics Division (UNSD) 1998, *Principles and Recommendations for Population and Housing Censuses*, Revision 1. Series M, No. 67, Rev. 1, UNSD, New York.
World Commission on Environment and Development 1997, *Our Common Future*, Oxford University Press, Oxford.

PART II

Understanding
social life

3

SOCIAL DOMAINS

In the context of manifold crises across the globe, questions of sustainability are now more crucial than ever. And it is critical that our understandings of sustainability are both theoretically engaged and systematically translated into practice. This means going back to basics in a number of ways. As has been suggested, the present approach works across four *domains of social practice*. But it is important to now elaborate this in a way that makes the *Circles of Sustainability* method both practically useful and grounded in very strong analytical foundations. Often approaches to sustainability expose only the superstructure of their activities, leaving the rest hidden and secret – or simply hidden and never interrogated. The assumptions that form the foundations of their methods remain underground. Here we want to begin to expose as much as the reader of a book such as this can comfortably bear.

If we begin at the level of empirical description, even such a simple thing as saying that economics is a different domain of social life from politics needs to be handled carefully. Demarcating social domains in this sense is a way of categorizing the 'parts' of social life in general. It is a way of making claims about empirical life in the broadest possible sense. The four domains chosen as primary in the Circles approach – economics, ecology, politics and culture – have been derived as the minimal number of domains that are together useful for giving a complex sense of the whole of social life. Each the domains are understood as always located in relation both to each other and to nature.

Certainly other domains could have been added – for example some approaches work with technology or infrastructure or knowledge as further social domains. But this complicates things. For example, adding the domain of technology could lead to issues of skewed weighting, with dominant contemporary emphases such as technological innovation in urban development being given undue methodological emphasis in a world where it is already massively overemphasized. The most overblown example today is the emphasis on 'smart cities'. It tends to prioritize the so-called knowledge industries as a separate and dominating domain of social life. The current fetish for smart cities is oriented around economic return and knowledge for profit's sake. The *Circles of Sustainability* broadens such fields as knowledge, infrastructure and technology and treats them seriously within the terms of the four-domain model without succumbing to singular fashions. Certain technological innovations offer much, but unfortunately current ideologies tend to fetishize the communications and information technologies *per se* as if it is simply a case of the more the better. To the contrary each practice and each domain of social practice needs to be judged for the nature of what is done rather just the amount of activity.

The shorthand phrase 'domain of social practice' is an abbreviation of the larger concern with 'domains of social practice, meaning and material expression'. This set refers to a series of critical questions for mapping sustainability. First, what is the way in which we do things now, and how could those practices be reorganized? Second, how are meanings given to practices and objects, both current and projected? And, third, how are we to understand the material objects themselves, now and into the future? The approach always tries to emphasize that these questions are only truly meaningful in terms of interconnected broader social and natural systems changing across time.

Demarcating social domains as a lived reality in everyday life is a relatively recent phenomenon. Indeed, it is a profoundly *modern* phenomenon. For example when Aristotle wrote what we now call *The Politics* (1962) he focused on affairs of the polis in general – not on politics as a separate realm. He treated the *oikos*, the co-residential household, as the basic unit within the polis and therefore the household economy as embedded in interconnected processes (see Roy 1999). He simultaneously distinguished political affairs as different from household management (*oikonomia*) – the name of which was to become much later the etymological root of two related terms, *economy* and *ecology*.

These two concepts are now treated as two obviously separate domains of practice – but Aristotle devoted most of his writings to drawing out their homologies and interrelations. In settings characterized by the dominance of customary ontologies – rural Rwanda or remote Papua New Guinea, for example – domains such as politics or economics, ecology or culture are not normally recognized as distinct areas of life. Except perhaps for the purpose of translation across settings or dealing with cross-cultural encounters, these domains remain embedded in the larger sense of the social. It is in only contemporary modern urban life that tends to lift them out as separate. And it is this – combined with a national imaginary (now overlaid by a global imaginary) that treats well-being as based on market relations – that leads to the domain of the economy being seen as the one to rule them all. It's the economy, stupid.

Although the categories of ecology, economics, politics and culture are modern, so long as the limits of the historically specific *modern* standpoint that makes the analysis possible is kept to the fore, the metaphor of domains can nevertheless be coherently deployed for analysing sociality and sustainability across the human condition, both present and past. This entails a reflexive qualifying of the modern tendency towards defining other ways of life in terms of modernity as the contemporary normality: 'We are modern and they are premodern'; 'We are now and they are in the past, or residual hangovers from the past'.

In other words, this conception of a social matrix of domains can be useful if it recognizes it own limits. For example in Port Moresby or Dili, or even Johannesburg, modern economics and politics rule at one level, but other forms of economic market relations and political authority continue to be important to local life. It is easier to say than to enact. The sensitivity needed to research with any depth the contemporaneous importance of very different ontological formations across different places in the world is profound. Words and concepts do actually mean different things in different settings, and not just because of the technical question of different languages.

A few paragraphs earlier we said that a social practice should be judged in relation to the nature of what is done rather than just the amount of activity. What then is the basis for judging the method that is being developed here? Two criteria for judging the value of an analytical consideration have already crept into the previous paragraphs: coherence and usefulness. It is important to make explicit the criteria of judgement for making such an analytical move in the first place before laying out definitions of our chosen domains. The key concepts here for considering the designation of domains and the development of any overall approach include the following: (1) practical usefulness, (2) analytical coherence, (3) simple complexity and (4) normative reflexivity.

Judging the value of any method

The test of practical usefulness

In relation to the notion of usefulness, it needs to be recognized that the mapping of the social world into domains is no more than a heuristic device. It is a device for learning and acting. This is the case for all approaches whether they admit it or not. The *Circles of Sustainability* approach is no more than as a process for learning. The four domains are treated as *useful* for analysing and learning about the patterns of social life, considered primarily at the level of empirical analysis. They are used in a way that allows for resolution into related elements or constituent parts – precisely the modern definition of *analysis* as a process – the breaking down of an object of enquiry into its elements.[1] The ultimate test of usefulness depends on long-term use and the positive outcomes of that use, and it can only be judged over time.

The test of analytical coherence

In relation to the test of coherence, we argue that the four-domain model of social life provides a much richer, less reductive, less skewed method than most mainstream approaches. For example many approaches tend to treat economics as if it is completely distinct from the social. It is amazing how, across almost every field of practice, phrases such as 'economic, environmental and social sustainability' or 'economic, environmental and social concerns' roll off the mainstream production line of naturalized expressions. Only critics of market-dominated politics ask why economics has come to be treated as the master domain separated from its social foundation. Very few people ask why the environment tends to be reduced to an externality of the economic or why the environment is separated from human activity. Even fewer people ask why the social is treated as grab bag of extra things that are left over after the economic and environmental are designated and demarcated.

The dominant global paradigm today is the Triple Bottom Line approach which sets out a three-domain model – economic, environmental and social (Hendriques & Richardson 2004). This model uses the category of 'the social' to incorporate all of those facets of social relations not tied to the primacy of the economic (qualified by the environmental). For all its good intentions this tends to blind sustainability reporting in relation to the fact that existing structures of power and narratives of meaning might themselves be contributing to unsustainable development. For example a deeply illegitimate polity or deeply xenophobic culture may not be conducive to sustainable development, even if all externalities are internalized into the cost of production and the over-exploitation of non-renewable natural resources is minimized. It also tends to blind its proponents to the ideological assumptions built into the approach. For example, the Triple Bottom Line approach tends to lead to what some critics have argued are incoherent practices such as the drive to growth in a world that is currently threatened by the ecological consequences of a growth machine. This goes back to the usefulness test – the question of outcomes and to what ends a method tends to lead? (see Figure 3.1)

The problem with the nested circles version of the Triple Bottom Line approach is that it centres economics and gives it a prominence that threatens to expand to consume the realm called society. The coherence of the model would quickly be

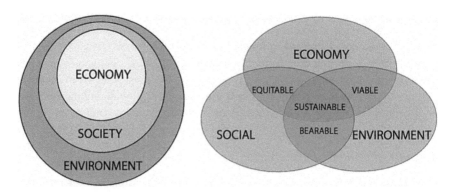

FIGURE 3.1 Different Ways of Representing the Triple Bottom Line Approach

tested if one asked what is the relationship between other domains of society such as culture and politics. The problem with the Venn diagram version, amongst many other considerations, is that sustainability is reduced to a small area of overlap at the centre of the three ovals.

In setting up an alternative approach we need some ways of analytically judging what is coherent. The coherence test can be judged around a number of questions:

- Can each of the domains in an approach be understood in categorically coherent relation to each of the other domains? One way of testing whether this is working within a given approach is to ask whether the various domain names can be used as adjectival in relation to each other. For example the *Circles of Sustainability* approach allows one to talk of the 'cultures of the economy' – for example the culture of desire for consumer goods and the culture of economic status. The Triple Bottom Line approach does not pass this test of analytical coherence. It does not make sense to talk of 'the social of economics', and not just because the grammar does not work. The four-domain approach, by comparison, allows an investigator for instance to focus on how economic practices or material expressions such as commodities are given cultural meaning and fetishized as having exchange value (Puma & Lee 2004).[2] Or to take a more familiar example, the approach allows one to discuss the economics of culture – namely the question of the economic sustainability of certain cultural practices. Is the library in your city economically sustainable? Is the way in which the annual jazz festival is managed economically sustainable? However, these questions do not automatically imply, as some methods emphasize, that judgements about what constitutes economical sustainability can be ascertained just through direct financial cost accounting. As will become clear, the domain of economics is much more complex that the current emphasis on financial return on investment would suggest.
- Can each of these domains be systematically divided into subdomains that are more than a miscellany of related subthemes? Systematic division of the domains becomes important for giving a sense of the complexity of each of these domains and in turn of the human condition in general. It is against these subdomains for example that we can map social indicators drawing a connection between qualitative issues and quantitative metrics. Having begun with the Triple Bottom Line division, the Global Reporting Initiative has then tried its best in its fourth iteration to escape incoherence, but to do so 'the social category' in their system now has four unwieldy subcategories – 'labour practices and decent work', 'human rights', 'society' and 'product responsibility' – while 'the economic category' and 'the environment category' have none (2013). Why 'product responsibility' is one of the major subcategories of the social alongside 'society' is more than perplexing.
- Can each of these domains be understood in both objective and subjective terms? In subjective terms can contemporary ideas, ideologies and imaginaries be mapped across the domains? In objective terms, can empirical indicators and metrics be mapped across the domains? Most approaches do not allow this.

The test of simple complexity

How can an approach be as simple as possible, particular at the top level of its presentation to local communities and urban practitioners? How can it be as simple as possible without becoming simplistic? This test can be expressed in longhand as the Test of Relative Simpleness in Rendering a Complex Social Whole. This is the social theory version of Ockham's razor. Ockham tells us that theories in science should move towards the simplest form where explanatory power is not sacrificed. The difference here is that the dimensions of social life can never be isolated as singular or standalone systems, and therefore the social whole always has to be kept in mind.

In relation to simply rendering complexity, the *Circles of Sustainability* mapping works in a way that attempts to solve the problems that many other ways of defining fundamental domains tend to treat either reductively or factorially. It works with a simple top-level figure expressive of a city or a locality (see Figure 3.2) that is used to highlight strengths and weaknesses in the sustainability of a particular urban area, and yet it is based on a complex underpinning.

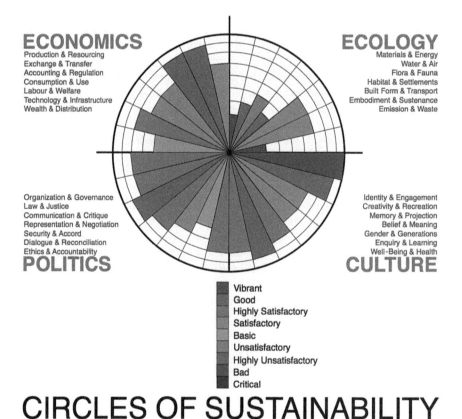

FIGURE 3.2   *Circles of Sustainability*

Here the question of complexity intersects with the notion of the 'social whole'. Many sustainability and impact assessment processes have as their focus a specific dimension of the social whole. This is not a problem so long as it is acknowledged. What we are attempting to do here goes much further. Problems arise when the social whole is oversimplified or misrepresented. From a Triple Bottom Line standpoint, the cultural and the political can be considered subsets or subsystems of an imperative primarily understood as the intersection of the economic market and the ecosphere on which it has an impact. Thus, the social is treated as an extra domain – supposedly very important but, in practice, relegated to those extra considerations, such as ethics and identity, that do not quite fit into the domain of economics. It is through this prism that ecological economics theory conceptualizes sustainable development.[3] The problem here is that either the model fails to deal adequately with the complex *whole* of human engagement or all those complexities are loaded into the extra domain of the social.

The second problem is that although the condition of human welfare continues to be treated as an end of sustainable development, the issue in contention is nevertheless reduced to the question of changes in the marginal value of resources. Key dimensions of the human condition tend to be subordinated, including the consideration that people have agency and construct alternative meanings and, therefore, can act in ways that contest or counter the dominant economic-ecological systems and values.

The third problem is that economics dominates the sense of what is important in understanding the social whole. For all the economic sophistication of methods that arose at the end of the twentieth century for measuring the 'non-market components of the value of ecosystem services', economics assumed the dominant measure of all things. The dominant sense of nature has tended to become what Martin Heidegger calls a 'standing reserve' – 'everything is ordered to stand by, to be immediately at hand', to be used as a resource (1977, p. 17). Trees become timber, cows become livestock and nature becomes a gene pool. Perhaps the turning point was the Clinton presidential campaign of 1992 when the electoral strategist James Carville popularized the phrase 'It's the economy, stupid'. Here, ironically, the very obviousness (or the dominance) of the domain of economics was deployed as a political resource. The joke was that we already knew it to be true. Meanwhile, human agency continued to contribute to undermining the capacity of the ecosphere to sustain civilization – confirming the issue that the social is not only the subject within but also an agent of economic and ecosystem change. Humans have the capacity to reflect on the effects of agency and, therefore, to plan and steer a new course of action over time. Moreover, humans can and must articulate amongst themselves ethical-moral reasons for acting or not acting in particular ways. In short, humans are social animals.

The test of normative reflexivity

It is in recognition of the human capacities for political-cultural agency and ethical-moral reflection that the need for an alternative to the current dominant three-domain framework becomes particularly apparent. That is, the three-domain model does not provide a basis for reflexively assessing the social constitution of unsustainable forces within and upon the social or natural environment. Nor can it provide a guide for negotiating sustainable resolutions to the problems associated with such driving forces. The alternative that is presented here addresses directly the presence of relations of political power and cultural meaning as well as economic resourcing and ecological engagement. In this view, it is necessary to recognize the existence of a minimal 'rule'[4] for assessing sustainable development. This minimal rule necessitates the holistic measurement of such considerations as political authority and legitimacy and cultural meanings and narratives in conjunction with economic values and ecological conditions within society (see Scerri & James 2010). In this view, trade-offs in the reporting process would need to be agreed on, subject to the constraint that economic and ecological drivers were assessed for their interaction with political and cultural drivers.

Of course, such decisions are inherently normative.[5] By making them explicit and measuring them as such, rather than burying them implicitly under the category of the social, it is argued that this approach will better capture the full spectrum of possibilities for developing policy for sustainable development in general. For these reasons, it is recommended that driving forces – and, it follows, critical issues and the indicators of states associated with them – be classified in terms of four domains of social practice. The four domains are understood as fields of social practice that, often but not always or necessarily, come into in tension with each other in attempts to implement policy and practice for sustainability. In this sense, the approach reframes sustainability as a social issue that requires some technocratic input, rather than first and foremost as a technocratic or economic issue requiring only measurement, assessment, predictability, administration and control.

The approach that we are developing is based on a two basic drives: first, that it should be principled, linked to contested and negotiated normative concerns about how we should live and, second, that it should be issue driven, locally adaptable and tied to practical outcomes. The method aims to have the following features:

- *Accessible* – At one level, the approach should be readily interpretable to non-experts, but at deeper levels it needs to be methodologically sophisticated enough to stand up against the scrutiny of experts in assessment, monitoring and evaluation and project management tools.
- *Graphic* – The approach needs to be simple in its graphic presentation and top-level description, but simultaneously have consistent principles carrying through to its lower, more complex and detailed levels.
- *Cross-locale* – The approach needs on the one hand to be sufficiently general and high level to work across a diverse range of cities and localities, big and small, but at the same time sufficiently flexible to be used to capture the detailed specificity of each of those different places.
- *Learning based* – The approach should allow cities to learn from other cities and provide support and principles for exchange of knowledge and learning from practice.

- *Comparable* – The approach should allow comparison between cities but not locate them in a league table or hierarchy.
- *Tool generating* – The approach needs to provide the basis for developing a series of tools – including web-based electronic tools (compatible with various information and communications technology platforms). These range from very simple learning tools to more complex planning, assessment and monitoring tools.
- *Indicator generating* – The approach needs to provide guidance for selecting indicators as well as methods for assessing their outcomes.
- *Relational* – The approach needs to focus not only on identification of critical issues and indicators that relate to those critical issues but also on the relationships between them.
- *Cross-domain* – The approach needs to be compatible with new developments that bring 'culture' in serious contention in sustainability analysis – such as the United Cities and Local Governments' four pillars of sustainability. The approach therefore uses a domain-based model which emphasizes interconnectivity of economic, ecological, political and cultural dimensions, each of which are treated as social domains.
- *Participatory* – Even if it is framed by a set of global protocols, the approach needs to be driven by stakeholders and communities of practice.
- *Cross supported* – The approach needs to straddle the qualitative/quantitative divide, and uses just enough quantification to allow for identification of conflicts.
- *Standards oriented* – The approach (and its methods) should connect to current and emerging reporting and modelling standards.
- *Curriculum oriented* – The approach needs to be broad enough to provide guidance for curriculum development and therefore useful for training.

Defining social domains

Defining such fundamental terms as *economy, ecology, politics* and *culture* is extraordinarily difficult. It is not just because they are essentially contested concepts such as 'democracy', 'justice' or 'aesthetics'.[6] This contestation is largely confined to academic debates. It is also paradoxically because for most people they have become taken for granted as the fields across which we walk, as the basis of our understanding of our world. People assume that they know what is meant by economy or culture, and we are rarely called on to define these terms. It is increasingly rare for even academics to actually try to define these basic terms. The classic text *Keywords* for example only explores one of these four concepts (Williams 1976).[7] We still hear the phrase 'It is the economy, stupid' as if the economy is completely self-evident as a domain of activity.

In summary then, the approach to understanding sustainability presented here begins with the social. If positive sustainability is defined as practices and meanings of human engagement that project an ongoing lifeworld of natural and social flourishing, then sustainability is a *social* phenomenon long before it is an economic or even just an ecological phenomenon. It is analytically possible to divide the social into any number of domains. Social domains are dimensions of social life understood in the broadest possible sense. In this case we have chosen the minimal number of domains that are useful for giving a complex sense of the whole of social life: namely ecology, economics, politics and culture. Each of the subdomains constitutes a placeholder. The particular words that we use to name each of the domains are less important than the social space that the combinations of those words evoke. The 'social domains', as we name and define them here, are analytically derived by considering the human condition broadly across time, across different places and across different ways of life. In practice, the four domains remain mutually constitutive.

Taking into account the many earlier controversies over defining these concepts, the following are our definitions.

Ecology

Ecology is defined as a social domain that emphasizes the practices, discourses and material expressions that occur across the intersection between the social and the natural realms.

The natural realm includes a spectrum of environmental conditions from the relatively untransformed to the profoundly modified. The distinction between the social realm and the natural realm, with the natural as a *context* for human action, is common in traditional (cosmological) and modern (scientific) understandings, but we are adding a further dimension. Our definition recognizes this usage but lays across both terms the important dimension of human engagement with and within nature, ranging from the built-environment to so-called wilderness areas. This means that the ecological domain focuses on questions of social-environmental interconnection, including human impact on, and place within, the environment from the unintended consequences of living on the planet to issues of the built environment. The ecological is thus not treated as a background context but a place of being.

Economics

The economic is defined as a social domain that emphasizes the practices, discourses and material expressions associated with the production, use and management of resources.

Here the concept of 'resources' is used in the broadest sense of that word, including in settings where resources were/are not instrumentalized or reduced to a means to other ends, including accruing exchange value. Although the domain of economics was only abstracted as a named area of social life *and* self-consciously practised as a separate domain in the early modern period,[8] this definition allows it to be used across different places and times. Questions of power are ever present in the economic domain in relation to contested outcomes over the use of resources.

Politics

Politics is defined as a social domain that emphasizes practices and meanings associated with basic issues of social power as they pertain to the organization, authorization, legitimation and regulation of a social life held in common.

The parameters of this area thus extend beyond the conventional sense of politics to include social relations in general. They cross the public/private divide; itself in formal terms a modern construct. The key related concept here is a 'social life held in common'. Although it is true that not everything that is done in the private or the public realm is political just because it may have consequences for issues of the organization, authorization, legitimation and regulation of a social life held in common, many issues of politics bear directly on the sustainability of a city.

Culture

Culture is defined as a social domain that emphasizes the practices, discourses and material expressions, which, over time, express the continuities and discontinuities of social meaning of a life held in common.

In other words, culture is how and why we do things around here. The 'how' is how we practice materially, the 'why' emphasizes the meanings, the 'we' refers to the specificity of a life held in common, and 'around here' specifies the spatial and, by implication, the temporal particularity of culture from the local to the global. The concept of culture had its beginnings in agriculture and cultivation, with subsidiary senses of 'honour with worship' of *cultura*, which in the sixteenth century were linked to understanding of human growth and development (Williams 1976). Questions of power are ever-present in the cultural domain in relation to contested outcomes over social meaning.

By way of background, the *Circles of Sustainability* approach, developed across the period from 2007 to the present, suggests that social life should be understood holistically across these interrelated domains. This bypasses either the dominant Triple Bottom Line approach or the narrower carbon-accounting approaches. Our alternative is intended to offer an integrated method for deciding on the critical issues associated with responding to complex problems and then acting on them. It takes a city, a community or an organization through the difficult process of deciding on the terms of its approach and guides the engagement. It allows for an understanding of competing issues and tensions. It then provides continuing feedback and monitoring in relation to implementation difficulties and successful outcomes. And it supports a reporting process, including a graphic presentation of the sustainability of a city or locale (Figure 3.2). The approach provides a way of achieving urban sustainability and resilience that combines qualitative with quantitative indicators. It sets up a conceptual and technology-supported approach with guiding tools for investigating problems faced by communities and does so in such a way as to be flexibly applicable across the very different contexts of a city, a community or an organization. It is particularly sensitive to the need for negotiation from the local level to the global.

Defining perspectives and aspects

Each of the social domains – ecology, economics, politics and culture – can analytically be divided in the 'perspectives'. In an earlier stage of our thinking, these perspectives were called subdomains, but the less formalistic metaphor of perspectives works better to register the interconnected nature of any of these provisional subdivisions. It emphasizes the issue that the subdivisions are *points of view*, not categorically separate or standalone categories. For example the cultural perspective of enquiry and learning reaches out to all the other domains in relation to enquiring about economics, politics and ecology, even though we have located its primary home in the domain of culture. This can be seen graphically in the figure of the *Circles of Sustainability* (Figure 3.2). All perspectives are interrelated through the centre point of the circle, sometimes tellingly in mathematics called the origin of the circle.[9] Each of the perspectives, such as 'organization and governance' or 'habitat and space', is analytically derived using the same process that is used for working through broad considerations of the human condition to derive the four social domains.

This division, we suggest, becomes *useful* – and no more or no less than useful – for giving a sense of the complexity of each of these domains and in turn of the human condition in general. It is against these perspectives for example that we map the questions in the urban profile and the social indicators drawing a connection between the qualitative and the quantitative. We understand that the process of setting up of a contingent 'order of things' has a long and troubled history (Foucault 1970).[10] There are always problems associated with any such ordering. Thus, we remain cautious about what can be claimed for such an order. Nevertheless, given that such ordering is conventionally done so badly in sustainability assessment approaches such as the Triple Bottom Line, it is important that we go back to basics so that a contingent but more adequately grounded matrix can be set up.

In choosing the different perspectives, a number of further considerations were kept in mind:

- Each of these domains and perspectives can be understood in both objective and subjective terms, but as soon as subjective issues or meaning are brought in, this entails a double thinking, connecting that domain or perspective to the relevant perspectives in the domain of culture.
- Each of these domains and perspectives can be understood in terms of ideologies, imaginaries and ontologies (see Chapter 5)
- Each of the perspectives is named in way that, as much as possible, makes them meaningful within social settings constituted through the dominance of very different ontological formations. For example exchange and transfer is a perspective rather than the more limited *modern* subdomain of finance and trade. By the same reasoning, air and water is designated as a perspective rather than greenhouse gases and ocean temperatures, where the latter is the more modern abstract (and particular) naming of air and water based on contemporary acute concerns about climate change.

TABLE 3.1 Social Domains and Perspectives

Economics	Ecology
1. Production and Resourcing	1. Materials and Energy
2. Exchange and Transfer	2. Water and Air
3. Accounting and Regulation	3. Flora and Fauna
4. Consumption and Use	4. Habitat and Settlements
5. Labour and Welfare	5. Built-Form and Transport
6. Technology and Infrastructure	6. Embodiment and Sustenance
7. Wealth and Distribution	7. Emission and Waste
Politics	Culture
1. Organization and Governance	1. Identity and Engagement
2. Law and Justice	2. Creativity and Recreation
3. Communication and Critique	3. Memory and Projection
4. Representation and Negotiation	4. Belief and Meaning
5. Security and Accord	5. Gender and Generations
6. Dialogue and Reconciliation	6. Enquiry and Learning
7. Ethics and Accountability	7. Well-being and Health

Based on this background thinking and extensive consultation across many cities we arrive at the set of four domains each with seven perspectives. This matrix is laid out in Table 3.1. Taking us back to the beginning, when applied to an assessment process, it gives us Figures 0.1 and 3.2.

Defining aspects of the social whole

Each of the *perspectives* is divided in seven *aspects*. The rationale for this is to generate a finer assessment process. While the figure of the circle, coloured according to levels of sustainability (Figure 3.2), gives a simple graphic representation of the outcome of an assessment process, there are a series of background considerations that need to be brought to the fore. A primary consideration involves having a way of assessing why, from a particular perspective, a city or a locale is judged to have a certain level of sustainability. In the background to the graphic circle are sets of questions linked to social indicators. To decide systematically on what is a good range of questions the *Circles of Sustainability* approach entails analytical dividing the perspectives into different aspects. For example one aspect of the economic perspective of 'production and resourcing' is 'manufacture and fabrication'.

Rather than seeing this subdividing process as setting up a classical Boolean tree, the concept of aspects is intended to emphasis the sense of an interconnected social whole. Each of the aspects has been made as generic and encompassing as possible. An explicit attempt has been made to make these aspects consequential for all kinds of urban settings across the Global North and Global South. Just as the definition of a perspective turns on a point of view, the classical definition of the concept of an aspect further brings out the notion of ways of looking. To extend the metaphor, we are concerned in summary with *aspects* of an integrated complex panorama. Depending on where one stands, an aspect can open a vision of the world, a vision that can be conceived in ways that are as broad as the *perspective* – which for current purposes frames that aspect of the panorama. For example the aspect of climate and temperature is included in the ecological perspective of water and air, but it also reaches beyond that perspective. To use a different analogy, this perspective is analytically treated as the originating location of this aspect rather than its resting place. That is climate and temperature is foundationally relevant to the human condition as a whole in relation to the possibilities of climate change, however, from that place in the circle, the aspect of climate and temperature reaches out to all other aspects of social life across the domains of economics, politics and culture.

The main reasons for setting up this panorama of interrelated aspects are firstly to provide a systematic basis for developing a series of questions for assessing sustainability as part of the Sustainability Profile Template. That is rather than choosing any old questions *that seem to align* to, or to have a common-sense affinity with, a particular perspective, designating aspects of each perspective allows for the questions to be chosen in a more methodological defensible way. (The sets of aspects will not normally be made visible in the template itself, except as a possible appendix for researchers or respondents who want to know more about the grounding of the method, but they do provide the means for choosing what questions will be asked about sustainability.) Second, it allows us to suggest, more systematically, possible indicators that can be used to assess sustainability in a holistic way. Indicators can be chosen to give a known range of possibilities by linking those indicators to each of the aspects of social life.

In choosing the different aspects, attention has been paid to urban settings across human history. For example within the economic perspective of production and resourcing, one of the listed aspects is extraction and harvesting. This binominal has been chosen rather than, for example, mining and agriculture, for one key reason. Although they sound as if they are referring to much the same field of activities, using the couple of extraction and harvesting allows a broader cross-society understanding of producing and resourcing from the non-human world – ranging from forestry to fishing, or from damming water to farming eels. It allows for the recognition of worlds of manual extraction rather than highly mechanized mining. Where this move no longer captures contemporary modern urban settings at all, the descriptors have been skewed to the contemporary. For example from the economic perspective of exchange and transfer, the aspect of trade and tourism has been included, even though tourism was not an active part of ancient or traditional cities and towns. This modern skewing has been done as little as possible.

An intriguing example is that of water. It highlights the issues of both ontological and language difference. The modern Western definition of *water* treats the concept as coterminous with the scientific understanding of H_2O, albeit in local context such as flowing down a river or a stagnant in a pond. Quite differently, for the Chinese the parallel term *shui* is less about the entity than about 'the being of fluidity'.

Water is the process of soaking downwards. *Shui* overcomes fire and is overcome by earth. Differently again, for most of the classical Greek philosophers, *hudōr* is a water category. But it is a very different one than understood by contemporary modern Western understanding of water. It is a foundational element. Aristotle for example considers glass and metals as belonging to the category of water. These differences do not mean that we necessarily descend into intelligibility or untranslatability. Although words and things belong to different registers, the basis here for our definitions is contemporary English with reflexive translation allowing for the delineation of what has been called the 'semantic stretch' of a concept (Lloyd 2012, pp. 87–90). To enhance that openness, we use couplets of words rather than single words – for example the perspective of water and air is linked to aspects such as waterways and rivers or air quality and respiration.

For reasons of consistency, elegance, and analytical discipline we have chosen to divide each of the perspectives into seven aspects. There is nothing magical about the number 7 in this system. The number, in part, has been chosen because it has cultural resonance in number of traditions. More important, it has been chosen as a number that gives sufficient range and complexity to the list without it becoming too long and unwieldy. There is no right number. Choosing a restrictive number has the positive effect of limiting the infinite number of possibilities and forcing the system to systematically prioritize the different domains, perspectives and aspects. Similarly the number 4 is used to as the other main numerical divider. It is used when we are looking for the smallest number that will still maintain a sufficient sense of analytical complexity. There is nothing intrinsically wrong with dualisms or trinities, but contemporary modern cultures have become so used to these groupings that they begin to naturalize these numbers as obviously true.

A series of other considerations came into play in developing the different aspects of the Circle of Social Life. For example, the seventh aspect of each perspective is always used to emphasize learning. In other words, because we are treating reflexive learning as fundamental to projecting a sustainable future, the theme of monitoring and reflection has been added as the seventh aspect of every perspective. It has been called monitoring and reflection rather than monitoring and evaluation (M&E) to avoid the sense that we are only talking about expert-driven techniques of M&E. The notion of reflection is intended to include not only formal monitoring but also interpretation and critique, both expert and lay.

The process has been worked in a dozen places in the world with very different constituencies. Beyond that a number of other approaches have been drawn on for considering categories for inclusion as aspects of the social – for example the Human-Scale Development approach (Max-Neef 1991), the 'Capabilities' approach (Nussbaum 2011), the Bhutan Gross National Happiness scale (2012), the UN–Habitat principles (2012) and others such as the Green City Criteria, amongst others. What we hope to achieve (laid out in Table 3.2 in the Appendix to this chapter) is a contingent, debatable but useful and coherent set of categories for mapping the human condition today.

APPENDIX

TABLE 3.2 Summary of the Matrix of Domains, Perspectives and Aspects

Domains	Perspectives	Aspects
Ecology	1. Materials and Energy	1. Availability and Abundance 2. Food and Sustenance 3. Minerals and Metals 4. Electricity and Gas 5. Petroleum and Biofuels 6. Renewables and Recyclables 7. Monitoring and Reflection
The ecological domain is defined as the practices, discourses and material expressions that occur across the intersection between the social and the natural realms, focusing on the important dimension of human engagement with and within nature, ranging from the built environment to the 'wilderness'.	2. Water and Air	1. Vitality and Viability 2. Water Quality and Potability 3. Air Quality and Respiration 4. Climate and Temperature 5. Greenhouse Gases and Carbon 6. Adaptation and Mitigation Processes 7. Monitoring and Reflection
	3. Flora and Fauna	1. Complexity and Resilience 2. Biodiversity and Ecosystem Diversity 3. Plants and Insects 4. Trees and Shrubs 5. Wild Animals and Birds 6. Domestic Animals and Species Relations 7. Monitoring and Reflection

Domains	Perspectives	Aspects
	4. Habitat and Settlements	1. Topography and Liveability
		2. Original Habitat and Native Vegetation
		3. Parklands and Reserves
		4. Land Use and Building
		5. Abode and Housing
		6. Maintenance and Retrofitting
		7. Monitoring and Reflection
	5. Built-Form and Transport	1. Orientation and Spread
		2. Proximity and Access
		3. Mass Transit and Public Transport
		4. Motorized Transport and Roads
		5. Non-motorized Transport and Walking Paths
		6. Seaports and Airports
		7. Monitoring and Reflection
	6. Embodiment and Sustenance	1. Physical Health and Vitality
		2. Reproduction and Mortality
		3. Exercise and Fitness
		4. Hygiene and Diet
		5. Nutrition and Nourishment
		6. Agriculture and Husbandry
		7. Monitoring and Evaluation
	7. Emission and Waste	1. Pollution and Contamination
		2. Hard-waste and Rubbish
		3. Sewerage and Sanitation
		4. Drainage and Effluence
		5. Processing and Composting
		6. Recycling and Reuse
		7. Monitoring and Evaluation
Economics	1. Production and Resourcing	1. Prosperity and Resilience
		2. Manufacture and Fabrication
		3. Extraction and Harvesting
		4. Art and Craft
		5. Design and Innovation
		6. Human and Physical Resources
		7. Monitoring and Reflection
Defined as the practices, discourses and material expressions associated with the production, use and management of resources	2. Exchange and Transfer	1. Reciprocity and Mutuality
		2. Goods and Services
		3. Finance and Taxes
		4. Trade and Tourism
		5. Aid and Remittances
		6. Debt and Liability
		7. Monitoring and Reflection

(Continued)

TABLE 3.2 (Continued)

Domains	Perspectives	Aspects
	3. Accounting and Regulation	1. Transparency and Fairness
		2. Finance and Money
		3. Goods and Services
		4. Land and Property
		5. Labour and Employment
		6. Taxes and Levies
		7. Monitoring and Reflection
	4. Consumption and Use	1. Appropriate Use and Reuse
		2. Food and Drink
		3. Goods and Services
		4. Water and Electricity
		5. Petroleum and Metals
		6. Promotion and Dissemination
		7. Monitoring and Reflection
	5. Labour and Welfare	1. Livelihoods and Work
		2. Connection and Vocation
		3. Participation and Equity
		4. Capacity and Productivity
		5. Health and Safety
		6. Care and Support
		7. Monitoring and Reflection
	6. Technology and Infrastructure	1. Appropriateness and Robustness
		2. Communications and Information
		3. Transport and Movement
		4. Construction and Building
		5. Education and Training
		6. Medicine and Health Treatment
		7. Monitoring and Reflection
	7. Wealth and Distribution	1. Accumulation and Mobilization
		2. Social Wealth and Heritage
		3. Wages and Income
		4. Housing and Subsistence
		5. Equity and Inclusion
		6. Redistribution and Apportionment
		7. Monitoring and Reflection
Politics	1. Organization and Governance	1. Legitimacy and Respect
		2. Leadership and Agency
		3. Planning and Vision
		4. Administration and Bureaucracy
		5. Authority and Sovereignty
		6. Transparency and Clarity
		7. Monitoring and Reflection
Defined as the practices,	2. Law and Justice	1. Rights and Rules
discourses and material		2. Order and Civility
expressions associated with		3. Obligations and Responsibilities
basic issues of social power,		4. Impartiality and Equality

Domains	Perspectives	Aspects
such as organization, authorization and legitimation.		5. Fairness and Prudence
		6. Judgement and Penalty
		7. Monitoring and Reflection
	3. Communication and Critique	1. Interchange and Expression
		2. News and Information
		3. Accessibility and Openness
		4. Opinion and Analysis
		5. Dissent and Protest
		6. Privacy and Respect
		7. Monitoring and Reflection
	4. Representation and Negotiation	1. Agency and Advocacy
		2. Participation and Inclusion
		3. Democracy and Liberty
		4. Access and Consultation
		5. Civility and Comity
		6. Contestation and Standing
		7. Monitoring and Reflection
	5. Security and Accord	1. Human Security and Defence
		2. Safety and Support
		3. Personal and Domestic Security
		4. Protection and Shelter
		5. Refuge and Sanctuary
		6. Insurance and Assurance
		7. Monitoring and Reflection
	6. Dialogue and Reconciliation	1. Process and Recognition
		2. Truth and Verity
		3. Mediation and Intercession
		4. Trust and Faith
		5. Remembrance and Redemption
		6. Reception and Hospitality
		7. Monitoring and Evaluation
	7. Ethics and Accountability	1. Principles and Protocols
		2. Obligation and Responsibility
		3. Integrity and Virtue
		4. Observance and Visibility
		5. Prescription and Contention
		6. Acquittal and Consequence
		7. Monitoring and Reflection
Culture	1. Identity and Engagement	1. Diversity and Difference
		2. Belonging and Community
		3. Ethnicity and Language
		4. Religion and Faith
		5. Friendship and Affinity
		6. Home and Place
		7. Monitoring and Reflection

(Continued)

TABLE 3.2 (Continued)

Domains	Perspectives	Aspects
Defined as the practices, discourses and material expressions, which, over time, express continuities and discontinuities of social meaning	2. Creativity and Recreation	1. Aesthetics and Design 2. Performance and Representation 3. Innovation and Adaptation 4. Celebrations and Festivals 5. Sport and Play 6. Leisure and Relaxation 7. Monitoring and Reflection
	3. Memory and Projection	1. Tradition and Authenticity 2. Heritage and Inheritance 3. History and Records 4. Indigeneity and Custom 5. Imagination and Hope 6. Inspiration and Vision 7. Monitoring and Reflection
	4. Belief and Meaning	1. Knowledge and Interpretation 2. Ideas and Ideologies 3. Reason and Rationalization 4. Religiosity and Spirituality 5. Rituals and Symbols 6. Emotions and Passions 7. Monitoring and Reflection
	5. Gender and Generations	1. Equality and Respect 2. Sexuality and Desire 3. Family and Kinship 4. Birth and Babyhood 5. Childhood and Youth 6. Mortality and Care 7. Monitoring and Reflection
	6. Enquiry and Learning	1. Curiosity and Discovery 2. Deliberation and Debate 3. Research and Application 4. Teaching and Training 5. Writing and Codification 6. Meditation and Reflexivity 7. Monitoring and Reflection
	7. Well-being and Health	1. Integrity and Autonomy 2. Bodies and Corporeal Knowledge 3. Mental Health and Pleasure 4. Care and Comfort 5. Inclusion and Participation 6. Cuisine and Emotional Nourishment 7. Monitoring and Reflection

CASE STUDY: VALLETTA AND PAOLA, MALTA

Valletta, Malta's capital city, is currently preparing for the European Capital of Culture 2018. It is a World Heritage City, famous for its imposing fortifications and holding out against the Great Siege of 1565. The built form of the city is the outcome of the dominance of European powers in the Mediterranean from the late medieval period. Although blitzed during the Second Siege in World War II, the city today thrives as a seat of government and administrative hub, a principal tourist venue and a cultural centre. Development in the postcolonial period has been marked by the shift from an imperially framed economy to a fragile local microeconomy. This is felt also in the Paola Township on the opposite side of the Grand Harbour, which remains predominantly industrial. Paola was affected significantly as a result of the departure of the British Mediterranean Fleet and the slow closure of its shipbuilding and dockyard. Paola, also an area important for its cultural assets predominantly the World Heritage Site of Hal Saflieni Hypogeum and the Kordin III Temples, is also seeking to regenerate a locally sustainable economy to create a better quality of life for its citizens. Here the domains of culture and economics are seen as bound up with each other.

In Valletta, flagship projects have been developed under the HERO (Heritage as an Opportunity) Action Plan (2010–15). The projects target vital areas around the Marsamxett quarters through a Cultural Heritage Integrated Management Plan (CHIMP) and consider culture and heritage as the main drivers for the area. The Action Plan for Valletta is based on a character appraisal and is considered a new approach through surgical interventions in the planning policies within the Valletta Local Plan. One of these projects is Cultural Urban Landscapes for Sustainable Tourism, which has been partly financed by the European Union through the European Regional Development Fund. The project involves revamping the dilapidated and abandoned Peacock Gardens into a recreational area, a *bel vedere*, a tourist hub and a World Heritage City Interpretation Centre. The project was delayed by new archaeological discoveries – namely a series of casemates wall segments, a World War I battery and a fortification wall – but over time will showcase the cultural heritage of the city and assist tourists in discovering the city's history through an interpretation centre. It will also be act as a gateway to the city from the west side and Marsamxett Harbour ferry landing.

Paola's 'Sustainable Planning through Urban Regeneration' projects have been developed as an integrated programme through the REPAIR Action Plan (2010–15). The Action Plan follows four main themes to spur sustainable development: (1) conservation, (2) tourism and recreation, (3) energy and waste and (4) local jobs for local people. In delivering these principles tangible projects were designed along the principle north–south axis of the town.

Based on a green corridor and heritage route the project targets the restoration and adaptive reuse of heritage assets and regeneration of gardens and public spaces. The corridor connects two of the most significant critical heritage systems: the Corradino Fortification Lines and the Hal-Saflieni Hypogeum.

The first phase of the Corradino Prison Museum was finished in October 2013, and works are underway on the interpretation section of the project. The Corradino Royal Navy Prison has been restored, and the east and central wings are being adapted to a museum. The project focused on the external and internal restoration of the wings, the chapel and central officers' quarters, the gatehouse and, most important, the south wing. In the south wing a crucial restoration project of a double roof with a Victorian ventilation system has been restored to guarantee energy efficiency and maintain microclimatic conditions. This project will enhance the master plan for the site, based on a triple-helix system with its current use as sports complex enhanced, a hostel developed and the museum developed to attract niche tourism to the area of Paola. In all these projects there exists evidence of multi-domain sensitivity.

Both action plans were developed with the support of the respective local councils but essentially with the intervention of the Urban Local Support Group (ULSG). The ULSG was significant in empowering people and to motivate citizens to participate in planning. The ULSG was a prerogative of the URBACT programme, but in Paola it was significant in creating an awareness that activated the founding of an NGO to promote local heritage, the Paola Heritage Foundation. The promotion of these projects was only possible through strong political will at the local council level, supported by European Union funding. In both cases the drive to encourage the implementation of the projects was only possible through a strong decentralized administration. What assisted the councils in Valletta and Paola was also the possibility to tap funding necessary to drive and complete the projects. In the compilation of the action plans the funding has supported integrated and long-term planning with heritage and culture as a fulcrum for sustainable conservation and development. The experience of these local council – driven projects supports the principle of subsidiarity and decentralization in a state where councils are still relatively young in the realm of city management. Moreover, the public participation in both projects shows keen interest of the local citizens to support local projects and democratization in planning and design is vital in ensuring wide recognition.

The assessment in Figure 3.3 was done in 2013 just for the domain of culture. Malcolm Borg and his team conducted cultural assessments using the *Circles of Sustainability* method for Valleta and Paola, as well as Conspicua, Floriana, Senglea, and Vittoriosa. The assessment for Valleta drew on background research, statistics and public data, as well as nearly 200 interviews within the areas earmarked for the Hero Valletta Action Plan. The interviews give a sense of the cultural strength of the city. Eighty of those adults interviewed attended and were attracted to local cultural activities and events, even when they were younger. Most of those interviewed were active within the Parishes of St Augustine's Church or St Dominic's Church, with eighty-eight interviewees directly involved with the preparation of the feasts or active in the church feast organizing groups. Out of those responding to the survey, 138 interviewees felt pride in contributing to the neighbourhood and 175 were proud to live within the area or neighbourhoods. More than 148 interviewees aspired to see more activities and would like to see more cultural events held within their location. These according to those interviewed should be aimed at families and the younger generation. More than 173 felt that cultural activities made their community feel closer. Many were aware of the increase of tourists within the locality, and 173 interviewees were happy to have more people visit these locations. The vast majority of interviewees knew that Valletta was a World Heritage City and were proud of it.

As shown by Figure 3.3 the weakness of Malta's capital city occurs in the area of education, and this has repercussions for losing young people

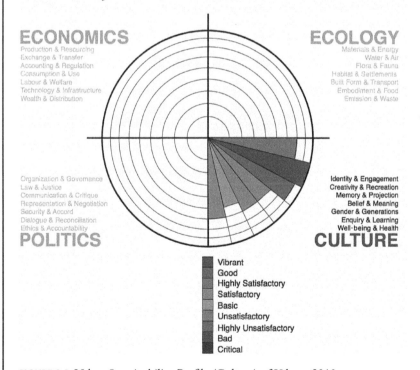

FIGURE 3.3 Urban Sustainability Profile (Culture) of Valetta, 2013

overseas, attracted by universities in Europe, North America and Australia. It also affects the flexibility, skill levels and sustainability of the workforce. For example for all of its strengths, Malta remains amongst the lowest-ranked member states of the European Union in some key areas of research and development. In 2010, Malta had 3.3 researchers (full-time equivalent) per thousand labour force compared to a European Union average of 6.5. Only four Member States had lower values. Malta has the lowest public expenditure on research and development as a percentage of gross domestic product in the European Union (0.25 per cent compared to an EU average of 0.75 per cent in 2010), with more than 80 per cent of all business enterprise expenditure on research and development is spent by foreign-owned companies. All this adds up to the importance of cultural questions in considering economic sustainability, as well as the overall sustainability of a city.

Notes

1 Modern usefulness does not sit alone, nor is it unproblematic. We recognize that the demarcation of these domains as separated spheres of life is only possible from an abstracted epistemological standpoint, usually associated with the dominance of the modern.
2 'The global expansion and power of capitalism are now bound up with its capacity to organize cultures of circulation' (Puma & Lee 2004, p. 9).
3 One of the earliest statements was Costanza's (1989). See also Daly (1999).
4 Whereas Weaver and Jordan (2008), advocates of Integrated Sustainability Assessment, argue explicitly for the embedding of such rules in the assessment, we contend that the disembedding of the category of the social makes it difficult to achieve such ends.
5 The environmental political theory literature justifies in detail the case for seeing sustainability and sustainable development in normative rather than technical terms (e.g. see Barry & Eckersley 2005).
6 The notion of essentially contested concepts comes from Walter Gallie (1955).
7 Politics, ecology and economics do not appear in Raymond Williams's (1976) list. The key to understanding why he leaves out politics, economics and ecology is that he is living in a period in which, already, the vocabulary has separated out the domain of the cultural, and his book is presented as a vocabulary of cultural concepts.
8 Charles Taylor provides a good summation of this process: 'perhaps the first big shift wrought by this new idea of order, both in theory and in social imaginary, consists of coming to see our society as an "economy", an interlocking set of activities of production, exchange and consumption, which form a system with its own laws and its own dynamic. Instead of being merely the management, by those in authority, of the resources we collectively need, in household or state, the "economic" now defines a way in which we are linked together, a sphere of co-existence which could in principle suffice to itself, if only order and conflict didn't threaten. Conceiving of the economy as a system is an achievement of eighteenth-century theory, with the Physiocrats and Adam Smith' (2007, p. 181).

9 The philosophical history of the centre point of the circle is extraordinarily rich and, for our purposes, provides a way of qualifying the modern tendency to treat geometrical ordering as a simple technical exercise. For classical Greek philosopher from Euclid to Aristotle a point is both the most abstract and the particular of entities. The tenth-century Persian mathematician Al-Nairzi, who wrote commentaries on Euclid and Ptolemy, responded that '[i]f any one seeks to know the essence of a point, a thing more single than a line, let him, in the sensible world, think of the centre of the universe and the poles' (cited in Heath 1956 p. 157). For the thirteenth-century Andalusian Sufi writer, Ibn Arabi, the centre point of a circle is the point of 'necessary being' while the circumference is the circle of 'possible' or contingent existence. 'The "possible" is the space between the point of the real and the circumference' (cited in Yousef 2008, p. 120).

10 'There is nothing more tentative, nothing more empirical (superficially at least) than the process of establishing an order among things' (Foucault 1970, p. xix).

References

Aristotle 1962, *The Politics*, Penguin, Harmondsworth.

Barry, John & Eckersley, Robin (eds) 2005, *The State and the Ecological Crisis*, MIT Press, Cambridge.

Costanza, R. 1989, 'What is Ecological Economics?' *Ecological Economics*, vol. 1, no. 1, pp. 1–7.

Daly, Herman 1999, *Ecological Economics and the Ecology of Economics*, Edward Elgar, Cheltenham.

Foucault, Michel 1970, *The Order of Things: An Archeology of the Human Sciences*, Tavistock, London.

Gallie, Walter 1955, 'Essentially Contested Concepts', *Proceedings of the Aristotelian Society*, vol. 56, pp. 167–198.

Global Reporting Initiative 2013, viewed 26 December 2013, <www.globalreporting.org/reporting/g4/Pages/default.aspx>.

Gross National Happiness 2012, viewed 18 January 2012, <www.grossnationalhappiness.com/>.

Heath, Thomas L. 1956, *Accompanying Euclid, the Thirteen Books of the Elements*, Dover Publications, Mineola.

Heidegger, Martin 1977, *The Question Concerning Technology*, Harper & Rowe, New York.

Hendriques, Adrian and Richardson, Julie (eds) 2004, *The Triple Bottom Line: Does it all add Up?* Earthscan, London.

Lloyd, G.E.R. 2012, *Being, Humanity and Understanding*, Oxford University Press, Oxford.

Max-Neef, Manfred A. 1991, *Human Scale Development: Conception, Application and Further Reflections*, Apex Press, New York.

Nussbaum, Martha C. 2011, *Creating Capabilities: The Human Development Approach*, Harvard University Press, Cambridge.

Puma, Edward Li T. & Lee, Benjamin 2004, *Financial Derivatives and the Globalization of Risk*, Duke University Press, Durham.

Roy, T. 1999, '"Polis" and "Oikos" in Classical Athens', *Greece and Rome*, vol. 49, no. 1, pp. 1–18.

Scerri, Andy & James, Paul 2010, 'Accounting for Sustainability: Combining Qualitative and Quantitative Research in Developing 'Indicators' of Sustainability', *International Journal of Social Research Methodology*, vol. 13, no. 1, pp. 41–53.

Taylor, Charles 2007, *A Secular Age*, Harvard University Press, Cambridge.

UN–Habitat 2012, last viewed 25 January 2012, <www.unhabitat.org/categories.asp?catid=671&q=Principles>.

Weaver, Paul & Jordan, Andrew 2008, 'What Roles are there for Sustainability Assessment in the Policy Process', *International Journal of Innovation and Sustainable Development*, vol. 3, no. 1–2, pp. 9–32.

Williams, Raymond 1976, *Keywords: A Vocabulary of Culture and Society*, Fontana and Croom Helm, Glasgow.

Yousef, Mohamed Haj 2008, *Ibn Arabi: Time and Cosmology*, Routledge, Abington.

4

SOCIAL MAPPING

Social mapping at its most complex involves working interpretatively across different layers of analysis. At the most basic level, good social mapping involves extensive
empirical work. This can take the form of collecting massive data sets, interviewing
selected individuals or just walking around a city and recording images, watch-
ing people and taking field notes as locals move through changing physical and
symbolic spaces. Such social mapping in the first instance will always be geared
towards the central focus of a given project. These maps are configured in relation
to the *social domains* and/or *themes* relevant to the project. For example, a project on
heritage might start with the *social domain* of culture, focusing on the subdomain of
memory and projection (see Figure 0.1) and mapping this against different ideological expressions of inclusion/exclusion or difference/identity. These could be then
interpreted in terms of a series of levels of *social analysis* that form the theoretical
apparatus of our methodology (see Table 4.2 on levels of analysis).

This method allows, for example, broader implications to be drawn out about
social formations at work in how people define their lifeworlds. Like constructing a
building, the approach does not entail using either every available tool – only those
most directly relevant to the project need to be used. Neither does it entail using
every available level of analysis. However, to avoid the sin of empiricism, it does
mean going significantly beyond just drawing some generalizations from the data
collection, and generating a theory based on unreflexively 'found' patterns – the
grounded theory misapprehension. The 'sin of empiricism' is not that empirical
data are treated as important. Rather, it is that such data are treated as the beginning
and the end of analysis. Data can never be theory or assumption free, and it is better
that we take data and theory together and mutual partners in analysis rather than
uncomfortable strangers.

If the focus of the analysis is on urban sustainability and development the initial
stage is to build up profiles of the different communities and places in the urban

region that will be involved in the project. These profiles can be developed and tested through bringing in different levels of analysis. If the focus is a theme or issue – for example climate change adaptation (see Chapter 10) – then a profile can equally be developed that gets beyond factorial analysis by testing empirical generalizations about that data. This is done by drawing on a range of sources through a variety of strategies, all within an integrated framework that allows on-the-ground detail to be mapped and assessed across increasingly abstracted modes of analysis. Engaged Theory moves from the empirical to the abstract and back again in a constant journey of return – testing each level of analysis against other levels (Table 4.2).

As an aside it needs to be said that, in contradistinction to Grounded Theory, this back-and-forth movement between the concrete and the abstract does not begin with the empirical. In the words of one commentator, '[b]ecause grounded theory focuses on the generation of theory that is grounded in data, it begins with emersion in data, using inductive logic. That is, it begins with data collection and generates theory out of the data' (Oktay 2012, p. 17). By comparison, Engaged Theory does not fetishize empirical data collection as the ground of good theory or act as if there is the possibility of pre-theoretical access to the 'real world'. Insofar as contemporary researchers we were all once children educated through *modern* education systems, and given that we were born into layers of ideologies, imaginaries and ontologies of meaning – all informed by contested theoretical debate – we are always already theoretically informed. Why do we think that classes or nation-states exist in the world? Why do we think of ourselves as 'having' an unconscious? Why do we talk of a domain called 'the economy'? It is because these abstracted or theoretical categories are lived realities, already part of what has made us who we are.

Even the idea that there are facts in the world is a theoretical presupposition based on a modern epistemology. Social mapping, the process used here as part of the Engaged Theory approach, maps and analyses empirical patterns, but in doing so it recognizes that the work of collection and analysing is already theoretically charged. By contrast, Grounded Theory generates its theoretical claims by supposedly entering into a pre-theoretical or theoretically neutral stage – data collection.

In summary, instead of beginning with the empirical in order to develop the methodology, Engaged Theory moves back and forth between more empirical and more abstracted analytical work. Because of the diversity of research projects, we draw upon a flexible toolshed of methods for gathering research material, but these tools are already considered theoretically informed. Researchers and practitioners are most welcome to modify the tools and the levels of analysis as they feel necessary, but they should do so for theoretically informed reasons rather than based on a desire for difference. One of the strengths of keeping a relatively consistent set of tools is that comparative analysis is possible.

At the level of empirical date collection and analysis, the toolshed contains tools that range across the following techniques amongst others:

- Writing *social profiles*, including urban social profiles (see Chapter 7)
- Developing *project profiles*, providing background on a pressing social issue
- Conducting *community conversations*

- Conducting *interviews* and *strategic conversations* with individuals
- Eliciting *personal life profile and stories*
- Eliciting *photographic narratives* or artistic representations
- Distributing a *survey questionnaire* (see Chapter 8)
- Gathering *quantitative data* from official and unofficial sources
- Collecting *policy documents* and contextualizing official discourses
- Facilitating *scenarios projection* forums (see Chapter 11)

The key with using these different tools is knowing which tool is appropriate for what job under what circumstances. When might an in-depth interview be more meaningful than a generating survey data? This complicated question needs to be left to later discussion.

Researching social and project profiles

Researching a locale or city, a community or a person, entails some form of social mapping. For example, a community profile is used to develop a sense of the larger composition of the individuals and communities in a locale. This includes finding out when and how a given community or group of communities came to be. It encompasses understanding the impact of different formative events and processes on the locale, including both local and global processes. Social profiles can be singular essays or developed over time as a series of interconnected thematic essays.

Individual life profiles

A life profile in the way that we use the term, unlike an oral history or a biography, is more directed in that it is organized around a central theme. At the same time it is more open textured, leaving room for more dynamically contextualized stories of the individual and for substantial passages of their words. Life profiles are centred on themes of *change*, including shifting populations and social movements; *events* including major events that have joined or broken communities such as wars, local celebrations, festivals and catastrophes; *people*, including immigrants, refugees, children, the elderly and indigenous communities; and *places* incorporating social clusters and geographic boundaries; institutions and clubs organizations and civic forums. It should be noted that the examples given here are only intended as indicative, but are not exhaustive elements of life profiles. Life profiles are organized around individual life narratives that provide background and context to contemporary community life. They involve background research, lengthy interviews and collaboration with the subject to ensure that the story is told accurately and with a degree of depth and reflection relating to the lifeworld or social themes. They provide an opportunity to explore the 'lived experience' of changes over time and to capture dynamically contextualized stories of local city and community life. Such life profiles offer a deeply textured understanding of the mapping of person over time, through place, as well as enabling a dynamic history to be built without over-historicizing the project at the expense of the now.

Community life profiles

All kinds of stories already circulate in local communities and some untold stories deserve to go into broader public circulation. These can range from local histories and myths to oral histories to recent experiences and events. We are interested in eliciting local stories that are well crafted and communicated as concisely as possible without losing their narrative richness. Such stories can be collected by community members, by outside researchers, or by a combination of both. They can be collected in the form of written accounts or as digital stories (see the section on photo-narratives later in this chapter) that combine images and audio. In many cases they will touch on more than one of the social themes.

Community life profiles are developed as a snapshot of a local city and of community life as experienced by individuals. They can be researched through interviews of ten to fifteen minutes that follow a schedule of questions relating to the subject's direct experiences of the complexities and dynamics of local urban and community life (relevant to the lifeworld or social themes noted in Table 4.1). The interviewer turns this into a concise narrative that is returned to the subject for amendment and approval. Because this process is not very time-consuming it is possible to collect a large number of such community life profiles over time and they can be used as background data for a wide range of research interests.

Project profiles and urban profiles

Project and urban profiles can also be made up of a series of thematic essays, written over time, but in this case they directly concern different domains and social themes relevant to the chosen project or a particular city. These essays should ideally be more than just a description or plan of the project that is being undertaken by the locale or city. The essays should involve the writer or writers exploring some focused aspect of social history or contemporary social life in relation to the chosen area of the project. Writing thematic essays relevant to the project is a way of providing context for understanding the complexity of the contemporary social issue that the city is taking on as a major point of intervention. A thematic essay could for example directly address one or more of the social domains and/or one or more of the social themes. This might range for example from a focus on the cultural-political implications of the *social theme* of belonging and mobility – perhaps discussed in relation to pressing social issue of refugees or migrants – and then linked back to the domain of ecology, perhaps discussed in relation to place and habitat. A thematic essay might stretch beyond the immediate locale to explore issues in the region, the nation, or globally, relating to the project theme. Thematic essays can present the outcomes of thematic research, and/or they can include elements of creative or lyrical writing on a theme. Urban profiles can also be written in many different ways. A good example is a recent book edited by Ian Shirley and Carol Neill (2013) that presents profiles of cities across the Asia-Pacific. Our approach in developing an urban profile is to use the *Circles of Sustainability* map to orient the way in which the narrative is directed.

Community-based conversations

At least in grounded and close-knit communities it is important early on in project that a community-wide discussion is held, initially working through relevant community leaders and organizations in these places. There is no doubt that such conversations are difficult to manage well, and they tend not work at all in relation to mobile modern locales with weak community ties. Here engaging local organizations becomes even more crucial. Inviting individuals to a public forum is an act of good faith. Community forums provide an opportunity to discuss what form the research might take, to introduce the basic questions, and to outline the research methods in layperson's terms. Depending on the situation and the person, or persons, in dialogue, discussions should be held in local or common languages or with translation back and forth to the language of the researchers. The issues raised in these forums became important background for properly engaging in the 'strategic conversations' with individuals in that community around themes of particular importance to each community (see the next section). One of the important aspects of this research process is to be clear about the relationship with the community and about what the project could and could not offer them. Dialogue what the project is about and how the information would be managed and used should be treated as a negotiation, not a given. If there are higher authorities co-involved in the research, for example an organ of the state, it is important to state explicitly that there was no pressure for communities or community members to participate. At this point the community can decide that the research should not go ahead. If there is a mutual decision to proceed, later community conversations also became an opportunity to gather and record background information as the basis of a brief community profile or general story of that community by way of an introduction to it. Community-based strategic conversations are also an important way of sharing the outcomes of the research allowing it to be reviewed by the communities themselves.

Strategic conversations and interviews

Beyond community-based conversations we use two particular kinds of personal interviews to explore specific topics and themes with relevant people: the first kind of interview is a semi-structured interview as conventionally understood. It is framed by a series of interconnected questions designed to investigate a designated theme. The second kind is called a strategic conversation. It is still based on a set of semi-structured questions, but strategic conversions are developed as dialogical encounters across a longer process than the usual interview.

   Normally an interview occurs in a designated time frame and the process generates a verbatim transcript of questions and answers. By comparison, while a strategic conversation includes an interview stage and begins with a verbatim transcript, it is a more comprehensive process. In a strategic conversation the interviewer is more direct about what material being sought, for what reason and by what method. The interviewer is more engaged, more challenging and more probing. Then, by the last stage of the process – the writing up of the interview – the narrative of the interviewee has either been reworked as a first-person soliloquy, a two-way dialogue or a third-person narrative:

1. A *first-person narrative* has only the interviewee's voice carrying an interconnected narrative. It is a soliloquy in which the person explores various dimensions of a theme or themes.
2. A *two-way dialogue* is the most recognizable of these forms, retaining the structure of an interview with questions and answers.
3. A *third-person narrative* is written by the researcher or researchers as an interpretative essay but contains numerous long quotes from the interviewee to illustrate the interpretative line that is taken around that theme or themes. It can also contain quotes from their writings, other interviews and relevant public documents.

Until the last stage of the writing the process for developing a first-person or third-person narrative is the same:

Step 1. Develop the themes and structure for the interview and relate it to a background methodology. Just like a semi-structured interview, the process begins with a problem, a theme, or an issue to be elucidated by an interviewee who knows something about that theme or themes. However, in developing the terms of the strategic conversation this stage involves more explicit reflection than a normal interview on the relation between the terms of the interview and the underlying approach. For example if the interview were about a particular project in particular place and the interviewers were drawing on the *Circles of Sustainability* approach, then questions should be posed across all the domains of the social to include questions that elucidate economic, ecological, political and cultural concerns. If, to take another example, the interview was about a particular concept or ideology, and the interviews were drawing more deeply on the Levels of Analysis approach, then the interviewers should be explicit about what they are doing and should bring to the interview a clear schedule of questions linked to the overall methodology

Step 2. Choose the interviewees. With strategic conversations considerable thought needs to go into the choice of people to be interviewed in relation to the nature of the topic. This entails two aspects: first, determining the kind of person relevant to the project and, second, determining the most relevant particular individuals who represent the chosen profile. The interviews thus need to be preceded by background research, determination of the necessary profile of the interviewees, and discussions with others about key people that should be interviewed.

Step 3. Approach the interviewees. In approaching the interviewees they should be given briefing notes before the interview outlining the following: (a) the theme or themes and the schedule of questions that will sit behind the investigation of that theme or themes, (b) the interview method that will be used (notes such as the ones that you are reading now, or some variation, can be used), and (c) the underlying methodology that the researchers will be using. Although it is not always possible, preliminary discussions could be had with the intended interviewees before the interview to go deeper into those three aspects. In such cases the interviewees can play a proactive and strategic role in the discussion of the topic under research. In all cases, our thinking is that an interviewee is an active and knowing subject. There is no pseudo-Freudian attempt to gain spontaneous depth by either surprising an interviewee or by lulling him or her into slips of uncomfortable disclosure. We are seeking knowing reflection and, if possible, reflexivity about their views on the theme.

Step 4. Conduct the interview. The term *strategic conversation* indicates that an active dialogue has taken place in which the interviewers and interviewee have pushed each other, based on some prior understanding of each other's views on the subject. A strategic conversation in this sense goes beyond the usual research interview during which an interviewer faces an unknown or relatively respondent and asks him or her to answer a series of set questions on the designated topic.

Step 5. Transcribe the interview and begin the post-interview stage. After the interview is done, the recording of the interview is transcribed and kept as a record of the moment. The transcript is then edited for grammar, syntax and repetition. At this point the two kinds of narratives take a different course.

First-person narrative. The interviewers rework the transcript to develop a narrative structure that does not depend on the interviewer's questions being explicitly present in the final essay. In other words, the questions are taken out of the transcript, and the transcript is gently edited and rewritten to allow the interviewee's voice to come to the fore. If there are passages in which the interviewers feel that the interviewee can be pushed further then highlighted notes and queries are appended to the text asking the interviewee to fill out more detail or explain with more clarity. Subheadings are used if there are narrative breaks and thematic sections. The redrafted transcript is send back and forth between interviewers and interviewee (using tracked changes) until all parties are satisfied that the first-person narrative is developed, accurate and clear. One of the skills in this process is to create a hybrid outcome of the initial moment and the later reflections. The interviewee needs to be happy that the subtleties of their position have been appropriately expressed, and the interviewers need to be satisfied that both some of the initial energy of the oral form has been retained and that further depth has been achieved by interrogating specific points of contention in written form.

Two-way narrative. This form takes the original transcript but refines the dialogue from both sides, clarifying both the questions and the answers, until both the interviewers and interviewee believe it represents what they were trying to say.

Third-person narrative. The interviewers rework the transcript as a third-person essay with themselves as the interpretative narrators. This takes much more work that the first-person narrative, including additional background research. Long quotes are retained, but they are wrapped in an interpretative gloss that explains, interprets and critically develops the material. This is then sent back to the interviewee to respond to the points of interpretation and analysis. This is then incorporated into the penultimate draft. Thus, like the first-person narrative form, the redrafted transcript is send back and forth between interviewers and interviewee (using tracked changes) until all parties are satisfied that the third-person narrative is developed, accurate and clear. The difference here is that the interviewers as the 'authors' of the third-person narrative have ultimate responsibility for the interpretation and, as such, can take the penultimate draft and write into it again without taking it back to the interviewee for final approval.

Strategic conversations, we suggest, set the conditions for a more nuanced public expression of the interviewee's standpoint than the usual transcribed thirty minutes of semi-structured interviewing. These narratives lose something of the spontaneity of the initial moment, but they gain much in depth and acuity, becoming hybrid oral-written narratives that have been interrogated over a series of stages.

Interviews and strategic conversations are always used in conjunction with other forms of data collection. For example, sometimes they are used to capture deeper and more nuanced information about topics that are included in the Social Sustainability Questionnaire and sometimes to get a deep understanding of an issue in question that begins with library research.

Photo-narratives

There are two forms of photo-narratives. The first is where the researcher takes an interconnected series of photos of a community, and brings them together into an essay with an explanatory text. Another way draws community participants further into the project by using photography as tool for interviewing. The approach that will be used is known is reflexive photography or photo-narration. In this approach, community participant observers are given a camera and invited to take photographs of people, places and things in their communities in relation to a particular theme. Reflexive photography assumes that community members possess a great deal of inside knowledge about the communities to which they belong. Community participant observers will also be invited to supplement their photos with meaningful photographs from their own collections as well as other personal artefacts that they believe expresses something about their community. They will also be given a mini photo album and will be asked to arrange their photos and to think about the connections between them. The purpose of this is to encourage the community researchers to begin to construct reflexively meaningful narratives about the places and events depicted in the photos. Reflexive photography supplements one of the other research tools – *interviews* and *strategic conversations*.

Social life questionnaire

We have developed a questionnaire that is used as a quantitative indicator drawing on some of domain themes and social themes of the project. In other words, the questions in the survey are mapped against the four domains of the Circles of Social Life (see Figure 0.1). The questions are written in such a way as to allow for comparative analysis across the different places of research. The Social Life Questionnaire has been used in many countries around the world with a common core set of questions, and with modular additions developed for the key determined issue in each locale (see Chapter 8 for an extended treatment of this tool). The questionnaire lends itself to being extended with context-specific variables. For example when working in Timor Leste on livelihoods, we developed a module of additional questions on food production and food security.

Quantitative data and policy documents

Gathering qualitative date includes gathering a whole series of objective indicators that inform our interpretive work. Ideally, the indicators would go back as far as possible. Carrying through the themes of the project, these will include population and demographic data, rates of mortality, fertility rates, incidence of illness, pollution levels and measures of arts and economic activities of the communities involved in the project.

Gathering policy documents is also an important part of this process. Communities and cities are in part constituted via official documents and reports, including those put out by civic and professional organizations and representative bodies. These might include tourist brochures and pamphlets, information regarding cultural activities and events in the communities, business planning documents, health reports and information and the like. Official discourse might also include official mappings of community against which our own social mappings can be compared.

Defining social themes

The *Circles of Sustainability* approach and all of its empirically based methods for collecting and analysing data, including the social mapping methods just discussed, provide us with a framework for judging the quality of sustainability across the four domains. However, this does not provide us with a way of judging what is ethically good. Beyond the four-by-seven ethical propositions for a good sustainable city discussed in the first chapter, and instead of setting forth a series of standalone ethical principles, we have chosen instead to focus on a number of social themes that require ethical negotiation. At the heart of this set of themes is the tension between sustainability and change. Just as sustainability, the endurance of a particular practice or system, is not automatically a good thing, neither is change. Even 'progress', the concept that is most often reached for as a signifier of the good, needs to be fundamentally questioned. As do all of our dominant ideological claims about what it good.

For example over the last couple of decades, the tension between accumulation and distribution has, across most of the globe, been relatively 'settled', at least in mainstream thinking, with the dominant ideological standpoint today emphasizing the primacy of accumulation. Distribution has come to be a subordinate or secondary consideration. Although it is more than an inconsequential afterthought, distribution of wealth has become reduced to an amelioration of excess inequality – not a basic consideration of social life to be pondered in its own right. Our argument is that positive sustainability requires fundamental and deliberative negotiation of questions of discontinuity and continuity in how this basic question of the relationship between accumulation and wealth is organized and lived.

Seven social themes have been chosen as sufficient to give a sense of the complexity of the fundamental issues that affect the human condition. These are themes that, in effect, are constant issues in social life, even across different social formations. Although there is a tendency to valorize one side or other of the valencies, in the following thematic couplets they are presented as themes in tension:

1. Accumulation/Distribution (currently a dominant theme of contention in the domain of economics)
2. Security/Risk
3. Needs/Limits (currently a dominant theme of contention in the domain of ecology)
4. Autonomy/Obligation
5. Participation/Authority (currently a dominant theme of contention in the domain of politics)
6. Inclusion/Exclusion
7. Difference/Identity (currently a dominant theme of contention in the domain of culture)

Although for the present purposes the seven social themes listed are minimally sufficient for highlighting the complexity of social sustainability the list could be extended to include many others. The number of social themes contested across human history is open-ended. Other social themes that we could have chosen to focus on include obligations/rights, well-being/adversity, mobility/belonging, freedom/obligation, autonomy/subjection, engagement/mediation, equality/difference, play/order, and comedy/tragedy, order/serendipity and so on.

Each of these Janus-faced themes is embedded in existing debates that draw broadly from existing ethical traditions.[1] The concepts contained within the pairs are in tension, but they are not opposites. As set out in the list, the first named theme in each couplet is placed first because, at least in Western democracies, that first-named theme represents an ideologically assumed virtue. However, even within the various classical traditions ranging from socialism to liberalism and from

TABLE 4.1 Social Themes in Relation to Domains and Dominant Ideologies

Social themes	Social themes in relation to dominance within each domain	Social themes in relation to dominant ideological contestations (global and national) (see Chapter 5)
1. Accumulation/ distribution	**Economy**	Neo-liberal or market globalism and economic nationalism vs. justice globalism
2. Security/risk		Security globalism (and imperial globalism) and security nationalism vs. justice globalism
3. Needs/limits	**Ecology**	Market globalism and market nationalism vs. justice globalism
4. Autonomy/obligation		Market globalism vs. democratic globalism vs. jihadist globalism vs. political nationalism
5. Participation/authority	**Politics**	Market globalism vs. justice globalism and democratic globalism vs. jihadist globalism
6. Inclusion/exclusion		Market globalism vs. justice globalism vs. cultural nationalism
7. Difference/identity	**Culture**	Market globalism vs. justice globalism vs. jihadist globalism vs. cultural nationalism

Note: Distinguishing different domains of the social requires moving across different levels of analysis, but once having defined those domains, for the purpose of a particular project the analysis returns to the empirical task of collecting data about practices and meanings relevant to the project.

Confucianism to Christianity, there is no obvious answer to the question of what constitutes the good. Therefore, the key question is how are these tensions socially negotiated within different settings in order to enhance positive sustainability. Because of constraints of space, we limit ourselves to describing two or three of those social themes and showing how they might work as possible qualitative indicators of social sustainability. It bears repeating, that in each case the central issue is to work through in practices how the associate concepts with such social themes are being (and will be) negotiated.

Participation/authority

Across the tensions inherent in this social theme, participants need to think about how it is that autonomous involvement in sectors of social life is related to the authority structures of the body in question. The assumption here is not that participation is better than authority, or vice versa. Rather, what is being brought into question is the degree to which people participating actively and autonomously in social life can do so in a meaningful way, and how they do so meaningfully in relation to the forms of authority exercised within their community, city or organization. Participation without negotiated authority – however autonomously that participation is framed and presented – is frustrating, time-consuming and, in the end, counterproductive. One of the current problems with democracy is that the rhetorical emphasis on participation is only enacted in faux consultation processes or limited procedural practices such as elections. The participatory engaged democracy of a city such as Porto Alegre through what they call 'participatory budgeting' (see the case study in Chapter 6) is still only a very partial process even in the city in which it was born.

Difference/identity

Across this tension, participants are called on to think about how it is that notions of difference are related to social identity. The aim here is to elicit an understanding of how well communities, cities or organizations cope with difference while being mindful of the fact that too much emphasis on difference can lead to fragmentation and dissolution of the strengths of a life in common. If a social identity is too strong, or too strongly enforced, this can give rise to an unsustainable and unjust xenophobia. On the other hand, if difference and diversity within a given body are given too much emphasis, then it may be weakened in political situations requiring a common voice, such as in negotiations over funding matters. For example, in terms of the political domain, this question is aimed at eliciting how power relations within the community might support a strong sense of identity that, as such, includes a capacity for coping with change. The key here is not how much diversity and how much commonality, but how the play of difference and identity is negotiated.

Inclusion/exclusion

Typically in contemporary debates, social inclusion is treated as a social good to be achieved. Calls for inclusion come thick and fast. Exclusion is said to be necessarily bad thing, one to be avoided at all costs. The issue that this very common conception of the problem elides is that in certain circumstance, exclusion leads to a social good or that it always necessary for good inclusion. For example, in places where harassment is common or social difference is threatening, there may legitimately be a need to exclude 'outsiders' from certain activities or places – for example excluding other than Moslem women from a public swimming pool on Thursday afternoons. Sometimes even the open and mobile presence of others in a zone of difference – for example a customary sacred site – renders that site cultural and politically dead.

A second, and more abstract, point is that concentrating on overcoming questions of exclusion tends to leave issues of exploitation unaddressed. For example unless we take seriously the forms of poverty specific to being marginalized under contemporary conditions of globalization, exclusion is seen to have no perpetrator. Seen in this way, exclusion or exploited inclusion 'is the form that poverty develops in conditions where the realization of profit occurs through organizing economic

TABLE 4.2 Levels of the Social in Relation to Levels of Theoretical Analysis

Levels of the social	DOING	ACTING	RELATING	BEING
Levels of analysis	I. Empirical	II. Conjunctural	III. Integrational	VI. Categorical
		Increasing epistemological abstraction of the standpoint of analysis		
Objects of analysis				
I Levels of social **MEANING**	Instances and patterns of social Ideas	Patterns of social Ideologies	Patterns of social Imaginaries	Patterns of social Ontologies
II Levels of social **RELATIONS**	Instances and patterns of social Activity	Patterns of social Practice	Patterns of social Integration	Categories of social Being
	E.g. • Institutions • Organizations • Fields • Disciplines • Regimes	E.g. • Production • Exchange • Communication • Organization • Enquiry	E.g. • Accumul./Distribution • Needs/Limits • Identity/Difference • Autonomy/Authority • Inclusion/Exclusion	E.g. • Temporality • Spatiality • Embodiment • Performativity • Epistemology
III Levels of social **FORMATION**	Domains of social Activity	Modes of social Practice	Modes of social Integration	Modes of social Being
	E.g. • Ecological • Economic • Political • Cultural	E.g. • Techno-scientism • Capitalism • Bureaucratism • Mediatism	E.g. • Face-to-face • Object-extended • Agency-extended • Disembodied	E.g. • Customary • Traditional • Modern • Postmodern
		Increasing ontological abstraction as a dominant formation		

operations in [globalizing] networks'. It represents the 'exploitation of the immobile by the mobile' and therefore, suggests that a city, community, or organization act to tie-down the perpetrators of such exclusion-inclusion exploitation (Boltanski & Chiapello 2005, pp. 354–5). The point is that only by coming to grips with how – on what terms and who – a city, a community or an organization includes *and* excludes some and not others that sustainable development in its most meaningful sense can be implemented.

Table 4.2 is a summary of the entire method of Engaged Theory. It provides a map of all the secrets of this book. The approach thus begins by presuming the importance of a first-order analytical abstraction, here called *empirical analysis*. It entails drawing out and generalizing from on-the-ground, detailed descriptions of what people do across time and in places. This does not mean accepting that what the person in the street says is an adequate explanation of a particular phenomenon. However, it does take such descriptions seriously as expressive of their experience of the world.

All social theories, whether they acknowledge it or not, are dependent on such a process of first-order abstraction. This first level either involves generating empirical description based on observation, experience, recording or experiment – in other words, abstracting evidence from that which exists or occurs in the world – or it involves drawing on the empirical research of others. The first level of analytical abstraction involves an ordering of 'things in the world', usually before any kind of further analysis is applied to those 'things'. Positing four domains of social life – ecology, economy, politics and culture – is simply one way of ordering the world. It is no more than a heuristic device, but it is one that is both categorically consistent and grounded in analysis of how *modern* categories can best be deployed to describe how, across different times and places, we as humans order our worlds.

From this often taken-for-granted level, many approaches work towards a second-order abstraction, a method of some kind for ordering and making sense of that empirical material. At the very least they occasionally move to an unacknowledged second level either to explain or rationalize the first. As we move to this more abstract level of analysis we remain agnostic about how this is done. The steps of analysis listed below are just one possible way and have both a hermeneutic dimension (meaning focused) and structural dimension (pattern focused).

The second level of analysis, *conjunctural* analysis, involves identifying and more importantly examining the intersection (the conjunctures) of various patterns of practice and meaning. Here we draw on established sociological, anthropological and political categories of analysis such as production, exchange, communication, organization and enquiry. At this level of analysis it makes sense to map ideological patterns (see Chapter 5 for a discussion of the various ideologies of globalization). Ideologies of exchange for example include consumerism, the assumption that commodity consumption is good and drives progress. One of the dominant contemporary ideological assumptions of communication, for example, is that faster, more transparent and more immediate connectivity is good and makes life better. Any limits to communication are thus bad.

The third level of entry into discussing the complexity of social relations, *integrational analysis*, examines the intersecting modes of social integration and differentiation. These different modes of integration are expressed here in terms of different ways of relating to and distinguishing oneself from others – from face-to-face relations to relations of disembodied extension such as mediated by communications technologies. Here we see a break with the dominant emphases of classical social theory and a movement towards a post-classical sensibility. In relation to the nation-state, for example, we can ask how it is possible to explain a phenomenon that, at least in its modern variant, subjectively explains itself by reference to face-to-face metaphors of blood and place – ties of genealogy, kinship and ethnicity – when the objective 'reality' of all nation states is that they are disembodied communities of abstracted strangers who will never meet. In relation to globalization, we can distinguish between different kinds of global connection from the embodied movement of people to the disembodied interchange of electronic images and text. What we can also do is distinguish dominant social imaginaries.

Finally, the most abstract level of analysis to be employed here is what might be called categorical analysis. This level of enquiry is based on an exploration of the ontological categories such as temporality and spatiality. Here we are interested in modes of being and the dominant forms that they take in different social formations. If the previous level of analysis emphasizes the different modes through which people live their commonalities with or differences from others through such categories as blood, soil and history, at the level of categorical analysis those same categories are examined through more abstract analytical lenses. Blood, soil, history, ritual and knowledge are thus treated as phenomenal expressions of different grounding forms of life: respectively, embodiment, spatiality, temporality, performativity and epistemology.

At this level, generalizations can be made about the dominant modes of categorization in a social formation or in its fields of practice and discourse. It is only at this level that it makes sense to generalize across modes of being and to talk of ontological formations, societies as formed in the uneven dominance of formations of tribalism, traditionalism, modernism or postmodernism.

Defining ontological formations

In the first chapter we defined different forms of settlement in terms of spatial distance and geographical configuration – urban to rural. However, these ways of thinking about locales need to be complemented by deeper layers of analysis. Unlike the Actor Network Theory for example which emphasizes networks of spatially extended relations as its basic category of analysis, Engaged Theory works across various levels. If we left our earlier description of the spatial-extension understanding of urban to remote communities without further development, it would also remain a flat understanding of spatiality. Such analysis needs to be accompanied by recognition of the possibility of the changing and layered nature of spatiality across all kinds of locales. In other words, beyond the question of the extension of social relations across space, there is also the question of how that space is lived. This includes the various *forms* of spatiality that constitute how one inhabits that space: the *lifeforms*. Here briefly we define some terms that are used loosely in the literature to distinguish different modes of living. As a shorthand designation, ontologically different dominant patterns of living are distinguished here as different ontological formations: the customary, the traditional, the modern and the postmodern (see Table 4.3).

Concepts such as 'the modern' or seemingly innocuous adjectives such as 'traditional' pass very easily into narratives of development. With the exception of 'the customary' – including 'the tribal', which is usually retranslated and hidden away under the heading of 'the indigenous' or the 'traditional' or is put in inverted commas – such categorizations tend sneak into many commentaries without definition or comment.

There is a profound danger in leaving this complicated area as ill-defined or subject to implied reference. All too often, academic and popular narratives carry

TABLE 4.3 Ontological Formations in Relation to Dominant Imaginaries

Ontological formations	Conjunctural formations	Imaginaries
Customary	• Tribal, hunter-gatherer • Reciprocal exchange • Peasant based, etc.	Mythological imaginaries • The Yolgnu story of kinship • The Trobriand story of origins, etc.
Traditional	• Slaveholding • Feudalism • Patrimonialism, etc.	Cosmological imaginaries • The Christian unfolding • The Islamic *Umma*, etc.
Modern	• Capitalism • Communism • Mediatism, etc.	Generalizing imaginaries • The national • The global, etc.
Postmodern	• Unbounded techno-scientism • Abstract fiduciary capitalism • Open social media networks, etc.	Relativizing imaginaries • Circuits of relativized meaning • A post-human condition, etc.

a taken-for-granted conception of 'the modern'. The modern is counterposed against other ways of life that are defined in the negative as 'the pre-modern'. In other words, those persons living as members of pre-modern communities do not have their dominant formations named except in the negative or in relation to the higher order held in place by the prefix *pre–*. By inference, pre-moderns become those who are on an inevitable or anticipated civilizational climb. They are defined as peoples but are treated as those who are yet come to a modern realization of their past identities and future potentialities. The political implications here are so important that we need to take an uncomfortable dive into the depths of social theory for a few paragraphs.

The usual first step in overcoming this problem is to set up a divide between the traditional and the modern. However, this quickly sets up the need to grapple with an earlier tendency across many fields of enquiry from political science to history and anthropology to set up a Great Divide between these ways of living. Most attempts to overcome bifurcation between the pre-modern and the modern are associated with a second form of blurring. The term *modernity* is often problematically used as an epochal period without recognizing that that can *only* have meaning as an ontological dominant – never as a completely encompassing or homogenizing formation. In the period that many called modernity, customary and traditional relations continue to be important. Witness the way in which jihadist globalism or cultural nationalism are at once modern ideologies and draw on older traditional cosmologies of meaning. When a method treats the modern as all encompassing it makes it impossible to conceive of an alternative projection of a politics, other than as subsumed by dominant modern ideologies such as progress and development. Pierre Manent's recent book *Metamorphoses of the City* provides a good example. The first sentences of his book set the tone for a confusing one-dimensional journey: 'We have been modern now for several centuries. We are modern and we want to be modern. This is the orientation of the entire life of our societies in the West' (2013, p. 1). That is an incredible claim. Who is the 'we' in such a claim? Why is the claim so totalizing? Such an argument makes the West the centre of a project for change. It relegates the rest of the world to a backwater that can only develop by entering the mainstream, and it ignores the ontological complexity of the West itself. It leads to a second untenable presumption: 'The city is that ordering of the human world that makes action possible and meaningful' (2013, p. 4). With such a claim, the nature of politics becomes the projection of the polis, and the domain of politics becomes *the* master category. Just as in this book we are battling against those economists who want to make economics the central consideration, here we must challenge a political philosopher who wants to make politics primary.

What can we retrieve from such an analysis? Not much. But there is a concept central to Manent's approach that is also a key term in our analysis – *projection*. This is the idea that the good change depends on a project, a projection of what is conceived to be possible.

This leads to a possible further complication. Any reflexive politics, any politics which 'recognizes' itself as it enacts its political project, is by definition drawing on a standpoint made possible by a process of lifting knowledge out of customary and traditional ways of understanding. But that is only at one level. And it is only done in relation to one mode of practice – namely enquiry. It is true that the epistemologies of modernism and postmodernism are formed in the analytical abstraction of knowledge. They force a process of constant reflection on the meaning of things rather than providing a relatively stable set of analogical or cosmological answers. Our fundamental point here remains. The 'encompassing' of a social dominant, or what can be described as a constitutive overlaying of different levels-in-dominance, can never be totalizing, however much it tries. This encompassing, including the contemporary dominance of modern life, is always just one level of the social. It may reconstitute prior practices and understandings and substantially dominate them. But, it tends to generate ontological contradictions across the various intersecting levels of social being rather than simply encompass or destroy all that has gone before.

In these terms, the best kind of city is one that draws on different ways of being and seeks to project a creative synthesis. It limits itself in relation to prior ecologies. It recognizes the prior existence of customary and tribal people who once were custodians of the landscape on which the city is built. It respects the architectural forms of its traditional past (and present) as more than touristic honey traps or archaic heritage. For example, when the city of Jerusalem portrays its *Jewish* traditional past in the Tower of David Museum, it needs to recognize that even the museum building itself is part of living history. The Islamic minaret that is now called the Tower of David cannot be ignored or relegated to an irrelevant past when the Ottomans dominated the landscape as an evil external empire.

Engaged Theory employs the concepts of customary, traditional, modern and postmodern as provisionally useful designations of ontological difference. This helps to make sense of the complexity of cities. These modes of social being, from the customary to the postmodern, are defined in terms of how basic categories of the human condition are practiced, understood and lived. This is not to suggest that customary tribalism is the same in the Trobriand Islands and Timor Leste, let alone in Rwanda, Bali or Australia. Nevertheless, the social form called here 'customary tribalism', distinguished as a mode of social being rather than as a distinct social practice, is thus defined by the dominance of particular modalities of space, time, embodiment, performance and knowing.

While much more could be said, the key intention of this brief discussion is simply to begin to evoke different life ways (modes of social being) and different patterns of practice (modes of practice). Continuing the example of the form of knowledge, *traditionalism* (as distinct from customary tribalism) abstracts from embodied nature and reframes the analogical and perceptual practices of tribalism in cosmological terms through entities such as Allah, God, Yahweh and Nature. That is, some kind of Being or set of Beings with a capital B come to connect and make sense of prior forms of more fragmentary mythological thinking and practice. Such cosmologies are extended through metaphorical and political reworkings of kinship or culture-nature such as the Line of David or the Great Chain of Being that are constantly re-embedded within the social whole. In terms of modes of practice (see Tables 4.2 and 4.3), traditionalism tends to be associated with different dominant modes of production (overlaying manual production with techniques that abstract from direct muscle power) of exchange (extended barter and trade relations), of communication (scriptural and written forms of address) of organization (patrimonial role-divided relations) and of enquiry (cosmological framing of nature and culture). Islamic financing systems or even property relations continue to be based on this formation, and it causes tensions as modern real estate law overlays sacred cosmologies of land.

The modern can in the same way be defined as carrying forward prior forms of being, but fundamentally reconstituting (and sometimes turning upside down) those forms in terms of technical-abstracted modes of time, space, embodiment and knowing. For example, time becomes understood and practiced not in terms of cosmological connection but through empty calendrical timelines that can be filled with the details and wonders of history – events made by us. Space is territorialized and marked by abstract lines on maps. Places drawn by our own histories become subordinated, at least in terms of objective power, to cadastral surveys, private property lines and anonymous transport routes. Embodiment becomes an individualized project separated out from others and used to project a choosing self. And knowing becomes an act of analytically dismembering and re-synthesizing information. In practice, modernism is associated with the dominance of capitalist production relations, commodity and finance exchange, print and electronic communication, bureaucratic-rational organization and analytic enquiry, but there is no necessary connection here. This historical connection lurches from periods of thriving to periods of crisis. In all cases it naturalizes itself as the taken-for-granted pathway to 'development'.

CASE STUDY: PORT MORESBY, PAPUA NEW GUINEA

In 1975, Port Moresby became capital of an independent Papua New Guinea. Originally the low-rise administrative centre for an Australian colonial government, it was not until after independence with the departure of most of the Australians that Melanesians became the majority of the city's population. Port Moresby was a tough city to live in then and is still a tough city, particularly for women (see Figure 4.1).

In ontological terms, the subject of this case study, the reality was that over the last generation or so the Melanesian *customary* layer of the city has been slowly relegated to the informal settlements and tribal urban villages, while the overt face of the city has been cut through by new modern developments framed by national plans, modern roads, concrete buildings and modern regimes of power. Across the mid- to late 1970s, traffic accidents

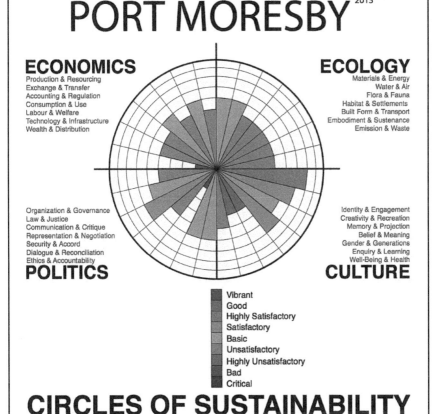

FIGURE 4.1 Urban Sustainability Profile of Port Moresby, 2013

for example accounted for more than half of all traumatic fatalities in Port Moresby General Hospital.

The most obvious visual signify of the *modern* overlay came two decades later with the 1995 Poreporena Freeway project. Amid allegations of abuse about government contracts, it bisected the city, cutting through a mountain from Waigani to the downtown area saving twenty minutes on the road trip between two centres of power – political and commercial. In *modern* geological terms, the freeway cut through an accretionary prism above a late Eocene–Oligocene, North-East dipping subduction system. But it customary terms it also cut through the land of the Motu Koitabu people. Today, nearly three decades after independence, based on a natural gas mining boom the city is going through a new stage of frantic building. Five-star hotels are being constructed, roads are being resurfaced and local urban villages are being modernized.

The demands of rapid uncontrolled migration, and the lack of affordable housing and other infrastructure, has seen the growth and overcrowding of the city's informal settlements. According to the 2000 census, 53,000 of Port Moresby's residents lived in the settlements, a number which has undoubtedly drastically increased since then. UN-Habitat (2012) estimates that 45 per cent of the city's residents live in settlements. Of the city's settlements, twenty are planned and seventy-nine are unplanned, forty-two are located on state land, and thirty-seven are on customary land. The settlements often lack even the most basic amenities and infrastructure such as sanitation, water and electricity. Inadequate government responsiveness to these problems is in part due to the absence of any ministry devoted to dealing with settlement issues, an arrangement dating back to a policy change in 1986 that deregulated housing development.

From a more positive perspective, Port Moresby is a city of small urban communities with *grounded-community* connections stretching to their rural relatives. It is a city of villages, a meeting place of cultures, a tropical capital located on the eastern coast of the beautiful Port Moresby Harbour. Overall, the complexity of Port Moresby is attributable to myriad factors including the Australian colonial legacy, vast wealth inequalities, intense movements of people, high rates of formal unemployment, a variably sustaining informal sector, ongoing destabilization of cultural values and ways of life and rising tensions between ethnic groups.

Port Moresby was established on the traditional lands of two interrelated peoples now known collectively as the Motu-Koita. The growth of housing settlements, infrastructure and industry in the city has led the Motu-Koita to feel acute social marginalization and deep anxiety about losing their cultural identity and land. This provides a point of entry for what can be called *ontological design for sustainability*.

The indigenous villages and the urban settlements of Port Moresby could become the focus of a revitalization of the city. This will require a cultural and political reinvigoration of social engagement in those settlements, and it will be much more than just an infrastructure and technology exercise. Nevertheless, some planning steps can be laid out, all of which presume considerable community representation and negotiation using deliberative democracy processes.

If we begin with basic questions of the relationship between the natural and the social, then paradoxically modern planning with all its legislated restrictions and exclusions is necessary to bring settlement patterns back into more integral relationship with nature. This would require restraints, once in place, that have not been carried forward from indigenous customary cultures in the region concerning, for example, where houses can be built. Regulations to stop any further building on the hills above the city or into the littoral zone along the coastline would be part of this process. The Poreporena-Napa Local Development Plan, 2011, mentions the possibility of not building above the 90-metre contour as 'an identifying element for the city', but an ontological design proposal would something much more radical than an aesthetic design element and it would be less tokenistic.

Except in the immediate downtown area, the sloping hills above, say, fifty metres would need to be returned to a mixture of urban vegetable gardening and open eucalypt woodland forests, with green fingers stretching down into the valleys in ways that allow walking and limited vehicle access. In the valleys, some land should ideally be zoned for food growing, integrated with urban housing estates. Land use would need to be negotiated with the Motu-Koita, the original custodians of the land, and it would require considerable care about how plots of agricultural land were allocated and woodlands were set aside.

Filling in the Fairfax Harbour with landfill projects for yacht clubs and refineries is not ontologically sensitive design. The limits of natural boundaries, including coastlines are important. Indigenous urban villages on the coast such as Hanubada, presently built stretching out over the harbour, would need to be spatially limited so that they do not consume any more waterfront space, but more important, industrial waterfront developments would need to be restricted to allow substantial green ribbons along the foreshore, crossed with public walking paths. Re-establishing mangroves ecosystems along the coastline needs to be a priority, both for practical reasons of responding to possible storm surges with climate change and for re-establishing a deep sense of nature as more than a standing reserve for human exploitation. Achieving even the beginnings of this will require amongst other initiatives, extensive community engagement and support in nurturing the new plantations, policing of the use of mangroves and trees for firewood and installing appropriately scaled and distributed sewerage and waste-water systems to stop the massive outflow that currently goes into the bay.

Turning to the genealogical valence of customary relations, the importance of cultural *identity and engagement* of family, language, tribe and region come to the fore, and what needs to be done is far from easy. The city of villages is associated with tension and violence.

It has become increasingly recognized that Port Moresby is tied by lines of deep genealogical connection back to the rural villages as far away as the Kerema, Mount Hagen or Alatou districts. However, what is to be done about this remains completely perplexing for mainstream planning. The importance of such relations could be brought into the centre of Port Moresby public life by instituting a calendar of events that recognize urban–village ties. Exchange and trading relations between such places could be brought to the fore, including through negotiating spaces in designated open-air, sheltered food markets. There are some important examples currently such as Koki Market, but the construction of modern malls and supermarkets is increasing (with all the increased prices for basic goods that this entails).

Across the city, land needs to be set aside near major transport nodes for farmers' markets that are built into the urban fabric, designed with open stalls, but sheltered from the sun and monsoonal rain under two- to four-storey buildings, offering increased residential density. The mix of street accessibility, open-air ground-floor spaces and increased residential density in otherwise commercial or dead zones, would enhance both the vitality and street security of the city.

Handled badly, this has potentially dangerous consequences for ethnic conflict. Thus, the negotiation of the use of space would need to be linked at the highest level to the symbolic politics of negotiation between different customary groups currently at odds with each other. Although urban villages will tend to remain more culturally homogenous, contestation over these public spaces could be source of positive diversity. This brings us the question of the mythological valence – the relation between social practice and oral expressions of what that practice means, expressed through stories, art, images, building design, festivals, public rituals and street symbolism.

Note

1 The closest philosophical recognition that we have found in relation to this setting out of dialectical themes is in Simone Weil (1952). There are, however, profound differences. She begins with the prior standing of obligations over rights with obligations coming 'from above': they are not treated as in a dialectical relation. Second, she treats obligations as only pertaining to individuals, not to collectives or organizations such as states or cities. Third, she then treats a series of themes as singular in the first instance – order, liberty, obedience and responsibility, among others – before qualifying them in unspecified 'antithetical pairs'.

References

Boltanski, L. & Chiapello, E. 2005, *The New Spirit of Capitalism*, Verso, London.

Manent, Pierre 2013, *Metamorphoses of the City: On the Western Dynamic*, Harvard University Press, Cambridge.

Oktay, Julianne S. 2012, *Grounded Theory*, Oxford University Press, Oxford.

Shirley, Ian & Neill, Carol 2013, *Asian and Pacific Cities: Development Patterns*, Routledge, London.

UN-Habitat 2012, *State of the World's Cities 2010/2011: Bridging the Urban Divide*, Earthscan, London.

Weil, Simone 1952, *The Need for Roots: Prelude to a Declaration of Duties towards Mankind*, Routledge and Kegan Paul, London.

5

SOCIAL MEANING[1]

How can we better understand the powerful subjective dynamics that occur in different social formations? Why is that when discussing issues of sustainability certain things are on the table and others are not? As a way of approaching this question, this chapter provides further entry into understanding the circles of social life by working across four interrelated levels: ideas, ideologies, imaginaries and ontologies (see Tables 4.1 and 4.2). Each of these four layers of lived meaning is constituted in practice at an ever-greater generality, durability and depth. For example ideas can be passing thoughts, and ideologies tend to move in and out of social contestation. Imaginaries move at a deeper level and, in different ways, enter the commonsense of an age. What is contested about them tends to be their ideological expressions. Most deeply, ontologies, such as how we live temporally or spatially, constitute the relatively enduring ground on which we walk. Whether we recognize it or not, cities are formed in terms of ontologies of time, space and embodiment, from the lines on our roads to the website presentations of urban centres. Material processes of globalization have been changing all of these three layers – at times, even at revolutionary speed. Rapid processes of urbanization have intensified this change. However, the deeper the processes of change, the slower the tendency for a new pattern to take hold as dominant and encompassing.

At the risk of oversimplifying the four principal concepts, the following minimal definitions are offered as a working summary:

1. *Ideas* are thoughts, opinions, beliefs and concepts. They can be held individually, but they tend to swirl around communicating segments of meaning.
2. *Ideologies* are patterned clusters of normatively imbued ideas and concepts, including particular representations of power relations. They are conceptual maps that help people navigate the complexity of their social universe. They carry claims to social truth as for example expressed in the main ideologies

of the national imaginary: liberalism, conservatism, socialism, communism and fascism.

3. *Imaginaries* are patterned convocations of the social whole. These deep-seated modes of understanding provide largely pre-reflexive parameters within which people imagine their social existence – expressed for example in conceptions of 'the global', 'the national' and 'the moral order of our time'. They are the convocations that express our inter-relation to each other.

4. *Ontologies* are patterned ways of *being* in the world. They are lived and experienced as the grounding or existential conditions of the social. For example modern ontologies of linear time, territorial space, and individualized embodiment frame the way in which we walk about the modern city. It is only within a modern sense of time that the ideologies of progress or economic growth can make sense. Even if prior ontologies affect how we see things such as sacred spaces and events, they tend to be reconstituted in terms of such dominant understandings.

In this chapter these four layers of social meaning are discussed and linked to dominant frames for understanding our contemporary world: globalism and modernism. All have consequences for how we think and act in relation to urban development and issues of sustainability.

Like other major social phenomena, ideas about sustainability are associated with patterns of meaning related to and about forms of material practice. The relationship between those practices and meanings is extraordinarily complicated and mutually constitutive. Here the key proposition is that, as full-blown ideologies are patterned and laid over each other, they become conceptually thick enough to form relatively coherent and persistent articulations of the underlying social imaginary. Just as the formation of nations is associated with the ideologies of the national imaginary, processes of globalization are associated with ideologies expressing the global imaginary that both influence and make sense of globalizing practices.

Thus in relation to sustainable development there are four layers of meaning: (1) ideas of sustainability; (2) ideologies of sustainability, with both framed by (3) imaginaries and (4) ontologies. Contemporary ideas about sustainable development come to us framed by two counter-images within the dominant global imaginary. On one hand, there is Spaceship Earth, Gaia, and the image of planet Earth connected to the relatively new globalizing self-consciousness about locality. Accordingly, the projection of planet Earth as a vulnerable globe suspended in space is central to most claims about sustainability, as are sayings such as 'think global, act local'. On the other hand, and in contention with the first set, there is a counter-image of the global so powerful that it has a single reference point – *the market*. There is no more powerful global metaphor today than the market. Markets have been so naturalized as an active globalizing force that it is now treated in the singular, with cities understood as nodes in a network of exchange. It no longer needs the adjective *global* in front of it to carry that meaning. In this context, it is no wonder that the Triple Bottom Line approach begins with the economic, adds the environment, and then turns to the social as the grab bag of extra considerations that do not fit into the first two domains.

Going deeper than the global imaginary is the long-term and continuing onto-logical dominance of modern ways of life. Thus, both the ideologies and objective realities of global vulnerability are currently tied to the ideologies and objective realities of both the Left and the Right. The modern Left enunciates modern pro-gressiveness and justice. The modern Right proclaims the necessity of progress and economic growth. This means that the way in which sustainable development con-verges on a common understanding of progress and change. There are significant crossovers in the concepts of being 'progressive' and supporting 'progress'. The con-cept of modernization thus thuds to earth with an ideological weight that links progress, development and modernity as intertwined necessities. The city is the locus where these ideas of progress and development become most intense.

Ideas and ideologies

Ideologies are patterns of ideas. One or two statements of contention do not an ideology make. It takes many ideas and the voices of many people to make an ide-ology. These patterns are formed through such processes as the power of repetition, the status of the speaker or source of the idea and the 'given' sense that some ideas are right or wrong. Expressed in terms of globalization specifically, four clusters of ideas are conceptually thick enough to warrant the status of mature ideologies (see Table 4.1): market globalisms, justice globalisms, imperial globalisms and religious globalisms.

Market globalisms constitute today's dominant set of ideologies. The chief codi-fiers of market globalism are corporate managers, executives of large transnational corporations, corporate lobbyists, high-level military officers, journalists and public relations specialists, intellectuals writing to large audiences, state bureaucrats and politicians. These global power elites assert that, notwithstanding the cyclical down-turns of the world economy, the global integration of markets along laissez-faire lines not only is a fundamentally 'good' thing but also represents the given outcome and natural progression of the human condition. This has obvious consequences for approaches to sustainability. The morphology of market globalism is built around a number of interrelated central claims: that globalization is about the liberalization and the worldwide integration of markets (neo-liberalism); that it is powered by neutral techno-economic forces; that the process is inexorable; that the process is leaderless and anonymous; that everyone will be better off in the long run; that glo-balization furthers the spread of democracy in the world; that the city, the so-called engine of growth, is its natural home; and that sustainability and growth economics are relatively compatible through technological innovation.[2]

Justice globalism, by comparison, can be defined by its emphasis on equity, rights, diversity and a more demanding sense of sustainability. Championed by forces of the political Left, it articulates a very different set of claims. It suggests that the process of globalization is powered by corporate interests, that the process can take different pathways, that the democracy carried by global processes tends to be thin and procedural and that 'globalization-from-above' or 'corporate globalization' is associated with increasing inequities within and between nation states, greater environmental destruction and a marginalization of the poor. Although the alter-globalization movement argues for an alternative form of globalization, it is globalization nevertheless. And as such, more than just another description of the world, the core concepts and the central claims of justice globalism constitute, we suggest, one lineage in a family of contesting ideologies. That makes justice globalism akin to its main competitors in the sense that it draws upon a generalizing, deep-seated imaginary of global connectedness. For a time, one line of justice globalism was associated with an anti-urban back-to-country sensibility, but this has changed fundamentally over the past few decades and urban justice and urban sustainability is central to the concerns of almost everybody.

The third constellation includes various *religious globalisms*, mostly of the political Right. Its most spectacular strain today is jihadist Islamism. Based on the populist evocation of an exceptional spiritual and political crisis, jihadist Islamists bemoan the contemporary age of *jahiliyya* (ignorance and pagan idolatry) and call for a renewed universalism of a global *Ummah* or a reworked meaning of a global Islamic community. In the Christian version, the City of Man is sinful and requires a renewed orientation to the City of God, but here again, although half the world's population still lives in the countryside, the city is the primary site of symbolic intensity. Jerusalem is one prominent city that holds this tension of globalizing religions together, albeit in a less and less sustainable way. Under extreme duress – Jerusalem during the intifadas, Sarajevo during the Serbian Siege, New York after 9/11, Colombo during the Singhalese-Tamil War – this tension with its previously creative possibilities has over the last couple of generations come to become less resilient.

A fourth variant, *imperial globalism*, has been weakening over the last few years as a result of the Obama administration's renewed multilateralism and the fracturing Washington Consensus in the wake of the global financial crisis. Developing out of market globalism and still retaining some of its central features, imperial globalism is the *publicly* weakest of these ideological clusters, even though for a time it informed the so-called Global War on Terror and the joint actions of the Coalition of the Willing spearheaded by the unilateralist Bush administration. Despite the waning influence of these hawks, imperial globalism still operates as a powerful background force. Its central claim – that despite the coming 'Asian Century', global peace depends on the global economic reach and military care of an informal, US-led Western empire – is still taken for granted within many governing groups and elite circles.

For all their complexity as ideologies, and despite the obvious tensions between them and the differences across different settings, these four globalisms are part of a complex, roughly woven, patterned ideational fabric that increasingly figures *the global* as a defining condition of the present. This is the case even as we remain entangled in the national. People who accept their central claims – whether from the political Right or Left – internalize the apparent inevitability and relative virtue of global interconnectivity and mobility across global time and space.

However one might seek to understand global history, and whatever reversals we might face in the future, the perception of intensifying social interconnections have come to define the nature of our times. Even though proponents of justice globalism strenuously insist that 'another world is possible', they hardly question that growing global interdependence remains a central part of most, if not all, alternative futures. Indeed, one unmistaken sign of a maturing ideological constellation is that it comes to be represented in discourse as post-ideological. It is just the way that it is.

Imaginaries

The buzzword *globalization*, part of common twenty-first-century parlance, reflects a generalized recognition that global processes inform social life. Globalization affects most of everyday life, from the way in which we borrow money and source basic commodities to the way we use digital modalities to keep in touch with friends and family via social networking sites such as Facebook, Twitter and MySpace. In this sense the various ideologies associated with globalization have come to coalesce around a new sense of a global social whole. A *global social imaginary* has formed with profound, generalizing and deep impact. This imaginary 'compels' many city leaders to feel that their city needs be a 'global city'. It engenders the current competition between cities for comparative global status. Why else would cities take the various league tables and prizes so seriously?

In the last decades, a number of prominent social thinkers have grappled with the notion that an *imaginary* is more than an ideologically contested representation of social integration and differentiation. Claude Lefort, for example, argues that, '[i]n this sense, the examination of ideology confronts us with the determination of a type of society in which a specific regime of the imaginary can be identified' (1986, p. 197). Cornelius Castoriadis takes the concept of an *imaginary* in a different direction that provides, nonetheless, a useful means of indicating how in this book we are *not* using the term. For Castoriadis (1991), the imaginary is that which expresses the creative excess of our human condition. It always exceeds the possibilities of the material conditions of life. Our use of the term is more akin to Pierre Bourdieu's conception of the *habitus* – that is 'systems of durable, transposable dispositions, structured structures predisposed to function as structuring structures, that is, as principles which generate and organize practices and representations' (1990, p. 53).

However, the concept of the habitus is too normatively driven to be the same as what we are trying to get at. The concept of the social imaginary in our use has a stronger sense of the social whole or the general 'given' social order. Nevertheless, what is important to take from Bourdieu is a sense of how patterns of practice and ideas can *be seen* to be *objectively* outside of the particular practices and ideas of persons, even as those patterns were generated subjectively by persons acting in and through the habitus.

Charles Taylor provides perhaps the most useful way forward in defining the social imaginary. It is the 'ways people imagine their social existence, how they fit together with others, how things go on between them and their fellows, the expectations that are normally met, and the deeper normative notions and images that underlie these expectations'. These imaginations set the common-sense background of lived social experience (2004, p. 23).[3] In Taylor's exposition, the *modern* social imaginary has been built by three dynamics. The first is the separating out of *the economy* as a distinct domain, treated as an objectified reality, something that we have criticized for being assumed to be the natural state of things. The second is the simultaneous emergence of *the public sphere* as the place of increasingly mediated interchange (counterposed) to the intimate or *private sphere* in which ordinary life is affirmed. The third is the sovereignty of *the people*, treated as a new collective agency even as it is made up of individuals who see self-affirmation in the other spheres. These are three historical developments, among others, that are relevant to what might be called a *modern* ontological formation (of which more later).

Our definition of the social imaginary contains another crucial insight, namely that it constitutes patterned *convocations* of the lived *social whole*. The notion of convocation is important since it is the calling together – the gathering (not the self-consciously defending or active de-contesting activity associated with ideologies) of an assemblage of meanings, ideas, sensibilities. The concept of the social whole points to the way in which certain apparently simple terms such as 'our society', 'we', 'the city', and 'the market' carry taken-for-granted and interconnected meanings. This concept allows us to define the imaginary as broader than the dominant sense of community. A social whole, in other words, is not necessarily coextensive with a projection of community relations or 'the ways people imagine their social existence' (Taylor 2004). Nor does it need to be named as such. It can encompass a time, for example, when there exists only an inchoate sense of global community. There is today paradoxically an almost pre-reflexive sense that at one level 'we' as individuals, peoples, urban communities and nations have a common global fate. Put in different terms, the medium and the message – the practice of interrelation on a global scale and the content of messages of global interconnection and naturalized power – have become increasingly bound up with each other.

As recently as a generation ago, notions of the social whole – including 'the market' – were stretched across relations between nation-states and would, therefore, have been seen as co-extensive with the nation-state. Hence, the then widespread use of the term *inter*national *relations*. When most sociologists and political scientists analyzed 'society', they tended to assume the boundaries of the nation – in the relevant literature this is referred to as 'methodological nationalism'. In other words, the social whole was a national imaginary that tended to be equated with the community of the nation-state. Now we find either that such concepts as city and society have become terms of ambivalence because they have become stretched between two contesting yet interdependent imaginaries: the national and the global. This helps to explain the contemporary excitement about cities. With the emerging dominance of the global, cities have come back into contention as having both local vigour and globalizing significance beyond their national settings. This is experienced as newness.

Novelty is perhaps most obviously expressed in the proliferation of the prefix *neo–* that has attached itself to nearly all major isms of our time: neoliberalism, neoconservatism, neo-Marxism, neofascism, and so on. Despite continuities there is then something new about political ideologies: a new global imaginary is on the rise. It erupts with increasing frequency within and onto the familiar framework of the national, spewing its fiery lava across all geographical scales. Stoked, among other things, by technological change and scientific innovation, this global imaginary destabilizes the grand political ideologies codified by social elites in an earlier period. Debates over sustainability of the urbanizing planet are at the centre of this firestorm.

To summarize: thus far, we have suggested that ideologies of globalization are part of an extended family that translate a generalized global imaginary into competing political programs and agendas. Political impact is redoubled by the spectacular rise of communications technologies. This has profound consequences for how debates about sustainability are conducted. It also has consequences for how people think about cities. The term *global cities* partakes of this consolidating imaginary, based on the idea that global cities are those that channel the flow of capital and communications.

But it goes further. When Jeb Brugman (2009), for example, proclaims the existence of an urban revolution that has already transformed the planet into a single *City* (with a capital *C*), a single converging urban system, he has taken this global imaginary to be everything. His analysis breaks down on almost every level. Obviously there are still non-hinterland rural zones. Obviously, new and intense competition has developed between globalizing cities, competition which means that the notion of a single urban system cannot be conflated with a globalizing social interrelations. Globalization and urbanization have not become the same process, even if the orbits of cities have become increasingly globalized.

Nevertheless, the problems with his analysis point to the emerging dominance of a global imaginary. This explains why for him and others the City thus becomes the globe. What is accurate in his analysis is that the dual forces of urbanization and globalization are changing the planet. But to understand this compounding change we need a very different kind of methodology that can (1) recognize dominant patterns of change *and* continuity, (2) distinguish different and contradictory layers of change/continuity and (3) explain why contemporary approaches to urban life emphasize the virtues of change above all else. It is understandable, given the force of the global imaginary, that writers are now saying that the City is the world, but how does that allow for the development of a more sustainable and complex social imaginary? In Brendan Gleeson's words, '[t]he imaginaries that [should stand] the test of time are, logically, those that do not refuse history or nature – ideas such as human solidarity, our dependence on nature, the possibility of failure and the frailty of human endeavour' (2010, p. 9).

Ontological formations

Why is development – or change – readily seen as both necessary and virtuous? Why is 'change for change's sake' and an obsession with 'moving onward and upward' so often confused for change as purposeful innovation. To understand this, moving to the final layer of our investigation of the dimensions of social meaning, we must grapple with ontological categories such as time and space. As discussed in the previous chapter, we use the concept of ontologies here as a shorthand term referring to the most basic framing categories of social existence: temporality, spatiality, corporeality, epistemology and so on. These are categories of being-in-the-world. They are historically constituted in the structures of human interrelations. If questions of ontology are fundamentally about matters of being, then everything involving 'being human' is ontological. Still, we are using the concept more precisely to refer to categories of human existence such as space and time that, on one hand, are always talked about and, on the other, are rarely interrogated, analysed or historically contextualized except by philosophers and social theorists.

In this context, let us note that we employ the concepts of the customary, the traditional, the modern and the postmodern as provisionally useful designations to refer to fundamentally different ontological formations.[4] These are different ways of life, with the term *ways of life* meaning something much deeper than lifestyle choices. Customary ways of life, including tribalism, are defined by the dominance of particular socially specific modalities of space, time, embodiment, knowing and performance that can be characterized by analogical, genealogical and mythological practices and subjectivities. For example this would include notions of genealogical placement and kinship, the importance of mythological time connecting past and present and the centrality of relations of embodied reciprocity between persons who spend most of their time in each other's presence.

Traditional ways of life can be characterized as carrying forward prior ontological forms from customary relations, but reconstitutes them in terms of universalizing cosmologies and political-metaphorical relations. An example here is the institution of the Christian Church. It carries forward older customary meanings and rituals – times of feasting, orientations to the sacred, and so on. At the same time it meets the modern world ambiguously. Christian denominations may have modernized their practices of organization and may have become enmeshed in a modern monetary economy, but the various lineages of the church, and most manifestly its Pentecostal variations, remain deeply bound to a traditional cosmology of meaning and ritual, including the traditional notion of dominion over nature. This helps to explain why sustainability did not become an issue for Christian-imbued cultures until recently. Revelation and the end of the world were in God's hands, and nature was the dominion of humankind.

A brief discussion of the themes of time and space will help bring to the surface this largely taken-for-granted connection between ontological categories, globalization and the concepts of development and change. Let us start with the ontological category of spatiality. Focusing on spatiality is crucial, because globalization is obviously a spatial process and issues of sustainability are taken to refer to places from the local to the global. Cities are nothing if not spatial configurations. The academic observation that to globalize means to compress time and space has long been part of public discourse. However, to be more historically specific, *contemporary* globalization is predominantly lived through a *modern* conception of spatiality linked to an abstracted geometry of compressed territories and sovereignties.

Modern space tends to subsume rather than replace traditional cosmological senses of spatiality held together by God or some other generalized Supreme Being. In other words, different formations are layered in dominance rather experiencing a simple epochal shift from an older form of temporality. Modern spaces overlay older forms with networks of interchange and movement. This accords with our presentation of contemporary globalization as generating new hybrid modernities anchored in changing conceptions of time and space. For example, those ideological prophets who espouse a jihadist or Pentecostal variant of religious globalism tend to be stretched between a modern territorial sense of space and a neo-traditional sense of a universalizing *Ummah* or Christendom, respectively. In their neo-traditional layer of understanding, the social whole exists in, prior to, and beyond, modern global space. It means that, *for those who believe*, the cities of Jerusalem, Rome or Mecca lie at the various centres of different universalizing spaces that link other urban and rural places around the world in a singular cosmology.

At the same time, particularly in fast-moving urban settings, we also find instances of ambiguous modern spatialities sliding into postmodern sensibilities that relate to contemporary globalization. For example take airline-advertising maps that are post-territorial (postmodern) to the extent that they show multiple abstract vectors of travel – lines that crisscross between multiple city nodes and travel across empty space. These are maps without reference to the conventional mapping expressions of land and sea, nation state and continental boundaries. To such a backdrop and with no global outline, an advertisement for KLM airlines assures potential customers that 'You could fly from anywhere in the world to any destination'. Our contention here is that one comfortably knows how to read those maps despite the limited points of orientation, and one also knows that they are global before reading the fine print – 'anywhere in the world'. This is the basis of the so-called network society. In this context, politics change. As Sofie Bouteligier (2012) has argued, globalization both gives rise to networked urban organizations and exposes the weaknesses of such organizations.

The modern category of temporality is also important to the contemporary global imaginary, even if the notion of time does not seem to be contained in the concept of globalization. More than that, it is crucial to underpinning the modern ideology of progress. Modern time is the demarcated, linear and empty time of the calendar and clock. It is *the* time of change, progress and development. This ontological sense that time moves 'forward' one second per second is a modern convention rather than being intrinsically natural. It is neither scientifically verifiable (except as tautology) nor continuous with older cosmological senses of time. Modern time is abstracted from nature. It is sustained by a particular mode of modern analytical enquiry – the Newtonian treatment of time as unitary, linear and uniform. This 'scientific' time reached one of its defining moments in 1974 when the second came to be measured in atomic vibrations, allowing the post-phenomenal concept of nanoseconds – one-billionth of a second.

The dual sense of forward moving and time precision has been globalized as the regulative framework for electronic transactions in the global marketplace. It drives the billions of transactions on Wall Street just as much as it imposes a non-regressive discipline on the millions of bidders on eBay, at a local real estate auction or waiting at a red traffic light. This then becomes a crucial point: a modern sense of time has been globalized and now overlays older ontologies of temporality without fully erasing them. It is the dominant time of the contemporary city, and it lives in contradiction with older forms of time.

Modernism carries forward prior forms of being including time and space but fundamentally tends to reconstitute them. It remakes them in terms of technical-abstracted modes of being. Thus, even religious time becomes understood and practiced not primarily in terms of cosmological integration but through linear timelines that can be filled with the ritualized details of the past and present, as well as events *made by us* with an eye toward a 'better' future. Indeed, one of the key dynamics of modernity is the continuous transformation of present time by cultural and political designs for the future. This dynamic, linked to the scientific idea of the arrow of time moving inexorably second by second, means that change and development become seen as both necessary and good. Being left behind or stagnating (both temporal-spatial metaphors) become 'obviously' bad conditions to avoid. This dynamic makes it hard to sustain good development, which sometimes entails keeping things the same.

A further crucial point is that ideologies tend to draw upon an assumed connection between modern time and globalizing processes to project their truth claims. These claims link together such concepts as progress, development, growth, efficiency, new, fashionable and just in time. They are not just any words. They are also temporal concepts used to promote mainstream urban change. In this context, concerns about sustainability and vulnerability mingle with extraordinary claims about the renewing capacity of technologies. It is part of a consciousness of modernity that arose as a vision that human beings can create urban life in a new image. Our argument here is not to criticize change or innovation *per se*. It is to challenge the un-interrogated dominance of change for change's sake or sustainable development seen as essentially good, simply because it involves change.

With the emerging dominance of the global imaginary, the city has become *the* hotspot of change. Urban life now signifies a *world* of changing possibilities. While particular nation-states and federated polities continue to legislate for each city's day-to-day activities, the feeling is that the city is post-national. A global city is now its own centre within a globalizing network, just as it provides spaces for individual movement. Modern spaces from cities to nation-states remain territorialized and marked by abstract lines on maps – with places drawn in by our own histories. At the same time, modern embodiment has become an individualized project used to project a choosing self. This self can choose to live sustainably or not. He or she can choose to live in this city or not. As modern epistemology (the nature of knowing) becomes an act of analytically dismembering and re-synthesizing information, our faith in the information technologies thus tends to redouble despite massive evidence that this faith got us into trouble in the first place. Hence, the idea of the 'Smart City' abounds. Unfortunately it is unthinkingly tied in practice to a form of modernism that is associated with the dominance of capitalist production relations, techno-science and commodity and finance exchange. None of these processes has a glowing record in relation to sustainability questions. However, in the context of such a *world* of possibilities this record matters less than what frames our ideas, ideologies and imaginaries. Just as there may be multiple intelligences, not just IQ, so there are multiple ways of being 'smart', not only by putting in massive and complicated urban IT systems.

Giving illustrative urgency to the previous discussion, we can say that while contemporary urban development overwhelmingly works within a *modernizing* paradigm of regularization, risk management and monitored efficient change, its effects are complicated by the *actual* layered nature of cities. In today's globalizing world despite the dominance of the modern, we actually find different formations of customary relations, traditionalism, modernism and postmodernism in complex intersection with each other. Thus, despite its promise, urban development produces both new freedoms and new oppressions. Just as modern ideologies of liberal freedom and subjective autonomy can be associated with objective figures of oppression, exclusion and displacement, so it is with modernizing urban change.

To the outskirts of many Global South cities come once-rural denizens autonomously and freely seeking work, only to find themselves squatting in the junk-filled interstices of the expanding built environment. From within bloating urban precincts, indigenous populations, still at one level practising customary lives, are given the freedom to assimilate or be pushed aside – at best into cultural reserves. In the city of Curitiba, a bus rapid transit system has become a global beacon of positive sustainability, but during the same period most of the indigenous population have been pushed out to live in zones well beyond rapid bus access. Three tribal groups, once living along the airport road, have since 2008 been relocated to Campo Santana, 25 kilometres from the city. Here they live in a forlorn camp of basic cement-rendered bungalows. Curitiba is a Janus-faced city, both good and bad.

Be'er Sheva provides an even-more stark example. In the early part of the twentieth century the town was predominantly Arab Bedouin. In the 1950s a murky amalgam of Jewish Zionism and the celestial 'Garden City' concept – associated with Ebenezer Howard and his book *Garden Cities of Tomorrow* – became the basis for planning. Now the population of the city is 98 per cent Jewish or other non-Arab residents. The Bedouin market has been reduced to a quaint reminder of the past, relegated to a car park on the outskirts of the city. This is a reprehensible outcome. A positively sustainable city, by contrast, should be able to creatively bring together such different worlds into a negotiated complex whole.

Contemporary ideologies of freedom or inclusion do not provide an adequate answer to these deeper issues of ontological displacement. A number of writers from Jane Jacobs (1961) and Richard Sennett (1994) to David Harvey (2012) and Sharon Zukin (2010) have argued that contemporary cities – rather than becoming just 'spaces of abstract freedom' – need to be built in such a way as to encourage enriching forms of embodied friction between different peoples. They argue that social life needs to return to the streets as more than simulated or commodified authenticity. Locals and strangers should rub shoulders, sometimes painfully, as they move through in locally defined *places*. This is a fine argument. The present argument goes further in the same direction to argue for the deepening of reflexively understood ontological friction – that is for the creative facilitation of positive and painful intersections of engagement, allowing for different ontological orientations to be present in the same place. As Tony Fry (2012) has emphasized, this includes in our relation to others and our relation to nature. The modern town square and the creation of urban commons – Tahrir Square in Egypt, Taksim Square in Turkey, Tiananmen Square in Beijing, Shahbagh Square in Dhakar, or Washington Square in New York – might allow for strangers and locals to rub shoulders. It is a minimal condition of positive friction. We have seen how urban commons provide the setting for both short-lived political revolutions and quiet relaxing afternoons in the park. But the politics of the town square tends to remain largely one-dimensional. In the context of complex globalization, the urban project has to go much deeper.

Designing for creative ontological friction entails building cities in a way that explicitly and reflexively recognizes ontological difference across different social formations – such as between relations of customary tribalism, cosmological traditionalism, constructivist modernism and relativizing postmodernism. It entails building for ontological friction across the social/natural divide. Yes, urban spaces should facilitate people rubbing shoulders. But good design and positive engagement should also explicitly take into account the different ontological meanings that rubbing shoulders or confronting nature have for different people. In short, it is not globalizing modern urban development in itself that is the problem, but rather that modern conceptions of development have come to overwhelm all other ways of living in the city. It is in the light of these considerations that the next part of the book turns to applied questions of how we might act otherwise.

Notes

1 Manfred Steger is the main co-author of this chapter with Paul James. The ideas for this chapter were first developed as an article by Steger and James (2013).
2 For a sustained discussion and critical analysis of these claims that draws on hundreds of examples, see Steger (2005).
3 This formulation dovetails to some extent with Antonio Gramsci's notion of cultural hegemony.
4 For a more detailed discussion of this subject, see Paul James (2006).

References

Bourdieu, Pierre 1990, *The Logic of Practice*, Polity Press, Cambridge.
Bouteligier, Sofie 2012, *Cities, Networks, and Global Environmental Governance: Spaces of Innovation, Places of Leadership*, Routledge, New York.

Brugman, Jeb 2009, *Welcome to the Urban Revolution: How Cities Are Changing the World*, University of Queensland Press, St Lucia.

Castoriadis, Cornelius 1991, *The Imaginary Constitution of Society*, Polity Press, Cambridge.

Fry, Tony 2012, *Becoming Human by Design*, Berg, London.

Gleeson, Brendan 2010, *Lifeboat Cities*, University of New South Wales Press, Sydney.

Harvey, David 2012, *Rebel Cities: From the Right to the City to the Urban Revolution*, Verso, London.

Howard, Ebenezer 1902, *Garden Cities of Tomorrow*, S. Sonnerschein, London.

Jacobs, Jane M. 1961, *The Death and Life of Great American Cities*, Random House, New York.

James, Paul 2006, *Globalism, Nationalism, Tribalism: Bringing Theory Back In*, Sage, London.

Lefort, Claude 1986, *The Political Forms of Modern Society*. Polity Press, Cambridge.

Sennett, Richard 1994, *Flesh and Stone: The Body and the City in Western Civilization*, Faber and Faber, London.

Steger, Manfred B. 2005, *Globalisms*, Rowman and Littlefield, Lanham.

Steger, Manfred B. & James, Paul 2013, 'Levels of Subjective Globalization: Ideologies, Imaginaries, Ontologies', *Perspectives on Global Development and Technology*, vol. 12, no. 1–2, pp. 17–40.

Taylor, Charles 2004, *Modern Social Imaginaries,* Duke University Press, Durham.

Zukin, Sharon 2010, *Naked City: The Death and Life of Authentic Urban Places*, Oxford University Press, Oxford.

PART III

Developing methods and tools

6

ASSESSING SUSTAINABILITY[1]

Sustainability assessment is now thoroughly on the agenda. This deepening attention to issues of sustainability and sustainable development goes back to the release
of the Club of Rome *Limits to Growth* report in 1972. Then came the influential
Brundtland report and the UN Conference on Environment and Development's
subsequent Agenda 21. In recent years, this attention has translated into the increasingly widespread organizational practice of sustainability assessment. However, the
means by which this is happening is fraught.

Financial accounting is unfortunately taking over the world of sustainability
assessment. The problem is not with accounting in itself. Good accountancy is a
foundational discipline based on tested practice in relation to money and capital.
The overwhelming problem is with extending of the methods of financial accountancy to colonize every other area of social life. It is as if financial proxies can always
be found to measure value and outcomes, including in one bizarre project the
financial value of planet earth. Good critical accountants are beginning to criticize
this process themselves:

> For the accounting profession to be able to meaningfully contribute to
> extending accountability beyond investors, lenders, and creditors (and it
> undoubtedly serves these interests well) it will need to abandon many core
> accounting conventions and principles – something that is deemed unlikely
> to occur – at least in the readers' lifetime.
>
> (Deegan 2013, p. 448)

Sadly, rather than recognizing the need for a paradigm shift in the field of assessment, the accounting profession has embraced the new possibilities of sustainability assessment without significantly changing their way of thinking. By contrast
the method developed here takes each of the domains of social life has having its

own integrity – and well as having interconnecting consequence. The concept of sustainability assessment is used in this chapter to cover the manifold activities of monitoring, evaluating, reporting and providing an evidence base for policy development in relation to sustainability problems and outcomes.

At one end of the spectrum, there are formal methods of top-down assessment and reporting against standardized indicator sets. These are often conducted annually with varying degrees of auditing assurance. They may or may not lead to policy outcomes, but they have become an important part of the public face of many organizations. Regularized corporate reporting practices such as One Reporting or the Global Reporting Initiative exemplify this end of the spectrum.

At the other end of the spectrum are qualitative assessments derived from bottom-up and locally grown measures. These assessments have been increasingly adopted by non-governmental organizations (NGOs), sub-national or municipal authorities, and community groups. Cities such as Seattle and Vancouver have headed towards this end of the spectrum. This chapter focuses on what has hitherto largely seen as impossibly difficult. How can urban governments and communities continue to use bottom-up processes that reflect their conditions and interests without altogether sacrificing the rigour of top-down assessment protocols?

Common to both top-down and bottom-up approaches are various, more or less explicit, *frameworks* – collections of processes, measures, procedures, tools and principles that guide assessment practices. As a number of studies suggest, frameworks may not be sufficient but they remain necessary to the development of robust and relevant sustainability assessments. They are important to guiding associated planning, decision-making, monitoring and implementation activities. Prominent examples of top-down frameworks for sustainability reporting and indicator sets include the Global Reporting Initiative, the ISO 14031 and the AA1000. These were largely developed for and by corporate and government organizations. However, they typically suffer poor translation when applied to urban communities, municipal governments and small NGOs. This poses a common dilemma in choosing the appropriate approach to pursue.

On one side of the assessment dilemma, while some level of assessment of sustainable development is unequivocally important, the difficulty for many would-be reporting entities is that they invariably define sustainability in terms that are radically incommensurable with existing standardized definitions. In many local or smaller-scale contexts, sustainability definitions do not necessarily lean towards universality, comprehensiveness, comparability or defensibility beyond contextual limits. To the contrary, definitions in these contexts are often *desirably* local, partial and particular. Such an approach tends to best reflect a given community's qualitative and interpretative understandings of what sustainability means to local people. A further source of apprehension in relation to using existing sustainability frameworks in community settings is that they are frequently synonymous with complex and techno-scientifically oriented standards. And they are often associated with insidious forms of control. Such complexities can limit genuine participatory and deliberative efforts towards consensus and action.

On the other side of the assessment dilemma, although rigid interpretations of the notion of a 'framework' have lent it bureaucratic overtones, avoiding frameworks altogether has its own problems. It can all too readily yield reporting procedures that are unrepeatable, unreliable, and subject to various forms of unrecognized distortion. This in turn leads to disenchantment. People feel exhausted, apathetic and/or simple overwhelmed by the difficulty of measuring and reporting on sustainability initiatives in anything more than subjectively conditioned terms. Accordingly, the entire apparatus dedicated to improving community or organizational sustainability should, we contend, be capable of being erected within terms elaborated by that community or organization itself. But it must simultaneously have an objectifiable and generalizing capacity. In other words, the method needs to work *both ways* – from the general to the particular *and* back again.

Is this impossible? No. The task of this chapter, following the terms of the broad *Circles of Sustainability* framework elaborated in Part I, is to respond to the bottom-up/top-down assessment dilemma by providing suggestions for a way forward. We start by briefly surveying existing work in the development of sustainability assessment approaches. The chapter then discusses the *Circles* conceptual method and process as allowing *both* for global or generalizing protocols *and* for engagement of local constituencies in sustainability development projects. A further case study at the end of the chapter outlines how the method has been used in Porto Alegre, Brazil.

Problems with top-down assessment processes

Considerable attention has been directed towards the development of robust top-down measures of national, transnational and global sustainability. The literature devoted to establishing generalized frameworks, processes, indices and indicators for measuring sustainability – all examples of bird's-eye, expert-driven processes – has in recent decades become voluminous. Well-known indexes include the ecological footprint index, the surplus bio-capacity index, the environmental sustainability index, the wellbeing index, human development index and gross domestic product index. What all of the critical literature points to is the growing complexity and maturation in standardized sustainability assessment. However, none of this work mitigates the need for locally applicable measurement tools or for linking them systematically to community-engagement processes.

The criticisms of assessment tools and processes are many. One set of criticisms concerns internal logic and validity. Processes of data normalization and weighting are commonly found wanting. Such failings limit index validity. Crucially, they often lead to skewed policies overly reliant upon index values. A second set of criticisms concerns the usability and usefulness of generalizing tools in a local context (see the set of value criteria for a method in Chapter 3). This is closely related to the capacity of a team to carry out sustainability assessments over the long term. It concerns to the ongoing availability of resources, both in relation to expertise and financial support. A third set of criticisms concern the normative and ideological framing (see Chapter 5). There are good reasons for questioning the purported adherence of certain indices to modern scientific principles and measures alone. In the usual Triple Bottom Line approach, the third domain of 'social' desiderata often becomes a category to embed or relegate inherently normative dimensions. These considerations are then often largely ignored in the apparently value-free construction and administration of economic and environmental indices.

As many writers have suggested, any conception of sustainability is bound up with a desired state of affairs. Uncritical and unreflexive use of indicator sets can, at worst, mask their normative foundations in another permutation of what Foucauldian theorists define as 'governmentality'. That is, it can hide the pervasive expression of power through institutions that monitor, measure and control. Top-down indicators can serve in this way to replicate or extend hegemonic central-local power relations, institutionalizing the very meaning of sustainability and instrumentalizing hitherto common discourses. This finds its practical correlation in the difficulties of applying top-down indicators at different scales and in different settings. Efforts to implement policy based on indicator sets and reporting frameworks frequently run headlong into a range of political, cultural and economic considerations, as well as technical and operational constraints.

Problems with bottom-up assessment processes

Bottom-up assessment processes have their own distinct set of problems. Apart from the issue of non-comparability already discussed, there is, secondly, a tendency for the concepts of community or stakeholder to be concretized within a bounded geographical frame or reified as a singular group of integrated individuals. As we have discussed in Chapter 2, many changes in the contemporary world, including the rapid adoption and penetration of communication technologies, suggest, however, that communities need to be understood along less contiguous and singular lines. Communities can cross-cut each other in geographical spaces, can operate across virtual spaces or interconnect by social movement and are constantly changing. Thirdly, the literature currently provides insufficient guidance for communities and localities looking to bridge the gulf between specific feedback elicitation techniques, and deeper social learning and change. Any comprehensive approach, we suggest, should encourage reflection and engagement within a community or organization, beyond the mere collation of information or monitoring of policy.

Fourthly, although there are many examples in the literature of studies devoted towards bottom-up approaches that aim to counter some of the criticisms of top-down indicator application and to capitalize on the merits of community engagement, there are concerns about the nature of that engagement. In this regard, a number of studies highlight the need for systematic feedback from locals on sustainability policy. Emerging from these findings is a clear need for methodological guidance over the process of people's engagement. Reed goes so far as to suggests that participation 'must be institutionalised, creating organisational cultures that can facilitate processes where goals are negotiated and outcomes are necessarily uncertain' (2008, p. 2,417). Moreover, there is strong need for integrating sustainability assessment with process of social learning. All of this echoes the concerns of recent efforts to apply structured and systemic approaches to the facilitation of indicator projects in the public sphere. This broader outlook, which views sustainability challenges as arising from conflictual elements within interconnecting domains, heavily informs the approach adopted here.

At an operational level, an array of different techniques has been deployed to identify community and constituency-based issues. As discussed in Chapter 5, these include community mapping, mixed expert and citizen panel-groups, iterative expert consultation and conventional forums, interviews and questionnaires. All have been used to identify community concerns, issues and in many cases, actual sustainability indicators. However, in spite of the proliferation of specific techniques for structured and systematic engagement, there is a general absence of holistic methodologies for framework development that are *generic in form but allow for context-dependent specificity with regard to content.*

There remains a need, in other words, for methods that not only are capable of being deployed in widely differing reporting contexts but also permit locally developed sustainability interpretations and indicators. Arguably, the seemingly irresolvable quandary between top-down and bottom-up approaches can best be negotiated by a substantial reorientation. Our reorientation begins by acknowledging the necessity of a general framework. Next it shifts the focus of that framework from the task of specifying *what* is to be assessed to *how* it might be assessed.

For example, it shifts the emphasis from using a given set of specific indicators common to the reporting standard to the analytical and practical articulation of *how* these indicators are to be selected and what we might learn from them. Within an appropriate process of community and expert engagement, and given a mechanism for informing those engaged in the choosing of indicators about their global comparability, this becomes a way of ensuring both ongoing relevance within a given urban community context and continuing global referencing. This reorientation also changes the nature of the categories within which any particular reporting indicators are chosen. It requires shifting the focus of the reporting categories from *specific* domains that happen fit the dominant requirements of the assessment constituency to *generalizing* domains that encompass the human condition in general.

The first move is simple. Rather than reducing sustainability to an economic-environmental condition, with a few social extras thrown in as the current dominant economically driven starting point has it, here sustainability is framed as a *social* condition. In this move, as has been expressed in a number of different ways across the course of the book, economics becomes 'just' another social category – as it was prior to the mid-twentieth century.

Secondly, rather than using the non-social category of the environment as defined in modern abstracted terms, we focus on the social category of ecology defined more generally and in an embedded way. Thirdly, we add in culture and politics, recognizing the broad conceptual histories of those terms in relation to power and meaning. As we have elaborated earlier, this gives us four categories of social sustainability: ecology, economics, politics and culture. Social sustainability is, in this conception, not one category among others, and it is not something that can be sacrificed in the pursuit of some element of economic or environmental sustainability. By the same method, we can handle questions of resilience, adaptation, security, reconciliation and liveability.

We have already argued that conceptualizing sustainability as fundamentally a condition of the social, avoids a key limitation of the approach inherent in the Triple Bottom Line metaphor. This can now be elaborated a little more. The Triple Bottom Line begins with corporations. It is corporate-oriented approach. It treats the social – that is, the way in which humans live and relate to each other and the environment – as secondary. Concurrently, economics is given an independent status that is ideologically assumed rather than analytically argued. In the most problematic versions, the economic is elevated to the master category and defined in terms that assume the dominance of a singular, historically specific, economic configuration – modern globalizing capitalism. Concurrently the environment comes to be treated as an externality or background feature. The environment becomes the externality that we can use as a resource, and the human dimension of ecological relations is defined only in terms of statistical costs and benefits. Thus, in many writings, even in those critical of the Triple Bottom Line approach, the social becomes a congeries of miscellaneous considerations left over from the other two prime categories. Once pointed out, it is startling how often one reads the taken-for-granted triplet of economic, environmental and social issues in texts that are otherwise quite reflexive about their assumptions.

Using the social as the frame of sustainability assessment better allows for a number of considerations. Firstly, and immediately, it makes the framework more relevant to urban communities for whom even the most critical economic and environmental issues are embedded in the resilience and wellbeing of the social unit as a whole. Local communities exist more obviously within a broader social matrix than corporations. Secondly, it brings to the fore questions of culture, allowing communities to relate their practices to values and meanings, histories and projections. Thirdly, by using the social as the general frame, issues of temporal and spatial extension in which particular economic, ecological, political and cultural objectives are pursued can be brought to the fore. Fourth, questions of social tension can be explicitly introduced, with these tensions in the pursuit of variable objectives explicitly negotiated and managed according to their temporal dimensions (the present, the near future and the far future) or spatial dimensions (local, neighbourhood, city, regional, etc.).

The classic trade-off between economic and environmental activity can thus, for example, be reformulated as a conflict between the short- and long-term demands of the social entity in question. This temporalized formulation, we suggest, better accords with the Brundtland Commission's definition of sustainable development as meeting the needs of the present without compromising the ability of future generations to meet their own needs.

Within this reorientation of the methodology and underpinning categories of sustainability reporting, certain lines of commensurability with other reporting contexts can be carried through very successfully. For a community to argue for its goals, and to establish its progress towards certain critical objectives, links between what can be termed 'the local sustainability reporting ontology' – the critical issues and indicators developed by the community – and the various globalized sustainability conceptualizations underpinning standards set by international agencies are needed. These links can assist people within communities and local government organizations to meet their own goals and yet conform to the ever-increasing imperatives to adopt standards, to ensure regulation compliance, to apply for funding and finance and to achieve transparency and accountability benchmarks. Supporting the development of these links also brings attention to the transparency and accountability of the indicator development and reporting processes themselves. It further supports comparability across time and space and with other community or organizational groups.

Building on these considerations, we present one possible approach for building a sustainability reporting framework. The method brings bottom-up sustainability processes and indicators into focus. At the same time allows for lines of concordance and commensurability with global reporting requirements. In the context of sustainability assessment, engagement involves a structured consultation with local communities about their issues and goals regarding development projects. However, engagement also covers two other aims of the approach. Firstly, engagement is required to mediate between the practical capabilities and needs of those communities, and the theoretical ideals of sustainability as expressed in global standards and protocols. Secondly, engagement also covers the communicative action inherent in the reporting activity itself.

Expressing the goals and representing the progress of sustainable development can be done in ways that speak both to those directly affected within a community and to those beyond who are required to support, sponsor and fund such development. In this sense, an *engaged approach* aims to coordinate the somewhat mechanical task of reporting and assessment within a broader political function of sustainable communication.

Towards a comprehensive assessment method

In our characterization of sustainability assessment, we distinguish broadly between the *process* and the *administration* of the framework. It is in keeping with our assertion that the process and not the indicators or KPIs (key performance indicators) themselves is most important. The discussion here is thus primarily directed towards elaborating the process within the overall approach. We assume that the administrative and measurement activities – the collection and the preparation and auditing of data, quantitative and qualitative – is field specific, governed by the specific nature (size, type, context) of the reporting entity. Although the *Circles* approach is oriented towards supporting community engagement, we acknowledge that our methods might still require the skills of experts who are able to facilitate the process by translating feedback into a coherent series of issues and indicators. We also acknowledge that the idealized presentation of the methodology here needs to be tailored to specific circumstances. In many cases, this will be contingent on the context and nature of the communities involved and the frequency and complexity of the reporting activity.

The method consists of a domain model comprising conceptual entities such as issues and indicators and a process for constructing the entities of the model according to a series of rules (e.g., an indicator must measure one or more issues). We begin by emphasizing how important it is to define what you are trying to do. This is such an apparently simple claim, but it is amazing how often this basic consideration of defining 'what is to be done' is assumed and quickly passed over.

An overview of the definition phase

Defining the terms of a project consists of a series of conceptual tiers:

1. Consider all the domains of social life.
2. Clarify the general issue and normative objective.
3. Clarify the critical issues and the associated objectives across all the domains.
4. Consider the relationships between different critical objectives.
5. Choose the indicators and targets.
6. Analyse the data collected against the indicators.
7. Reflexively monitor and learn throughout the process.

Consider all the domains of social life

The first tier consists of a claim about all urban projects. Wherever they start, whatever they focus on, all projects should work across all the domains of social life. Rather than assume for example that a project is only about the ecology of water because it is concerned with sewerage outfall, it is important to recognize that the culture of water use or the governance of water supply are just as important in the larger scheme of things. This suggests that a holistic domain model, consisting of domains and subdomains (or perspectives), and subdividing further into different aspects for additional fine-grained work, can provide guidance. The domains form the uppermost categories of a conforming reporting framework. The Circles of Social Life figure, discussed at length in earlier chapters, assumes that the domains cannot be simply treated as analytically distinct categories. Ecological, economic, political and cultural features all interrelate within different social formations. They are conceived as systems within, and inextricable from, the environment, which is the base of all life. This systemic and holistic focus transfers to the concern with understanding the relationships between different critical issues and indicators.

In this respect, the Circles of Social Life model – and, by extension, the general methodology proposed here – shares an affinity with integrated-assessment and transition-management approaches. It creatively seeks to fill the space that currently exists between those approaches such the Smart Cities movement that project a one-dimensional answer to basic urban problems – in their case, the answer is technologize, set up massive information systems and get big data – and alternative approaches, such as associated with the Global Justice movement, that suggest that in order to build comprehensive sustainability and resilience we have to attend to everything at once. The first is reductive, and the second is overwhelming.

Begin with a general issue

Given how overwhelming the complexity of managing change can be, it is suggested for the purpose of clarity that the focus of a project should be on a single *general issue*. However, rather than reductively assuming that an obvious 'problem' makes for a good project, the general issue and its main objective should be interrogated for their normative assumptions. A general issue can be defined as broadly or narrowly as the convening group decides. It can be as broad as 'the general social sustainability of our city' or as narrow as the cultural sustainability of a particular project in a particular quarter, for example 'the sustainability of street-art and social life along our waterfront'. A general issue can appear to be simple – such as 'resource-use by residents in the city' or 'constructing walking paths through the city'. Alternatively, a general issue can be posed as a direct technical question, such as 'Will the provision of infrastructure for electric vehicles bring about higher sustainability?' Even apparently simple or direct issues are usually more complicated than they appear. There are rarely obvious answers. Given the interconnection of all social issues, an adequate practical response needs to have the same cross-connection sensitivity. As with practical responses to all problems – from the seemingly simple to seemingly intractable – projects for social change benefit from careful management and active community and civic engagement. It is important to understand both the critical issues that have an impact on the general issue and those that are affected by it. This brings us to the third tier.

Move to defining critical issues and associated objectives

In the third tier we assume that the central concept of any assessment process is that of particular *critical issues*. An issue is a reporting category residing among the overall reporting context, the domain model and the specific variables or indicators for which data are collected. As distinct from a general issue – that is an issue encompassing the entire reporting scope – many, many particular issues bear back on any core concern. Critical issues are those which have been identified as critical to the overall project, and that require some level of attention. Issues can be varied. Notionally they represent some kind of concern that is expressed either by experts or by one or more local persons or groups – persons who directly or indirectly are affected by or have interest in the general issue at hand.

Corresponding to the general issue is some kind of normative goal or *general objective*, a consensually determined and shared aim or intention at the heart of the endeavour. Corresponding to subordinate critical issues are *critical objectives*, expressing some particular desirable state of affairs for a given issue. These objectives are determined, ideally, by a deliberative dialogue negotiated by the key constituencies supported by local and outside experts. If the context demands, issues can have further subsidiary components. These are aspects or features of an issue that in turn require separate specification. These, too, may have specific objectives. Of course, it should be noted that the meta-constraint of resources dedicated to the reporting project itself may begin to kick in at this point.

Do not treat critical issues as singular

The fourth tier consists of the importance of working through the relationship between different critical issues/objectives and different indicators, across all domains of social life. The most fundamental relationship describes the state of a critical issue/objective through some combination of indicators, typically once these have been appropriately normalized, weighted and aggregated. Assessing the compatibility of critical issues/objectives and resolving possible tensions between them is fundamental to the success of a project. This step in the process serves in particular to highlight the tensions between different objectives. Social contradictions abound in the world. Such tensions always exist in some way, but often they go unrecognized. For example, economic growth, to the extent that it is associated with increased use of non-renewable resources, is completely incompatible with environmental sustainability.

Cooling buildings as response to climate warming is potentially in a contradictory relation to greenhouse-gas emissions, the cause of climate change in the first place. Increasing the number of tourists to enhance income to enhance local's quality of life can become anathema to quality of life to the extent that it brings congestion, noise, distorts the economy and changes what is means to live in that particular place. Explicitly recognizing the most salient of these tensions and contradictions enhances the possibility that the city will be fully aware of countervailing forces and contradictory objectives, and thus policymakers, practitioners, and engaged locals can find ways to negotiate between these tensions or mitigate possible problems.

Treat indicators as indicators, not as performance targets

The fifth tier consists of choosing a series of *indicators*. Indicators are directly observable and measureable variables that indicate something about one or more issues. Relevant indicators can be taken from the collections of other agencies or from what is already collected locally. The term *indicator composition* is used to describe the process of modelling the relationship of one or more indicators to issues. Other kinds of relationships may be stipulated between two or more issues, between two or more indicator sets, or between two or more individual indicators. A common use-case for such relationships is the need to translate locally developed indicators to global standards, such as the Global Reporting Initiative or the UN Cities Programme. A relationship of *synonymy* can be made between a local and a standard indicator set to describe this. Taken all together, the set of relationships are as follows:

- *Issue categorization* – states that an issue belongs to a given domain or subdomain
- *Indicator categorization* – states that an indicator belongs to a given domain or subdomain
- *Issue composition* – states that one issue is a component of another
- *Indicator composition* – states that one or more indicators measure the state of a given issue. When more than one indicator is involved, the relative contribution or weight of each indicator to the measurement of an issue can be stipulated.
- *Indicator-set membership* – states that an indicator belongs to a particular indicator set
- *Issue, indicator-set and indicator similarity* – state that two given issues or indicators are semantically similar, or more strongly, synonymous

Correlate with other data and analyse

The sixth tier is composed of data collected during the administration of the reporting framework. As mentioned earlier, we envisage these data are collected during the ordinary administration of the framework, and, apart from mentioning the related questionnaire in relation to one of our projects elaborated in Chapter 8 we do not have the space to discuss the many dimensions of this process here.

Learn from the activity of doing the project

The seventh tier underpins all our work – namely reflexive learning. This entails more than just giving time for reflection. It means, first, reflecting on the nature of what is being assumed and the terms of what is being learnt. The call for 'evidence-based policy' is too often an excuse for reframing existing data to prove what one already assumes to be the case. Reflexive learning means asking why are we doing what we are doing. Why is this or that general objective assumed to be good? Why is economic growth assumed to be a positive general objective in the economic domain? Why is the concept of social inclusion used as the catch-cry for positive social engagement with the poor as opposed to the more difficult objective of relative equality?

Secondly, and more deeply, reflexive learning involves recognizing the strengths and weaknesses of modern knowledge systems. For example it is often said that 'knowledge is power', but, without reflection on the ontological layers of knowledge in different social settings, an unreflexive *modernist* response is to conclude that therefore increased dissemination of knowledge (read: information) will give those receiving all that information more power. It is one of the liberal modern illusions, among others, such as 'more interconnectivity will bring about stronger social integration' or 'more inclusion makes for stronger communities'. Information flows in our globalizing world in a way that is without precedent, big data opens ever-increasing sources, interconnectivity has become a constant refrain, and inclusion is written in most NGO manifestos and Western government mission statements, but all of this constitutes no more than a platform for *possible* reform. At worst, it provides legitimacy for new oppression.

Defining the stages of project management

Doing something of significance in the world can certainly be done haphazardly and serendipitously, but when acting together it is better acting with some sense of a common framework. The set of stages of practice presented here is mapped against the UN Global Compact 'Management Model' stages. The process pathway takes us through seven stages: commitment, engagement, assessment, definition, implementation, measurement and communication. When first presented (see Figure 6.1) it looks like a fairly conventional project management model. However, it goes much further than most similar tools. This is achieved by treating the Circles of Practice figure as a way of developing an integrated model that systematically locates all the tools and processes presented in this book and others. Again there is no magical number of stages. But by choosing seven stages as a constraining guideline we have given ourselves scope for elaborating the process with sufficient complexity while keeping the method sufficiently simple to be manageable and understandable.

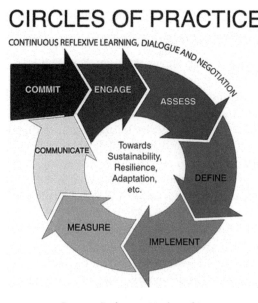

FIGURE 6.1 Process Pathway: Circles of Practice

Commit to responding creatively to a complex or seemingly intractable problem.

Without commitment there is little or nothing. Ideally commitment should be public and collaborative. Rather than held preciously in the corners of one's good intentions it should be communicated widely. The commitment should have content, a broadly conceived objective in relation to a fundamental issue. Ideally it should be linked to an affirmation of a set of principles for action and a set of broad proposals for moving forward.

Engage local and global partners in the process of responding to the provisionally identified main issue.

Engagement can be minimal or elaborate. In the *Circles of Sustainability* approach used by the UN Global Compact Cities Programme, the core group the purpose of going forward involves a management group, a project facilitator, and a critical reference group. The management group is responsible for the eventual application of the framework and overseeing the sustainability process. The management group should ideally include members from different constituencies: civil society, universities, government and business. The project facilitator acts as a facilitator for the application of the methodology and convenes any associated meetings and workshops. The critical reference group extends the circles of engagement. It never has to meet as a whole group, but ideally it comprises representatives of the main constituencies in question. It is used as a basis for individual advice or to draw people into face-to-face workshops. Typically the project facilitator and the management group are employed by the sponsoring organization, whereas the critical reference group is much broader and includes critics of the politics of the management group. Other roles – auditors, information technology support, executive and management teams – may be involved in various stages, according to available resources. Beyond the named critical reference group, it is essential to engage with the general community through the usual consultation processes.

Assess the nature of the problem, and analyse the current situation in relation to the general issue in contention across all social domains.

Assessment is crucial. It is the research phase of the process. The assessment team may need to consult specific members of the critical reference group, as well as source data, such as statistical and demographic surveys, key documents and other information artefacts. Because this stage has been described in general in Chapter 4 and will be developed further in relation developing an urban profile (Chapter 7) and conducting a social questionnaire (Chapter 8) there is no need to elaborate here.

Define the terms of the problem, and identify the most important critical issues that will provide the focus of action in relation to the general issue.

The task of defining a problem is often left to a few experts. One way of taking the process of definition further with better outcomes is to include members of different constituencies in the process. Having identified and invited members into the Critical Reference Group, facilitators can convene workshops for introducing the project, the general issue and the normative objective. Further workshops can be used for beginning the process of identifying a list of subsidiary critical issues and associated objectives. These issues are developed in consideration of the four-domain model of sustainability with a requirement that for any project and *general issue*, critical issues are spread across the four domains. The outcome of such workshops is, ideally, an exhaustive and comprehensive list of issues that matter most in realising the normative goal of the project.

In this fourth stage, to complete the composition of the framework, is a significant advantage to a series of examination of the relationships both between issues and between indicators. The *Circles* method uses a matrix tool based on a modified form of Grosskurth and Rotmans's Qualitative System Sustainability Index (QSSI) model to map critical issues in tension. Mapping these relationships provides the basis for interpreting eventual indicator data (Grosskurth & Rotmans, 2007, pp. 177–88). To take a simple example, a relationship that stipulates the use of available product-recycling approaches places additional cost pressures on waste disposal. Recognizing this can provide explanatory power to the eventual reporting model (in the form of alarm triggers and systematically generated notes that suggest ways of responding to the tension).

At the completion of this phase of the methodology, the management group should have a general project definition (comprising the general issue and associated normative objective), a series of subsidiary, critical issues and associated objectives, a database of indicators and associated targets and, finally, a series of relationships between issues and indicators. This definitional structure can then direct the fifth, sixth and seventh stages: implementation, measurement and communication.

> *Implement* measures to respond to the problem, and authorize the various aspects of the plan and its subprojects within project parameters.

> *Measure* and monitor activities, and assess progress towards achieving the normative goal and objectives of the project.

> *Communicate* progress and strategies in relation to the project through public documentation, publication and through engagement with stakeholders.

Communication should occur all the way through the project, including the implementation stage. However, it has been placed as the 'last' stage to emphasize the importance of reporting deeply and widely. The process as outlined pushed organizations towards the production of a sustainability report, based on responding to critical issues and measuring outcomes. Less obviously but equally critically, it pushes cities towards the generation of an interpretive mesh for understanding the often-complex constellation of relationships between issues and indicators. Coming to terms with the impositions, compromises, trade-offs and affordances around the general issue of the project allow stakeholders to employ the resulting framework in policy development and monitoring and in adjusting that framework to evolving issues.

These stages can be elaborated into increasingly detailed phases. When laid out in relation to the various phases, activities and tools through a process pathway the full method can be seen in one image. It is has a possible starting point and a logical set of steps, but it has no set end and no single, defined mandatory pathway. It is an iterative process that once begun will ideally spiral through the circle of sustainable development a few times. Moving through the process can be fast or slow; it can skip steps the first time and come back to them the second time around with more intense focus; and it can either be done with minimal or maximum engagement, or somewhere in between. Other tools can be added to the process pathway, and work already done can be assessed in terms of the process pathway and incorporated into the mix.

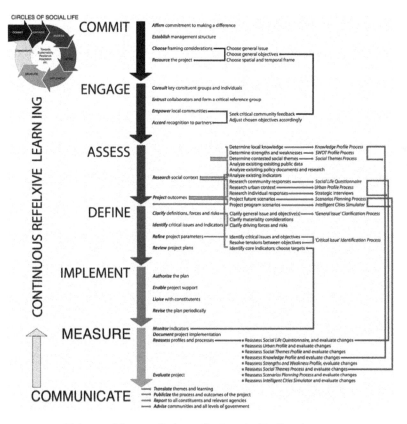

FIGURE 6.2 Elaborated Process Pathway for Sustainable Development

APPENDIX

All that we have done in elaborating the process pathway is open up the black box of planning so that the various possible stages and phases have been put into a visible, contestable and (hopefully) useful systematic framework. This sort of process consultants usually leave hidden and only make available to paying clients. It is not intended that a project attend to all of the phases as outlined in the process pathway, but it is part of the strength of the method that project managers and constituents know what is being left out of the project management process when it is used as less than the thick method it could be.

In spite of the apparent linearity of the presentation, the methodology can be employed both within and between reporting cycles, and at both micro and macro levels. In particular, critical issues, indicators and relationships can be continuously recalibrated with the aim of promoting a broader, consensual picture of sustainability among stakeholders. Similarly, the steps can be abbreviated to a minimal critical path or can be expanded to invoke richer sub-processes.

TABLE 6.1 Process Stages in Relation to the Tools

Process stages	Process phases	Process phases—possible tasks	Process tools—possible guidelines, and terms of reference
1. Commit	**Affirm** commitment to making a difference	**Affirm** a long-term commitment to taking on a significant project that responds to a complex issue and will potentially bring about positive social change. For example,	• Guideline 1.1. *Overview: Process Pathway*

Process stages	Process phases	Process phases—possible tasks	Process tools—possible guidelines, and terms of reference
		• affirm publicly a commitment to take on a significant project.	
		• affirm commitment to the ten principles of the United Nations Global Compact.	• Guideline 1.2. *Principles of the Cities Programme*
		• affirm agreement with the Cities Programme Principles of Action.	• Guideline 1.3. *Principles of Action*
		• affirm engagement with the Cities Programme.	• Terms of Reference 1.1 Signatory Cities 1.2 Leading Cities 1.3 Innovating Cities
	Establish the management structure	**Establish** a management group who can carry forward a process of social change. Ideally this should be based on a broad partnership of people from different levels of government, civil society and business. For example,	
		• establish a Management Group to run the project.	• Guideline 1.4. *Principles of Partnership* (in development)
		• establish a Local or Regional Secretariat of the UN Global Compact Cities Programme.	• Terms of Reference 1.4 Local Secretariat 1.5 Regional Secretariat
	Choose the framing considerations	**Choose** the framing considerations, including the general issue in question, the general objective of the project and the material scope of the project. For example:	
		• choose the general issue the city wishes to address.	• Guideline 1.5. *Project Profile Template*
		• choose the general objective(s) in relation to that general issue.	
		• choose the temporal and spatial scope of the project.	

(Continued)

TABLE 6.1 (*Continued*)

Process stages	Process phases	Process phases—possible tasks	Process tools—possible guidelines, and terms of reference
	Resource the project	**Resource** the project financially or begin to explore ways of sustaining the project through in-kind, personnel, infrastructural or financial support. For example, • resource the Management Group administrative costs taking into account the possibility of seconded staff, in-kind support such as office space or seed-funding. • resource the project costs for research and implementation or set up a mechanism for developing an unfolding budget.	
2. Engage	**Consult** key constituent groups and individuals	**Consult** as widely as possible and get advice on key people who should be appointed to a consultative reference group. For example, • consult locally with key constituent groups and individuals, including through meetings and public forums, based on the 'all-affected principle'. • consult with the Cities Programme Executive and its Global Advisors. • consult more broadly, including if necessary with professional consultants. • consult about who should be named as part of an honorary group of advisors to the project.	• Guideline 2.1. *Conditions of Engagement*

Process stages	Process phases	Process phases—possible tasks	Process tools—possible guidelines, and terms of reference
	Entrust collaborators and form a critical reference group	**Entrust** a group of advisors and name a consultative reference group, seeking to select a range of persons who are engaged across sectors relevant to the project and from across all domains of social life – economic, ecological, political and cultural. For example, • entrust a critical reference group by appointing key advisors and naming them publicly.	
	Empower local communities	**Empower** local communities who are in any way affected by the project through inviting them into an ongoing critical engagement. For example, • empower local communities by actively seeking critical and constructive feedback during this stage and all subsequent stages of the project. • empower communities through integrating the results of earlier consultations into a rough preliminary 'project description' to which local people can respond.	
	Accord recognition to partners	**Accord** recognition to the different partners and individuals who, in multifarious ways, are contributing to the project. For example,	

(*Continued*)

TABLE 6.1 (*Continued*)

Process stages	Process phases	Process phases—possible tasks	Process tools—possible guidelines, and terms of reference
		• accord recognition to institutional partners, contributing organizations and affiliated individuals through public naming, such as through publishing those names on a website. • accord recognition through developing memorandum of understanding.	
3. Assess	**Determine** knowledge and resources	**Determine** the available relevant information sets and the knowledge base of individuals associated with the project. For example,	
		• determine the knowledge base of the management group and the critical reference group (and bring in more expertise if necessary).	• Guideline 3.1. *Knowledge Profile Process* (in development)
		• determine what relevant data is already available in relation to the locale, map against the *Circles of Sustainability* domains and archive material in an accessible way.	• Guideline 3.2. *Local–Global Database*
		• determine strengths and weaknesses.	• Guideline 3.3. *Strengths and Weaknesses Profile* (in development)
		• determine what relevant indicators are currently collected. • determine if additional resources are required and seek to acquire those resources.	

Process stages	Process phases	Process phases—possible tasks	Process tools—possible guidelines, and terms of reference
	Analyse data and documents	**Analyse** the current situation in relation to the general issue in contentionacross all social domains – economics, ecology, politics and culture. For example, • analyse existing public data. • analyse existing policy documents.	
	Research social context	**Research** the background context to the general issue and seek to understand driving forces on the general issue. For example, • research driving forces • research the overall sustainability profile of the chosen urban locale. • research community responses through social questionnaires. • research individual responses through interviews. • research tensions in social life.	 • Guideline 3.4. *Urban Profile Process* • Guideline 3.5. *Social Life Questionnaire* • Guideline 3.6. Interviews and Conversations • Guideline 3.7. *Social Themes Profile Process*
	Project outcomes	**Project** current developments into future possible scenarios, based on current possible trajectories, as a way of anticipating the consequences of social change. For example, • project future social scenarios through eveloping stories about alternative pathways. • project program scenarios by anticipating the effects of the project in question on other aspects of social life in the urban locale.	 • Guideline 3.8. *Scenarios Planning Process* • Guideline 3.9. *Project Simulation Process: The Intelligent Cities Simulator*

(Continued)

TABLE 6.1 *(Continued)*

Process stages	Process phases	Process phases—possible tasks	Process tools—possible guidelines, and terms of reference
4. Define	**Clarify** definitions, forces and risks	**Clarify** definitions of the general issue in question and the key materiality considerations of the project. For example, • clarify the definitions of the general issue. • clarify the general objective in relation to that issue. • clarify the relation between the general objective and the ten United Nations principles. • clarify materiality considerations of the project in response to the general issues, including defining the time frame and spatial scope of the project. • clarify the driving forces affecting the general issue. • clarify risks and challenges involved in effecting social change.	• Guideline 4.1. *General Issue Clarification Process*
	Identify critical issues and indicators	**Identify** the most important critical issues that will provide the focus of action in relation to the general issue, and decide on the objectives and indicators of change in relation to each of those critical issues. For example, • identify the critical issues that affect the main issue. • identify the critical objectives in relation to the critical issues. • identify and resolve tensions between critical objectives. • identify key indicators.	• Guideline 4.2. *Critical Issues Identification Process*

Process stages	Process phases	Process phases—possible tasks	Process tools—possible guidelines, and terms of reference
	Refine project parameters	**Refine** the project directions and parameters in order to finalize plans for implementation. For example, • refine the project parameters in the light of the clarified definitions and risk assessments. • refine the budget parameters. • refine indicator targets. • refine and finalize the overall plan.	
	Review project plans	**Review** the strengths and weakness of the current overall plan through enlisting expert outsiders. For example, • review the overall plan through a peer-review process, bringing to your city people who have had experience of similar projects elsewhere, and/or • review the overall plan through a consultancy process.	• Guideline 4.3. *Peer Review Process* (in development)
5. Implement	**Authorize** the plan	**Authorize** the various aspects of the plan and its subprojects within project parameters. For example, • authorize coordinators and delegate authority to them. • authorize contracts to be signed. • authorize budgets and expenditure lines. • authorize approval processes for planned steps. • authorize procurement processes.	• Guideline 5.1. *Procurement Process* (in development)

(*Continued*)

TABLE 6.1 (*Continued*)

Process stages	Process phases	Process phases—possible tasks	Process tools—possible guidelines, and terms of reference
	Enable project support	**Enable** the various aspects of project support. For example, • enable appointments processes necessary to conducting the project. • enable necessary training processes and team development. • enable necessary procurement processes and activities. • enable necessary technology installation.	
	Liaise with constituents	**Liaise** with all relevant constituents (stakeholders and affiliates) through the implementation process.	
	Revise the plan periodically	**Revise** the plan periodically on agreed intervals, adjusting the details of implementation where necessary given changing circumstances and responses to project developments.	
6. Measure	**Monitor** indicators	**Monitor** the progress of the project throughout the period of its implementation and after. For example, • monitor activities, and assess progress towards achieving the main goal and objectives of the project. • monitor indicators chosen during the Identification and Refinement phases.	
	Document project implementation	**Document** the project implementation process. For example, • document the project implementation through written papers, and disseminate publicly, such as through a website or a Local–Global database.	• Guideline 3.2. *Local–Global database*

Process stages	Process phases	Process phases—possible tasks	Process tools—possible guidelines, and terms of reference
	Reassess profiles and processes	**Reassess** the way in which the project has broader impact by rerunning previously used assessment tools – or run them for the first time to generate baseline data for tracking longer-term changes over time. For example, • reassess by conducting an urban profile process again. • reassess by running the Social Questionnaire again. • reassess through a further round of interviews. • reassess Social Themes Profile.	• Guideline 3.4. *Urban Profile Process* • Guideline 3.5. *Social Life Questionnaire* • Guideline 3.6. *Interviews and Conversations* • Guideline 3.7. *Social Themes Profile Process*
	Evaluate overall project outcomes	**Evaluate** the overall project outcomes, including strengths and limitations. For example, • evaluate data from each of the processes run during the Reassessment phase. • evaluate the project internally through a major written report. • evaluate the project externally through a consultancy process.	
7. Communicate	**Translate** themes and learning	**Translate** the technical dimensions of the project into lay language for broad communication. For example, • translate the technical material including themes, critical issues, objectives and outcomes of the project into easily accessible language for broad public dissemination.	

(*Continued*)

TABLE 6.1 (*Continued*)

Process stages	Process phases	Process phases—possible tasks	Process tools—possible guidelines, and terms of reference
	Publicize the process and outcomes of the project	**Publicize** the process, outcomes and themes of the project and its subprojects. For example, • Publicize through meetings, in media releases, through dissemination of documentation and by archiving material in the Local–Global database, etc. • Publicize the themes and nature of the project through innovative learning tools.	• Guideline 7.1. *Fierce Planet Video Game*
	Report outcomes of the project	**Report** on the project in an ongoing way throughout its various stages. For example, • report on decisions and outcomes to all constituents, partners and relevant agencies through appropriate levels of documentation, including through web-based dissemination.	• Guideline 7.2. *Communication on Progress*
	Advise communities, partners and government	**Advise** communities, partners and all levels of government about next steps.	

CASE STUDY: PORTO ALEGRE, BRAZIL

The *Circles of Sustainability* methodology has been used in a number of projects, but for present purposes we present a community project in Porto Alegre, Brazil, called the Chocolatão Community Resettlement project. The project involved the resettlement of 800 or so residents of the inner-city favela in Porto Alegre, Brazil. The residents of the Chocolatão settlement maintained their living through garbage picking and selling the recycled matter to local buyers of waste paper, plastic, metals and glass. The slum was full of rubbish and the people were often sick.

How was it possible to relocate such a community without the usual profound problems? Normally we would recommend against relocating the residents of informal settlements at all. Instead, rehabilitation and upgrading of the basic infrastructure and gradual formalization of the area is a much better alternative. Normally, deep resentment arises from a displacement. The lives of the displaced community are not improved, even if their new houses are made of concrete rather than building waste. Normally, relocation is a counterproductive short-term 'solution', and over time, without an infrastructure of ongoing livelihoods in their new neighbourhood, the people drift back into new slums closer to the centre of the city.

In this case, relocation was necessary for health and security reasons, and the city was determined to handle the process quite differently from business as usual. Instead of giving notice and contracting bulldozers, the project was implemented steadily and progressively over a period of seven years, with the resettlement of residents finally occurring in May 2011. The project became part of a whole-of-city reconstruction of how it is possible to deal positively with slums.

At the inception of the project, the city of Porto Alegre and our team (through the International Secretariat of the United Nations Global Compact Cities Programme) worked collaboratively towards identifying synergies between the objectives of the municipality's Local Solidarity Governance Scheme and the Cities Programme. The scheme promoted participatory processes through which local communities in seventeen regions within the municipality conducted workshops that enabled citizens to vote on and prioritize categories of urban problems. Housing emerged as a key concern for citizens and was accordingly identified as the general issue for Porto Alegre's Cities Programme project. Although it would become much bigger, the overall normative objective of the project at the time was to devise a long-term, sustainable and ethical strategy for resettling the residents of the Chocolatão slum. The practical objective became one of moving them to a suburban region of Porto Alegre where new, modularized housing would be constructed.

In line with an early version of the present method, city hall assembled a critical reference group with representatives from government, the private sector and civil society. One month later, in December 2007, city hall hosted a workshop aimed at refining the project by allowing reference group members to identify critical issues and joint solutions to those issues involved in the resettlement. Representatives from the local community, various municipal government departments (Housing, Health, Waste, Water, Education, Local Solidarity Governance, Funding and Investments, Industry and Commerce, Finance, Security and Human Rights and the Office of the First Lady), the federal government and NGOs (Velásques, Martist Brothers and the Foundation for Assistance and Citizenship) participated in the first workshop.

A key outcome of the workshop was that participants recognized that the resettlement project would involve more than simply rehousing the Chocolatão residents. There were cultural and political themes that went far beyond the ecological subdomains of habitat and settlements and built form and transport. This was further reflected by the involvement of ten municipal government departments unrelated to housing. Although the workshop's ostensible aim was to focus on the resettlement project, it also served to address immediate concerns about garbage-exacerbated fires, children's health and community identity in the neighbourhood – and in all informal settlements. Children were getting sick from the garbage being recycled in their homes, and their schooling was intermittent. This not only indirectly highlighted the importance of the housing issue as a whole but also emphasized the subdomain of engagement and identity. Rather than be shifted into an anonymous housing zone the community wanted to stay together.

A second workshop was held with the same reference group six months later, in mid-2008. This addressed some of the perspicuous community concerns with the proposed resettlement, such as safety and livelihoods. The latter two issues were especially pertinent given the location of the resettlement in an outer suburban area. The main economic activity for residents in the community involved sorting and recycling waste produced by industry in downtown areas of the city. The resettlement threatened that activity. Here was the possible breaking point. Gradually an alternative pathway emerged. Recycling depots were to be built by local companies near the new location and supported by the municipality. Worker cooperative arrangements were suggested. The purpose of the cooperative was not only to allow recycling to be done more efficiently at the new site but also to provide sustainable livelihoods and take the recycling out of people's homes where children's health was being badly affected by the storage of rubbish.

Subsequently, regular, sometimes weekly, meetings occurred between representatives of Vila Chocolatão and city representatives. The workshops stopped, seen perhaps misadvisedly as having completed their role. The community meetings were initially riven with conflict, but over time trust developed, and a full local community consultation process developed. The ongoing representative process became the basis for treating local governance very seriously – issues in the political subdomain of representation and negotiation moved into underpin discussions of organization and governance. A local governing group emerged that was strong enough to carry the community through powerful counter-pressures, including from the drug cartels.

Looking back uncritically from the present, the project has been incredibly successful in rehousing a whole community of slum dwellers. Their lives have qualitatively improved and incomes have moved from wretched subsistence to living wages. More than that, because recycling depots were built across the city in relation to other settlement workers, the informal landscape has changed more comprehensively.

Nearly two years after the resettlement, the process is still working. One of the keys to the success was the way in which the project worked across the four domains of sustainability to restructure the garbage collection process of the entire city (linking the subdomains of emission and waste and organization and governance), set up recycling depots next to existing slums, and at the new Residencia Chocolatão. The cultural pride of slum dwellers was transformed, including by using identity-based graffiti linked to the subdomain of performance and creativity. That recognition meant that instead of bulldozing a community, with non-negotiable relocation into concrete blocks on the periphery of the city – only to find those people returning to the inner-city slum where their livelihoods were based – the new *residencia* has become an ecologically sustainable place where people are culturally proud to live *and stay*.

The case study exemplifies the role that passionate local management and strong community engagement can play in urban sustainability projects. Members of the affected community were, in effect, given opportunity to articulate the main issue addressed by the project, and identify subordinate critical issues that they saw needing to be addressed. They may not have explicitly thought of themselves as moving through clear steps, but the outcome covered the ground of clarifying and defining critical issues. Moreover, in accordance with our discussion earlier of the problems with treating communities as singular, the project sought out intersecting and conflicting community relations. In the case of Vila Chocolatão project, this included the communities in the area in which the people of Chocolatão would be relocated, people who were initially alarmed that a group of dirty rubbish pickers was moving into their clean suburban area.

Along the way, we learned much as researchers about the complexity of local projects, including the need for a more critical and ongoing assessment process which would provide illustrative material to show the success of that project to less community-engaged regions, but also to build on this first stage in Porto Alegre itself. The lack of *consistent*, ongoing consultation and monitoring across the different constituencies through the project confirmed, in our view, the need for more systemic engagement in the mechanisms of reporting and assessment. The lack of bottom-up reporting detracted from the substantive even extraordinary outcomes. Although community participation was fundamental to the successful relocation of residents to a new housing facility, our lack of capacity to carry forward the workshops and involve cross-community members together with local experts in ongoing sustainability assessment of their project meant this function continued to reside at a distance with local and state authorities. It clouded some of the transparency and, even for such a successful project, meant that state-based and municipally mediated housing policies restricted for example the creativity of the process to modularized-design houses that some residents now feel need modifying. At the same time, we appreciate the pragmatic and economic justifications for using top-down performance indicators and processes in each case. The world is not a place for theoretical purity. In almost all terms this was an inspiring outcome.

Note

1 Andy Scerri and Liam Magee are the main co-authors of this chapter with Paul James. Lin Padgham, James Thom, Hepu Deng, Sarah Hickmott and Felicity Cahill also contributed substantially to the conceptual development of the chapter.

References

Deegan, Craig 2013, 'The Accountant will have a Central Role in Saving the Planet . . . Really? A Reflection on "Green Accounting and Green Eyeshades Twenty Years Later"', *Critical Perspectives on Accounting*, vol. 24, no. 6, pp. 448–58.

Grosskurth, J., & Rotmans, J. 2007, 'Qualitative System Sustainability Index: A New Type of Sustainability Indicator, in Hák, T., Moldan, B., & Dahl A. L., eds, *Sustainability Indicators: A Scientific Assessment*, Island Press, Washington, pp. 177–88.

Reed, M. 2008, 'Stakeholder Participation for Environmental Management: A Literature Review', *Biological Conservation*, vol. 141, no. 10, pp. 2,417–31.

7

GENERATING AN URBAN SUSTAINABILITY PROFILE[1]

The Urban Profile Process is intended as a way of developing an interpretative description of the sustainability of an urban region and its immediate hinterland. There are many such tools for measuring sustainability, but most of those tools either depend on developing hugely expensive banks of statistics or on turning to one-off, narrow and limited surveys. As cities become larger and more complex places, located in a world slipping into unsustainability, the complexity of measurement has redoubled. Measurement needs to be equally attuned to things as different as carbon emissions and the spirit of place. The lyrics of Leonard Cohen's song 'The Future' point to this complexity with a particular poignancy: we have crossed a threshold; the order of the soul has been overturned.

The Urban Profile Process uses a systematic series of qualitative questions organized around the four-domain model laid out earlier in Chapter 3. By answering these questions across the full range of the social practices and meanings it is intended that a simple figurative representation can be developed of the complexity of a given situation at a given time (thus meeting the requirement of *simple complexity* discussed earlier). The sustainability profile template laid out in this chapter is intended as a way of developing a comprehensive understanding of an urban region – a city, a metropolis, a town, a municipality or a village.

The depth of the analysis depends very much on who is enlisted to use the tool and how much time they put into it. Using the Urban Profile Process it is possible to generate a clear and simple graphic representation of the sustainability profile of that region in a very short time, but that does not mean that the graphic representation is anything more than a starting point. On the other hand, with sufficient time and resources, the tool can be used to frame a process that is thorough, deep and ongoing.

What we are trying to measure are basic questions across the four domains:

1. At what level and how sustainable is the ecological *resilience* of the urban region? Here the question refers the extent to which people's impact upon and involvement with nature can enhance both their own physical well-being and the capacity of the urban and hinterland environment to flourish in the face of external impact.
2. At what level and how sustainable is the economic *prosperity* of the urban region? Prosperity does not mean the level of wealth or material possessions. It is worth remembering that the term derives from Latin *prosperare*, according to expectation for, *pro*, and hope, *spes*. The basic question refers to the issue of what extent can local urban communities engage in activities relevant to their economic well-being and be confident about the sustainability of their local economies in the face of changing structures and pressures in and beyond their locale.
3. At what level and how sustainable is political *engagement* of people in the city? Here the urban profile gives an understanding of the extent to which members of communities can participate and collaborate meaningfully in structures and processes of power that affect them and others.
4. Finally, at what level and how sustainable is the cultural *vitality* of the urban region? This refers to the extent to which communities are able to maintain and develop their beliefs, celebrate their practices and rituals, and cultivate diverse systems of meaning, and its long-term sustainability.

Pilot studies have already been conducted in a number of cities across the world using the various drafts of the process tool in development. Some of those are represented in Figure 7.1.

Each of these figures represents a qualitative assessment by local and other experts of the sustainability of the respective urban areas. The quality and the standing of the assessment depend on the expertise of the persons who are conducting the assessment. Optimally, we suggest that the assessment group should comprise three to ten people with different and complementary expertise about the urban area in question. Deliberation, discussion and debate is ideally right at the heart of the process. Table 7.1 is intended for recording the names and expertise of the persons on the assessment panel.

The assessment panel should meet for a sustained period to conduct the assessment. The amount of time taken depends upon the nature of the assessment (see Table 7.2). Two hours is possible for a rapid assessment; 4 hours is minimal for an aggregate assessment, but a day would be better to allow for proper contestation and discussion. It might, however, take significantly longer for an annotated assessment. And a comprehensive assessment would take from a few months to a year, depending on how much dedicated time is given to it. Ideally, individuals on the panel should read through the questions before meeting as a panel and when necessary seek information about issues with which they are not familiar.

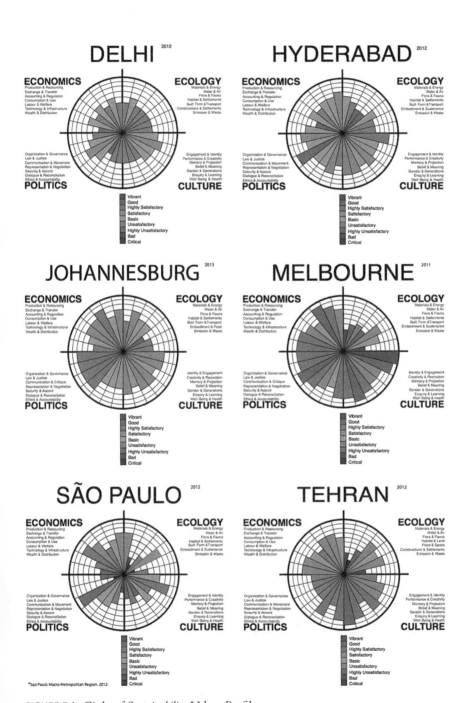

FIGURE 7.1 *Circles of Sustainability* Urban Profiles

TABLE 7.1 Urban Profile Assessors on the Assessment Panel

The profile mapping process can be done by different kinds of respondents. Different people have different knowledge sets, all of which can be valuable in making an urban assessment. In order to understand the nature of the assessment, we just need to know what kind of knowledge is held by each respondent in the Assessment Panel.	*Please indicate which kind of respondent(s) you are by adding names in the boxes below. Add more lines or more space to the list if necessary.*	
1. **Internal Expert Assessors** That is, individuals who live in the urban region in question and have expert knowledge* of that region or a significant aspect of that region. * Here 'expert knowledge' is defined as either being trained in some aspect of urban planning/administration, etc., or working in that capacity for some time.	Name	Position and/or Training
2. **External Expert Assessors** That is individuals who do not live in the urban region in question but have expert knowledge of that region or a significant aspect of that region.	Name	Position and/or Training
3. **Lay Assessors** That is, individuals who live in the urban region in question, and who have extensive local knowledge of the region or an aspect of the region, (without necessarily either being trained in urban planning, administration, or working in the field).	Name	Length of time having lived in the urban region

In approaching the tool, the following guidelines are given:

If you are conducting a rapid assessment only the general question in each set needs to be answered. That question works as a proxy question for that whole area of sustainability. If you are conducting an aggregate assessment at least six of the questions in each set of seven questions need to be answered. If one of the questions in each set is deemed to be particularly inappropriate for your urban area, you can either choose to replace that one question with an alternative question that you formulate for yourself or choose not to answer that question and leave the assessment blank.

In most cases, the questions will be weighted equally in finalizing the assessment – that is, unless a prior round of assessment is done to rank and weight the questions in each perspective in relation to each other.

TABLE 7.2 The Nature of the Assessment Process

The profile mapping process can be done at five levels:	*Please indicate which profile exercise you intend to complete by ticking the box or boxes below.*	
1. **Rapid Assessment Profile** By responding to the single 'general question' under each 'perspective' by marking the 9-point scale.	☐	
2. **Aggregate Assessment Profile** By responding to the 'particular questions' under each 'perspective' by marking the 9-point scale).	☐	and/or
3. **Annotated Assessment Profile** By completing the exercise at level 2 *and* writing detailed annotations about how the points on the scale were derived.	☐	and/or
4. **Comprehensive Assessment Profile, I** By completing the exercise at level 3 *and* writing a major essay on the urban area using the questions to guide the writing. and/or	☐	and/or
Comprehensive Assessment Profile, II By completing the exercise at level 3 and assigning metrics-based indicators to each point on the scale.	☐	and/or
5. **A Certified Assessment** By completing an Assessment Profile at one of the previous levels, and then negotiating with the certifying body – e.g., the UN Cities Programme Secretariat – to have their Global Advisors critical respond and certify that assessment.	☐	and/or

Definitions for the purposes of this questionnaire

- Sustainability is defined as activity that 'meets the needs of the present without compromising the ability of future generations to meet their own needs'. This is the minimal definition of what in the questionnaire calls a level of 'satisfactory sustainability'.
- Positive sustainability is defined as practices and meanings of human engagement that make for an ongoing lifeworld that projects natural and social flourishing or vibrancy.
- Urban area, or area, as used in the questionnaire means the area that you have defined as the basis for making this assessment. The concept of local is used to mean the space within the urban area.
- Urban region means the urban area and its immediate hinterlands, including its peri-urban extensions, adjacent agricultural and rural land, and its water catchment areas if they are in the immediate vicinity of the urban area.

- Broader region is taken to mean within two to three hours' land transport from the urban region.
- Concepts such as good and appropriate are to be defined in terms of the values of the sustainability assessment respondents, but in an annotated assessment these are the sorts of issues that would need to be defined by the assessment panel.

The scale for critical judgement

The questionnaire asks for critical judgement on a nine-point scale of sustainability from critical sustainability to vibrant sustainability. The period in question is the present (unless otherwise specified) and the limits of projection are the next thirty years or one generation, using the United Nations' definition of sustainable development as development that meets the needs of the people now, without compromising the needs of the next generation.

Critical sustainability, at the least sustainable end of the sustainability spectrum, means a level of sustainability that requires critical or urgent change *now* in order to be assured of continuing basic viability over the next thirty years and thus into the adult lives of the next generation.

Vibrant sustainability, at the other end of the spectrum, means a level of sustainability that is currently active in reproducing vibrant social and environmental conditions that augur well for long-term *positive* viability for the next generation and beyond.

Basic sustainability, the midpoint on the scale, signifies a level of sustainability that allows, all other pressures being equal, for a basic equilibrium over the coming period meeting the needs of the next generation (see Table 7.3).

The Urban Profile process works on the basis of a four-domain model with each domain is divided into seven perspectives, and seven questions are asked about each perspective (see the questionnaire in the Appendix to this chapter).

TABLE 7.3 The Scale of Sustainability

1	2	3	4	5	6	7	8	9
Critical	Bad	Highly Unsatisfactory	Unsatisfactory	Basic	Satisfactory	Highly Satisfactory	Good	Vibrant

APPENDIX: URBAN PROFILE QUESTIONNAIRE

Ecology

1. Materials and energy

General Question: How sustainable is energy production for the urban area?

1	2	3	4	5	6	7	8	9
Critical	Bad	Highly Unsatisfactory	Unsatisfactory	Basic	Satisfactory	Highly Satisfactory	Good	Vibrant

Particular Questions   *Number 1–9*
How sustainable are the following aspects of the urban area?

1. The availability of material resources in the broader region[2]
2. The availability of food grown in the immediate urban region[3]
3. The availability of minerals and metals sourced from the broader region
4. The proportion of electricity produced for the urban area by renewable means
5. The dependence of the urban area on fossil fuels
6. The use of recycled materials
7. The translation of resource-use monitoring into reduction strategies
   • *Optional alternative question:*

2. Water and air

General Question: How sustainable are the levels of air quality and water quality in the urban environment?

1	2	3	4	5	6	7	8	9
Critical	Bad	Highly Unsatisfactory	Unsatisfactory	Basic	Satisfactory	Highly Satisfactory	Good	Vibrant

Particular Questions   *Number 1–9*
How sustainable are the following aspects of the urban area?

1. The bodies of water in the urban region
2. The ready access of all to potable water distributed with minimum energy-use
3. The continuous presence of good quality air in the urban region
4. The liveability of the urban region's climate
5. The carbon footprint of the urban area
6. The development of climate-change adaptation strategies for the urban area
7. The translation of air and water quality in the area monitoring into quality-improvement strategies
    • *Optional alternative question:*

3. Flora and fauna

General Question: To what extent is biodiversity sustainable across the urban region?

1	2	3	4	5	6	7	8	9
Critical	Bad	Highly Unsatisfactory	Unsatisfactory	Basic	Satisfactory	Highly Satisfactory	Good	Vibrant

Particular Questions   *Number 1–9*
How sustainable are the following aspects of the urban region?

1. The resilience of regional ecosystems to past and present urbanization
2. The biodiversity of the region now by comparison with the time of its first major settlement
3. The rate of native plant species' extinction in the urban region across the last 100 years
4. The tree coverage of the urban region – native or otherwise

Particular Questions   *Number 1–9*
How sustainable are the following aspects of the urban region?

5. The continuing viability of native species of birds and animals in the urban region
6. The relation of people in the urban region to non-domesticated animals and birds
7. The translation of monitoring of flora and fauna into sustainability-improvement strategies
   • *Optional alternative question:*

4. Habitat and settlements

General Question: How well does the urban area relate *ecologically* to the landscape on which it is built?

1	2	3	4	5	6	7	8	9
Critical	Bad	Highly Unsatisfactory	Unsatisfactory	Basic	Satisfactory	Highly Satisfactory	Good	Vibrant

Particular Questions   *Number 1–9*
How sustainable are the following aspects of the urban region?

1. The human liveability of the regional topography
2. The extent of original habitat still viable in the urban region
3. The existence of natural spaces – either original habitat or parks and gardens – as integral and accessible to all local neighbourhoods[4]
4. The limiting of building in areas prone to natural risks such as flooding and landslides
5. The use of appropriate materials in buildings[5]
6. The retrofitting of buildings and infrastructure to respond to environmental issues
7. The translation of habitat monitoring in the urban area into robust conservation strategies
   • *Optional alternative question:*

5. Built form and transport

General Question: Does the form of the urban area and its transport system support sustainable living?

1	2	3	4	5	6	7	8	9
Critical	Bad	Highly Unsatisfactory	Unsatisfactory	Basic	Satisfactory	Highly Satisfactory	Good	Vibrant

Particular Questions: *Number 1–9*
How sustainable are the following aspects of the urban area?

1. The spread of the urban area – with particular concern in relation to urban sprawl
2. The access of people to the different social amenities across the urban area through overlapping transport modes
3. The accessibility of mass transit systems in the urban area – particularly as extending to the urban fringes and non-formal zones[6]
4. The degree of dependence on cars
5. The level of support for using non-motorized transport such as bicycles and walking through provision of safe walking paths, protected bike-lane networks, low-speed residential zones, etc.
6. The implementation of energy-use reduction practices for air and sea transport
7. The translation of transport monitoring into quality-improvement strategies
   • *Optional alternative questions:*

6. Embodiment and sustenance

General Question: How sustainable is the urban area in supporting the physical health of people?[7]

1	2	3	4	5	6	7	8	9
Critical	Bad	Highly Unsatisfactory	Unsatisfactory	Basic	Satisfactory	Highly Satisfactory	Good	Vibrant

Particular Questions   *Number 1–9*
How sustainable are the following aspects of the urban area?

1. The general physical health of residents
2. The rate of infant mortality in the urban area
3. The level of physical exercise enacted regularly by all people in the urban area
4. The hygiene of urban streets for all people
5. The nutrition of food generally eaten by residents
6. The level of urban agriculture in the urban area, including in people's home sites
7. The translation of physical health monitoring into quality-improvement strategies
   • *Optional alternative question:*

7. Emission and waste

General Question: How sustainable is the way that the urban area deals with emissions and waste?

1	2	3	4	5	6	7	8	9
Critical	Bad	Highly Unsatisfactory	Unsatisfactory	Basic	Satisfactory	Highly Satisfactory	Good	Vibrant

Particular Questions   *Number 1–9*
How sustainable are the following aspects of the urban area?

1. The level of carbon emissions in the urban area
2. The amount of hard waste produced by the urban area
3. The treatment of sewage, including the subsequent dispersal of the treated products
4. The storm-water drainage system in the urban area
5. The composting of household green and vegetable waste
6. The level of hard-waste recycling in the urban area
7. The translation of emissions and waste monitoring into quality-improvement strategies
   • *Optional alternative question:*

Economics

1. Production and resourcing

General Question: How sustainable are the broad patterns of production and resource access in the urban area?

1	2	3	4	5	6	7	8	9
Critical	Bad	Highly Unsatisfactory	Unsatisfactory	Basic	Satisfactory	Highly Satisfactory	Good	Vibrant

Particular Questions   *Number 1–9*
How sustainable are the following aspects of the urban area?

1. The general prosperity of the urban area
2. The local manufacturing base of the urban area for producing basic goods
3. The access in the urban area to necessary primary resources
4. The arts communities in the urban area[8]
5. The level of design expertise in the urban area[9]
6. The labour resources of the urban area[10]
7. The translation of economic monitoring into quality-improvement strategies
   • *Optional alternative question:*

2. Exchange and transfer

General Question: How sustainable is the current movement of money, goods and services into and through the urban area?

1	2	3	4	5	6	7	8	9
Critical	Bad	Highly Unsatisfactory	Unsatisfactory	Basic	Satisfactory	Highly Satisfactory	Good	Vibrant

Particular Questions   *Number 1–9*
How sustainable are the following aspects of the urban area?

1. The opportunity to participate in ethical trade – for example, locally through community gardens and produce markets or globally through fair-trade networks
2. The availability of basic goods, including through non-commercial and low-cost outlets
3. The fair redistribution of financial resources through processes such as the tax system
4. The resilience of external trade relations, including through bilateral exchange agreements between cities
5. The provision of material aid and social support to people in need beyond the immediate the urban area
6. The levels of debt carried by different sectors of the urban area – both public and private
7. The translation of financial monitoring into quality-improvement strategies
• *Optional additional question:*

3. Accounting and regulation

General Question: How robust are the various accounting and regulatory frameworks in the urban area?

1	2	3	4	5	6	7	8	9
Critical	Bad	Highly Unsatisfactory	Unsatisfactory	Basic	Satisfactory	Highly Satisfactory	Good	Vibrant

Particular Questions   *Number 1–9*
How sustainable are the following aspects of the urban area?

1. The transparency of public spending
2. The robustness of financial auditing systems that apply in the urban area[11]
3. The appropriateness of regulation of goods and services[12]
4. The application of consistent land-use regulation
5. The appropriate regulation of financial systems that affect the urban area

6. The appropriate regulation of labour practices,
   including health and safety considerations
7. The translation of the monitoring of regulatory systems
   into quality-improvement strategies
   • *Optional alternative question:*

4. Consumption and use

General Question: How sustainable are the current consumption patterns of the urban area?

1	2	3	4	5	6	7	8	9
Critical	Bad	Highly Unsatisfactory	Unsatisfactory	Basic	Satisfactory	Highly Satisfactory	Good	Vibrant

1. The reuse of goods, including through personal exchange and
   second-hand outlets
2. The development of responses to food security and vulnerability to
   seasonal shortages of food
3. The ongoing availability to all of goods and services deemed
   necessary for good living
4. The ongoing availability to all of basic utilities – such as water,
   electricity and gas
5. The capacity of local people to respond to peak-oil issues, including
   rising costs
6. The accuracy of advertising circulated locally in providing
   information about consumption goods
7. The translation of the monitoring of consumption patterns into
   strategies for enhancing good production and good use
   • *Optional alternative question:*

5. Labour and welfare

General Question: How sustainable are the conditions of work across the urban area?

1	2	3	4	5	6	7	8	9
Critical	Bad	Highly Unsatisfactory	Unsatisfactory	Basic	Satisfactory	Highly Satisfactory	Good	Vibrant

Particular Questions   *Number 1–9*
How sustainable are the following aspects of the urban area?

1. The range of livelihoods available in the area to those with appropriate skills
2. The possibility for all of meaningful productive vocations
3. The relative equity of access to secure employment in the area across differences of gender, age and ethnicity
4. The capacity of the labour force to work productively
5. The safety of workers
6. The comprehensiveness of general welfare support processes across the urban area[13]
7. The translation of the monitoring of labour practices into strategies for enhancing the comprehensiveness of good working conditions
   • *Optional alternative questions:*

6. Technology and infrastructure

General Question: To what extent is basic infrastructure in urban area appropriate and supportive of a broad cross-section of needs?

1	2	3	4	5	6	7	8	9
Critical	Bad	Highly Unsatisfactory	Unsatisfactory	Basic	Satisfactory	Highly Satisfactory	Good	Vibrant

Particular Questions   *Number 1–9*
How sustainable are the following aspects of the urban area?

1. The appropriateness of technologies and public infrastructure used to support the ongoing development of the urban area
2. The robustness of information storage systems available to people in the urban area
3. The adoption of new technologies in transport such as hybrid vehicles and intelligent transport systems
4. The quality of the building stock, both commercial and housing, in the urban area

5. The resourcing of the education system with appropriate technologies and infrastructure readily available to locals
6. The resourcing of the health system with appropriate technologies and infrastructure readily available to locals
7. The translation of the monitoring of technological use into strategies for enhancing positive technological application
   • *Optional alternative question:*

7. Wealth and distribution

General Question: Is the wealth of the urban area sustainable; and is it distributed in a way that benefits all?

1	2	3	4	5	6	7	8	9
Critical	Bad	Highly Unsatisfactory	Unsatisfactory	Basic	Satisfactory	Highly Satisfactory	Good	Vibrant

Particular Questions   *Number 1–9*
How sustainable are the following aspects of the urban area?

1. The public use of wealth of the urban area for maximum social benefit for all
2. The maintenance of the inherited social wealth of the urban area – for example the maintenance of heritage buildings or public spaces for maximum social benefit
3. The relative equity of wage levels for different groups – as categorized by job, but also across difference of gender, age and ethnicity, etc.
4. The affordability of local housing for all
5. The relative equity of accumulated wealth of the residents of the urban area
6. The effectiveness of processes for redistributing wealth in the urban area
7. The translation of the monitoring of wealth accumulation into strategies for enhancing the social benefits for all
   • *Optional alternative question:*

Politics

1. Organization and governance

General Question: How well does the current system of governance function to maximize benefits for all?[14]

1	2	3	4	5	6	7	8	9
Critical	Bad	Highly Unsatisfactory	Unsatisfactory	Basic	Satisfactory	Highly Satisfactory	Good	Vibrant

Particular Questions   *Number 1–9*
How sustainable are the following aspects of the urban area?

1. The political legitimacy of the various levels of government relevant to the urban area
2. The capacity of the leaders of the various kinds of governance relevant to the urban area
3. The visions projected by the relevant levels of government for positively managing the form of the urban region – for example in relation to managing urban growth

(Continued)

Particular Questions   *Number 1–9*
How sustainable are the following aspects of the urban area?

4. The capacity of the administrative staff in the various levels of bureaucracy
5. The authority of the various levels of governance to carry out policy
6. The transparency of decision-making processes
7. The translation of the monitoring of administrative practices into strategies for enhancing the quality of governance
   • *Optional alternative question:*

2. Law and justice

General Question: How well does the dominant legal system work?[15]

1	2	3	4	5	6	7	8	9
Critical	Bad	Highly Unsatisfactory	Unsatisfactory	Basic	Satisfactory	Highly Satisfactory	Good	Vibrant

Particular Questions   *Number 1–9*
How sustainable are the following aspects of the urban area?

1. The protection of human rights in the urban area
2. The civil order of the urban area
3. The responsiveness of local residents to legal requirements
4. The treatment of all locals as equal before the law – this includes the specified articulation of complementary systems of justice such as customary or traditional law
5. The fairness and circumspection of the dominant legal system
6. The appropriateness of legal judgements in relation to various levels of penalty and punishment
7. The translation of the monitoring of the legal system into strategies for enhancing the quality of legal administration
   • *Optional alternative question:*

3. Communication and critique

General Question: How sustainable is social communication access in the urban area?

1	2	3	4	5	6	7	8	9
Critical	Bad	Highly Unsatisfactory	Unsatisfactory	Basic	Satisfactory	Highly Satisfactory	Good	Vibrant

Particular Questions	Number 1–9

How sustainable are the following aspects of the urban area?

1. The level of positive freedom for political expression in the urban area
2. The range of newspapers, broadcasters and public communications systems circulating information relevant to people living in the urban area
3. The proportion of households with open access to mediated communications – including radio, television, Internet and other social communications
4. The quality of public political analysis – both mainstream and alternative – easily accessible in the urban area
5. The openness of the urban region to non-violent political protest being enacted and heard
6. The level of respect for privacy by public and private information gatherers
7. The translation of the monitoring of the media systems into strategies for enhancing the quality of media communication
   • *Optional alternative question:*

4. Representation and negotiation

General Question: How well are citizens of the urban area represented politically?

1	2	3	4	5	6	7	8	9
Critical	Bad	Highly Unsatisfactory	Unsatisfactory	Basic	Satisfactory	Highly Satisfactory	Good	Vibrant

Particular Questions	Number 1–9

How sustainable are the following aspects of the urban area?

1. The active membership of residents in non-governmental organizations and advocacy groups – trades unions, professional associations, clubs, religious affiliations, etc.
2. The active participation of local people in the political processes of the urban area
3. The power of local people to affect political decision-making processes relevant to the urban area
4. The availability of municipal representatives for consultation with residents
5. The active possibility of civil negotiation between groups with different interests – such as unions and business
6. The active and legitimate contestation of political power and office
7. The translation of the monitoring of the political systems into strategies for enhancing the quality of public participation
   • *Optional alternative question:*

5. Security and concord

General Question: How secure and peaceful is the urban area?

1	2	3	4	5	6	7	8	9
Critical	Bad	Highly Unsatisfactory	Unsatisfactory	Basic	Satisfactory	Highly Satisfactory	Good	Vibrant

Particular Questions   *Number 1–9*
How sustainable are the following aspects of the urban area?

1. The level of personal security in relation to human security issues – such as food security, natural disaster, economic crisis or military threat
2. The physical safety of workplaces
3. The level of personal security in relation to domestic violence or day-to-day street conflict
4. The provision of shelter for residents of the urban area without homes or those leaving behind difficult circumstances such as domestic violence
5. The provision of active support for immigrants from outside the urban area escaping conflict, persecution or poverty
6. The provision of affordable insurance processes supported by formal guarantees
7. The translation of the monitoring of security threats into strategies for enhancing the quality of personal security for all
   • *Optional alternative question:*

6. Dialogue and reconciliation

General Question: Is meaningful dialogue possible between groups with significant political difference in the urban area?

1	2	3	4	5	6	7	8	9
Critical	Bad	Highly Unsatisfactory	Unsatisfactory	Basic	Satisfactory	Highly Satisfactory	Good	Vibrant

Particular Questions   *Number 1–9*
How sustainable are the following aspects of the urban area?

1. The recognition of differences of identity – including, in particular, recognition of the original inhabitants of the urban region
2. The existence of active processes for negotiating different understandings of past events and histories of conflict
3. The existence of active processes – formal and informal – for handling tensions between communities distinguished by ethical, racial, religious, class, gender or sexual differences
4. The level of social trust in other people

Particular Questions	Number 1–9
How sustainable are the following aspects of the urban area?	

5. The possibilities for enacting rituals and processes of remembrance and renewal
6. The existence of processes – formal and informal – for welcoming new arrivals
7. The translation of the monitoring of political tensions into strategies for enhancing the reconciliation processes
   • *Optional alternative question:*

7. Ethics and accountability

General Question: How ethical is social life in the urban area?

1	2	3	4	5	6	7	8	9
Critical	Bad	Highly Unsatisfactory	Unsatisfactory	Basic	Satisfactory	Highly Satisfactory	Good	Vibrant

Particular Questions	Number 1–9
How sustainable are the following aspects of the urban area?	

1. The grounding of municipal policies in clearly enunciated ethical principles
2. The public accountability of powerful public figures – for example corporate, media and union leaders
3. The general integrity brought to day-to-day transactions in public and private life
4. The active role of public integrity and anti-corruption offices and organizations
5. The possibility of meaningful public debate over ethical principles and their interpretation
6. The institution of processes for responding consequentially to breaches in accountability
7. The translation of the monitoring of corruption issues into strategies for enhancing integrity processes
   • *Optional alternative question:*

Culture

1. Identity and engagement

General Question: Does the urban area have a positive cultural identity that brings people together over and above the various differences in their individual identities?

1	2	3	4	5	6	7	8	9
Critical	Bad	Highly Unsatisfactory	Unsatisfactory	Basic	Satisfactory	Highly Satisfactory	Good	Vibrant

Particular Questions
How sustainable are the following aspects of the urban area?

Number 1–9

1. The active cultural diversity of different local communities and groups
2. The sense of belonging and identification with the local area as a whole in a way that connects across community and group differences
3. The tolerance and respect for different language groups and ethnic groups in the urban area
4. The tolerance and respect for different religions and communities of faith in the urban area
5. The possibility of strangers to the urban area establishing and maintaining personal networks or affinity groups with current residents
6. The sense of home and place
7. The translation of the monitoring of community relations into strategies for enhancing identity and engagement
   - *Optional alternative question:*

2. Creativity and recreation

General Question: How sustainable are creative pursuits in the urban area – including sporting activities and creative leisure activities?

1	2	3	4	5	6	7	8	9
Critical	Bad	Highly Unsatisfactory	Unsatisfactory	Basic	Satisfactory	Highly Satisfactory	Good	Vibrant

Particular Questions
How sustainable are the following aspects of the urban area?

Number 1–9

1. The level of participation in and appreciation of the arts – from painting to storytelling
2. The level of involvement in performance activities such as music, dance and theatre as participants and spectators
3. The level of cultural creativity and innovation
4. The level of support for cultural events – for example public festivals and public celebrations
5. The level of involvement in sport and physical activity as participants and spectators
6. The affordance of time and energy for creative leisure
7. The translation of the monitoring of creative pursuits into strategies for enhancing creative engagement
   - *Optional alternative question:*

3. Memory and projection

General Question: How well does the urban area deal with its history in relation to projecting visions of possible alternative futures?

1	2	3	4	5	6	7	8	9
Critical	Bad	Highly Unsatisfactory	Unsatisfactory	Basic	Satisfactory	Highly Satisfactory	Good	Vibrant

Particular Questions   *Number 1–9*
How sustainable are the following aspects of the urban area?

1. The level of respect for past traditions and understanding of their differences
2. The protection of heritage sites and sacred places
3. The maintenance of monuments, museums and historical records
4. The active recognition of indigenous customs and histories
5. The sense of hope for a positive future for the urban area as a whole
6. The level of public discussion that actively explores possible futures
7. The translation of the monitoring of themes of past and future into strategies for enhancing positive engagement
   • *Optional alternative question:*

4. Belief and meaning

General Question: Do residents of the urban area have a strong sense of purpose and meaning?

1	2	3	4	5	6	7	8	9
Critical	Bad	Highly Unsatisfactory	Unsatisfactory	Basic	Satisfactory	Highly Satisfactory	Good	Vibrant

Particular Questions   *Number 1–9*
How sustainable are the following aspects of the urban area?

1. The level of knowledgeable engagement in cultural pursuits in the urban area
2. The possibilities for counter-ideologies being discussed and debated publicly
3. The level of thoughtful consideration that lies behind decisions made on behalf of the people of the urban area
4. The sense of meaning that local people have in their lives
5. The extent to which people of different faiths or spiritualities feel comfortable practicing their various rituals, even when their beliefs are not part of the dominant culture

(Continued)

Particular Questions   *Number 1–9*
How sustainable are the following aspects of the urban area?

---

6. The possibility that passions can be publicly expressed in
   the urban area without descending into negative conflict
7. The translation of the monitoring of ideas and debates into
   strategies for enhancing positive engagement
   • *Optional alternative question:*

---

5. Gender and generations

General Question: To what extent is there gender and generational well-being across
different groups?

1	2	3	4	5	6	7	8	9
Critical	Bad	Highly Unsatisfactory	Unsatisfactory	Basic	Satisfactory	Highly Satisfactory	Good	Vibrant

---

Particular Questions   *Number 1–9*
How sustainable are the following aspects of the urban area?

---

1. The equality of men and women in public and private life
2. The positive expression of sexuality in ways that do not lead to
   intrusion or violation
3. The contribution of both men and women to bringing up
   children
4. The availability of child care in the urban area – whether formal
   or informal, public or private
5. The positive engagement of youth in the life of the urban area
6. The availability of aged care in the urban area – whether formal
   or informal, public or private
7. The translation of the monitoring of gender and generational
   relations into strategies for enhancing positive engagement
   • *Optional alternative question:*

---

6. Enquiry and learning

General Question: How sustainable is formal and informal learning in the urban region?

1	2	3	4	5	6	7	8	9
Critical	Bad	Highly Unsatisfactory	Unsatisfactory	Basic	Satisfactory	Highly Satisfactory	Good	Vibrant

Particular Questions	Number 1–9

How sustainable are the following aspects of the urban region?

1. The accessibility of active centres of discovery – ranging from formal scientific research institutes to places of playful discovery for children
2. The active participation of people in the urban area in deliberation and debate over ideas
3. The accessibility of active centres of social enquiry – both formal and informal – ranging in focus from scientific research to interpretative and spiritual enquiry
4. The active participation of people in formal and informal education, across gender, generation, ethnicity and class differences
5. The existence of local cultures of writing – from philosophical and scientific to literary and personal
6. The setting aside of time in the various education processes – both formal and informal – for considered reflection
7. The translation of the monitoring of education practices into quality-improvement strategies
   • *Optional alternative question:*

7. Well-being and health

General Question: What is the general level of well-being across different groups of residents?

1	2	3	4	5	6	7	8	9
Critical	Bad	Highly Unsatisfactory	Unsatisfactory	Basic	Satisfactory	Highly Satisfactory	Good	Vibrant

Particular Questions	Number 1–9

How sustainable are the following aspects of the urban area?

1. The sense of control that people have in the urban area over questions of bodily integrity and well-being
2. The level of knowledge that people in the urban area have in relation to basic health issues
3. The availability of consulting professionals or respected community elders to support people in time of hardship, stress or grief
4. The capacity of the urban area to meet reasonable expectations that people in the urban area hold about health care or counselling
5. The participation of people in practices that promote well-being
6. The cultural richness of cuisine and good food
7. The translation of the monitoring of health and well-being practices into quality-improvement strategies
   • *Optional alternative question:*

Notes

1 Sunil Dubey is the main co-author of this chapter with Paul James.
2 Remember here that 'broader region' here means within 2 to 3 hours' land transport. 'Material resources' includes all resources from water, food and energy to concrete and steel.
3 Remember here that 'urban region' means the urban area and its immediate hinterlands.
4 Here 'natural spaces' means vegetated spaces – either original habitat or created natural settings such as parks.
5 Here 'appropriate materials' might be taken to mean such things as materials that are appropriate to the climate or materials that are recycled, locally sourced or sustainably produced.
6 Here 'mass transit systems' should be taken to include both public and private transport systems such rail and bus networks.
7 Here in the ecological domain the emphasis is on physical health. Mental health is considered to be in the cultural domain.
8 'Arts communities' might be taken to include different artists from musicians and painters to craft workers.
9 'Design expertise' might be taken to include architects and planners to graphic designers and jewelry designers and so on.
10 'Labour' includes both manual and intellectual labour resources, from artisans and physical workers to doctors and engineers.
11 Here consideration of the question should take in both public and private auditing systems.
12 Here, as elsewhere, the question of 'appropriateness' should be judged in relation to general public outcomes, including the poor or vulnerable, rather than outcomes pertaining to any one sectional interest.
13 'Welfare' is broadly defined here to include, on one hand, social security, pensions and in-kind state support to individuals or families and, on the other hand, support that comes from social networks, philanthropy and personal relations.
14 Here the 'current system of governance' includes nationally, regionally, municipally and locally.
15 Here the 'dominant legal system' includes the national, municipal and local levels of law and their intersection.

8

MEASURING COMMUNITY SUSTAINABILITY[1]

As we elaborated earlier, measuring community sustainability is a difficult process that is prone to subjectivism and lack of systemic rigour. In response to these kinds of problems there has been a tendency to move towards overly rigid and positivist mechanisms of enquiry. Moreover, measuring community sustainability tends to suffer from a fundamental tension that arises in developing a generally applicable mechanism of research that at the same time is able to handle local differences and requirements. The tension is redoubled when the surveys are used in various settings that cross the Global South and Global North. In this chapter, the development of a 'social life' questionnaire within the *Circles of Sustainability* approach is critically narrated. The first version of the questionnaire looked good and served our initial purpose, but beneath the surface the foundations of the questionnaire were naive and limited. The initial development was in many ways too ambitious, and the questionnaire was first rolled out at a time when we did not yet have the capacity to bring together cross-disciplinary skill sets. However, instead of suggesting that the project backtrack on its generalizing-particularizing ambitions, a series of steps were undertaken, described in this chapter, to begin to overcome profound structural limitations. The questionnaire appended at the end of the chapter is the outcome of that work.

The project faced significant challenges. How is it possible to develop a method that overcomes the subjectivism/objectivism divide? On one hand, some social researchers, anthropologists and ethnographers have progressively adjusted, refined and calibrated their tools of research to reflect the intricacies, sensitivities, and subject positions of the communities they have sought to understand, including acknowledging the effect of their own subjectivities on what they are trying to understand. However, this trend has too often led to an inability to say much about the patterns of social life beyond soft allusion, inference, or hermeneutic projection. On the other hand, recent attention to ecological and economic risks, and the corresponding rise of sustainability discourses, has led to an emphasis on rigorous objective measurement. Perversely, however, this search for objective understanding has often led to the re-projection of positivist universals into the categories and variables of different methodological frameworks, undermining the subtlety of such tools of analysis.

An alternative synthesis is clearly necessary. In broad terms, the search is on for methodologies that bring together both objective and subjective understandings through using both qualitative and quantitative methods. Part of that task is to generate sensitivity to local conditions has led to various forms of subject-centred methodologies that still maintain a strong interest in social patterns and structures. The growth of global ethnography, grounded theory, hermeneutically inspired strategies, even our own Engaged Theory, are at least in part responses to the limitations of either *postmodern* subjectivism or wholesale co-option of natural scientific method into *modern* empiricism.

In narrower terms, the key question is how else is it possible to maintain a subtle assessment of the viability, resilience and subjective sustainability of communities while using objectively measured indicators which are globally applicable across time and space, including across different dominant formations of practice – customary, traditional, modern and postmodern? This imperative is particularly critical for marginalized, at-risk communities and communities in the Global South where assessments of sustainability form – or ought to form – the basis for subsequent policy development and action. Moreover, it is equally important that indicators reflect not only objectively measurable conditions of the social and natural environment but also the subjectively understood sense of sustainability, as experienced by the community itself.

It is in this context that we discuss the development of the survey tool, the Social Life Questionnaire, which endeavours to convey a picture of the subjective attitudes of community members towards the sustainability, liveability and resilience of their communities. The Questionnaire was applied to about 3,300 members of various communities between 2006 and 2012, predominantly in the Southeast Asian region, but across very different settings, north and south. In aiming to be encompassing of all dimensions of sustainability, the indicator set is similar to other holistic approaches. However, it differs in a number of respects. One key difference is that we treat questions in a questionnaire as also constituting an index – in this case, an index that seeks to objectively 'measure' subjective beliefs that always needs to be correlated against other forms of data gathering such as the urban profile (see Chapter 4 on social mapping and Chapter 7 on generating an urban sustainability profile).

Secondly, and more profoundly, the underlying structural basis for understanding sustainability has been substantially revised in relation to other accounts, such as the Triple Bottom Line or Capabilities approach. The survey shares common features with the psychometric perspectives of the Australian Unity Wellbeing Index, the World Values Survey and the World Database of Happiness. And, indeed, certain constructs of the Wellbeing Index and World Values Survey are incorporated into our indicator set. But it is based on a very different framing consistent with the rest of the

Circles of Social Life approach. Thirdly, we further differentiate the approach by suggesting it aims to measure the *intersubjective* character of a community – not only how members of that community feel about their social and natural environment now but also how they view the future prospects of that social and natural environment.

Understanding how a community understands its own sustainability complements existing subjective and objective sustainability measures of a city as a whole, and, we argue, extends the *localization* of such measures to those for whom they are most relevant. Although, as we show, the questionnaire in its previous incarnation had limitations in terms of scientific validity and reliability, the exploratory analysis that follows demonstrates how the current iteration might complement a sustainability assessor's existing toolkit. The analysis also makes a contribution in its own right into understanding key factors and relationships of the sampled communities.

Developing the social life questionnaire

The Social Life Questionnaire was first developed and administered to a number of rural and urban communities in Victoria, Australia, in 2006.[2] Over the following years it has been further administered to a number of diverse communities in the Southeast Asian, South Asian and Middle Eastern regions, including Papua New Guinea, Timor Leste, Sri Lanka, India and Israel/Palestine, as well as Cameroon. The sites thus crossed the Global North/South divide, and the questions were formulated to make sense in cross-cultural contexts. Although using a similar apparatus to numerous other surveys, the aim was not to assess community sustainability in a benchmarking or simple comparative fashion.

Benchmarking surveys and models are frequently criticized as being of arguable utility to communities at greatest risk. There is little comfort in knowing how unsustainable one is relative to others. However, there are several affordances that arise out of the search for general assessment instruments:

1. For all the limitations of benchmarking, when coupled with other methods, qualitative questionnaires provide a basis for comparability across diverse communities. Such comparisons can in turn be provocations for further diagnosis and action.
2. Qualitative questionnaires provide community members with a quantification of their sense of sustainability. This can be contrasted not only with other communities but also with other objective and subjective sustainability quantifications – levels of air pollution, gross domestic product, corruption or psychological well-being assessments, for instance. Such contrasts can provide both internal members and external agents with advanced warnings of potential threats.
3. Qualitative questionnaires also provide some basis for longitudinal comparison.

In the case of the work in Papua New Guinea the results did become the basis for a sea change in the formulation of government policy around community development.

However, in Papua New Guinea as elsewhere, the results were intended as complementary to accompanying research interventions, including publicly available metrics. Additionally, the questionnaire was always used in relation to more extensive qualitative engagement through a series of ethnographic, interview-based and observational inquiries into urban sustainability (see Chapter 4). This was also notably the case in studies of sustainability in Sri Lanka in the aftermath of the tsunami from 2004 to the present.

At the same time, additional sets of questions were used in addition to a consistent core set of sustainability indicators to reflect regional, localized, project-based and time-based differences. For example, our work in Sri Lanka and India after the tsunami included a module of additional questions on disaster recovery. Nevertheless, the core set of questions was consistently measured across repeated applications of the survey, and these questions are the basis for the following discussion.

The core set of questions reflects a socially holistic conception of sustainability, evident in a range of approaches to sustainability reporting. Again, our conception adumbrates four domains against which social sustainability, liveability and resilience can be assessed. Consistent with all the other tools in our methodological shed the questionnaire is constructed around the domains of the economy, ecology, politics and culture. The category of the social is not erased by this move but, rather, is treated as imbricated in each of these domains. Sustainability, in this conception, is thus irremediably social in character. Most of the core set of questions represent one of these four facets of sustainability. The remaining common survey questions capture administrative and demographic variables – the complete set is listed at the end of this chapter.

In spite of the care undertaken in the data-aggregation process, a number of concerns remain concerning both validity and reliability. Although the survey in its current iteration makes few claims of hypothesis testing, these do compromise the extent of inference drawn from the findings. Addressing these concerns became important for the current redesign of the survey. Principal among the concerns are the following:

1. *Variables articulation:* What facets of sustainability are being measured?
2. *Variables mapping:* How can the different variable systems be mapped against each other?
3. *Construct validity:* Are the constructs separately necessary measures of sustainability?
4. *Construct comprehensiveness:* Are the constructs collectively sufficient measures of sustainability?
5. *Construct reliability:* Is the language sufficiently clear and capable of being reliably interpreted by a broad range of respondents, across different locations and times?
6. *Subjective–objective comparability:* How do perceptions of members of a community relate to other measures of its sustainability?
7. *Sampling strategy:* How wide a range of sampling forms can be adopted in different settings, including convenience, snowball, purposive and cluster sampling, before the statistical comparability between those settings breaks down?

A series of descriptive statistics were obtained for this set, both to observe tendencies in the data and to cross-check the data-cleaning process, to ensure absence of out-of-bound data. Similarly, a series of pairwise correlations were run for all scalar variables. We then conducted a factor analysis with varimax rotation to view whether variables clustered together intelligibly. We hypothesized that characteristic demographic data could be useful predictors for some of the behavioural and attitudinal data, and ran a series of regression tests to test this. Finally, an analysis of variance (ANOVA) and further correlation tests were administered to determine whether meaningful differences existed, for the core attitudinal variables, between the various communities participating in the survey. The interpretation of these tests on the viability of the questionnaire is discussed in the following.

Comparing different communities

After the data were consolidated, total sample size was 3,368. Country distribution was heavily oriented towards Papua New Guinea, Australia, East Timor and Sri Lanka. Gender distribution was approximately even (female = 49.4 per cent, male = 50.2 per cent), whereas age distribution skewed towards a younger demographic, with more than 75 per cent of respondents younger than age fifty. Self-assessments of health, wealth and education – variables related to indices such as the Human Development Index – reflect the application of the survey to the large number of Global South countries. The majority of respondents described themselves financially as 'struggling' (50 per cent), with only 9.1 per cent stating they were 'well-off'; 45.2 per cent of respondents stated they had primary school or no formal education at all, whereas only 18.4 per cent had completed secondary school. Conversely, 48.6 per cent of people assessed their health as being 'generally good'. A proxy Human Development Index variable was composed out of the normalized values of health, financial and education self-assessment variables. The frequency distribution of this composite variable demonstrates that in fact the relative skews of these variables collectively cancel out, leaving a close approximation to a normal distribution.

Of the fifteen common attitudinal variables, all but three had median, and all but one had mode values of 'agree'. As all Likert items were phrased in such a way that agreement tended to endorse the underlying variable being measured, this indicates a degree of correlation between responses is likely. The average mean value was 3.65, while the average standard deviation was 1.06, a relatively low dispersion, which confirms the clustering of responses on the positive end of the scale. Inferential tests suggest, however, that there are some interesting differences between communities sampled.

Both Spearman's rho and Pearson's correlation coefficient were obtained of all core scalar variables, twenty-two in total, and separately, of all attitudinal variables, fifteen in total. Of 231 possible scalar correlations, 179 (77.5 per cent) were significant at the 0.01 level, with a further 8 significant at the 0.05 level (81.0 per cent). Of the 105 possible correlations of the 15 attitudinal variables, 100 were significant at the 0.01 level. Together these results suggest a very high degree of dependence between the variables, a feature discussed later in both the factor analysis and survey redesign sections. Given the sample size, the use of five-point scales for attitudinal variables and the potential for skew in both wording of question probes and sampling strategy, such coalescence is perhaps not surprising.

A factor analysis was conducted on all attitudinal variables. Kaiser–Meyer–Olkin measure of sampling adequacy was 0.843, a very high level for conducting factor analysis. Varimax rotation was selected because of potential dependencies between discovered factors. The factors themselves have been interpolated as follows:

1. Satisfaction with various aspects conditions (life as a whole, involvement with community, personal relationships, the environment, sense of safety, work/life balance).
2. Trust and confidence in *political* conditions (ability to influence authority, belief decisions are in interest of whole community, trust in experts and government)
3. Trust and confidence in *cultural* conditions (enjoy meeting and trust in others, influence of history, importance and use of technology)

The three factors are interpreted here as accounting for each of the four domains in the underlying *Circles of Sustainability* model. The first factor combines all six *satisfaction* constructs, taken from the Australian Unity Wellbeing Index. These have been – very liberally – interpreted as reflecting general contentment with *economic* and *ecological* circumstances, where ecology is considered as both a social and a natural context. The following two factors more directly aggregate items reflecting political and cultural engagement, respectively.

Because missing values caused a large number of cases (1,593, or 47.3 per cent of 3,368) to be ignored in the analysis, a separate analysis was conducted with mean values substituted back in. The analysis showed a weaker sampling adequacy result, but no change in the variables or factors identified. A series of composite indices, termed, respectively, 'Attitudes towards Economy and Ecology', 'Attitudes towards Politics' and 'Attitudes towards Culture', were constructed from the normalized values of the relevant underlying indicators. These in turn were compiled into an overall 'Attitudinal Self-Assessment' index, similar to the HDI Self-Assessment variable described earlier. All five computed variables were then used in subsequent regression and ANOVA tests.

A series of regression tests were conducted to note the significance and direction of relationships between the principal component clusters of attitudinal variables, and demographic and self-assessment characteristics. For the Wellbeing Index satisfaction levels (interpreted, as suggested earlier, to cover economic and ecological domains), and attitudes relating to the political domain, only the financial self-assessment variable stands out as a strong – and negative – predictor, suggesting that those who assess themselves poorly in a financial sense nonetheless score highly against satisfaction and political engagement indicators. Conversely, all variables other than 'Financial Assessment' and 'Years lived in previous neighbourhood' have a strong predictive relationship on the aggregated cultural engagement indicator.

An ANOVA test was also conducted using the community as the grouping variable. Of particular interest was whether the first three principal components identified in the component analysis had significant differences between communities. Similarly we examined the composite 'Attitudinal Self-Assessment' and 'HDI Self-Assessment' variables across the groups. Each of the five computed variables showed significant differences across the different community groups at both 0.05 and 0.01 levels.

Table 8.1 compares both mean values and rank for the five composite variables across each of the seven communities (Melbourne [2009] and Timor are incomplete due to certain items not being included in their respective surveys). As the ranks make clear, Human Development Index self-assessment means appears to correlate with attitudes towards economy, ecology and culture, with Australian towns and Be'er Sheva ranking highly for each of these four variables. 'Attitudes towards Politics', on the contrary, correlates inversely. This suggest that communities which are generally satisfied and confident regarding economic, ecological and cultural dimensions are sceptical of prevailing power systems and structures; those which, on the other hand, self-assess poorly and are dissatisfied with present material conditions nonetheless have trust and confidence in political mechanisms.

TABLE 8.1 Composite Variable Mean Comparison

Mean values

Values	Attitudes towards Economy and Ecology	Attitudes towards Politics	Attitudes towards Culture	Attitudinal Self-Assessment	HDI Self-Assessment
AusTowns	24.2	11.5	21.4	72.8	65.5
Be'er Sheva	24.3	11.7	22.7	74.8	78.4
Malaysia	21.4	13.1	15.8	65.2	46.5
Melbourne	.	.	.	.	53.6
Papua New Guinea	24.2	13.8	17.1	70.9	41.6
Sri Lanka	22.5	13.5	19.7	72.7	38.4
Timor	.	14.0	15.3	.	36.0

Mean rank

	Attitudes towards Economy and Ecology	Attitudes towards Politics	Attitudes towards Culture	Attitudinal Self-Assessment	HDI Self-Assessment
AusTowns	3	6	2	2	2
Be'er Sheva	1	5	1	1	1

(Continued)

	Attitudes towards Economy and Ecology	Attitudes towards Politics	Attitudes towards Culture	Attitudinal Self-Assessment	HDI Self-Assessment
Malaysia	5	4	5	5	4
Melbourne	–	–	–	–	3
Papua New Guinea	2	2	4	4	5
Sri Lanka	4	3	3	3	6
Timor Leste	–	1	6	–	7

A further pairwise set of correlations was ran over the composite variables, which confirm the earlier findings across the whole data set – all variables correlate significantly at 0.05, 0.01 and even 0.001 levels, with 'Attitudes towards Politics' the only variable correlating negatively with the others.

Overcoming methodological limitations

Of greatest interest in the results was the strong relationship between the first three factors of the factor analysis, and the four domains articulated in the model. This suggests the survey instrument successfully measures community values towards these different domains of sustainability. Several confounding points need to be noted, however. First, these factors only account for 47.2 per cent of the total variation – leaving a large amount of attitudinal variance unexplained by the four-domain model. Second, the limitations around the survey design and administration discussed earlier suggest higher levels of significance testing are needed at the very least before results can be inferred to the broader community populations. Third, both economic and ecological constructs were coalesced in the primary factor identified. Given a key claim of the four-domain model is that each of the domains is at least potentially in conflict with others, the moderate sample size and range of communities ought to bring out greater variation between constructs measuring each domain. Of course, both the domain-construct relationship and the factor analysis have been conducted *ex post*; an important feature to exhibit in results of follow-up surveys would be a stronger correlation between *ex ante* and *ex post* alignment of variables to coordinating factors. Nevertheless, the coalescence of principal components with the independently derived domains suggests these remain a sound basis for the construction of future iterations of the indicator set.

While the aims of the survey were exploratory – and emphatically not intended to introduce ranking considerations – the correlation, regression and ANOVA tests do demonstrate a series of significant relationships and high degrees of deviance between the communities who have participated. The key finding from the exploration appears to be the inverse relationship between levels of political engagement and satisfaction and all other subjective indicators – economic, ecological and cultural. Results for Australian towns and Be'er Sheba, in particular, demonstrate that those with high levels of general satisfaction, education and material contentment tend to be more sceptical and pessimistic with regard to their involvement in structures of power. This clearly needs more robust study but points to a potential series of hypotheses to be tested in future rounds of the survey.

It is clear that the first version of the survey showed potential but did not yet deliver as an adequate assessment instrument of community sustainability. At best it could augment other methods of both quantitative, objective, and qualitative, subjective assessment. The questionnaire thus required serious revision to play a distinct role positioned against current indicator sets and their respective orientations by assessing sustainability at an *intersubjective* communal level. In additional to a series of methodological strictures discussed earlier, this major revision has required several further analytic distinctions to coordinate the structure of the questions in the revised survey.

The previous survey design was not considered sufficiently robust for fulfilling these extended aims. A number of criticisms were raised, both in the conduct and analysis of surveys. While counteracted items can be used control individual item bias – and indeed in the first version of the survey some effort had been made in this direction – no explicit strategy was adopted. This led to irregular and hard to identify sources of skew. Moreover, the extent of bias in some cases leads to lack of variance in response to items that already offer only a limited five-point range. Where most results cluster around 'Agree' to 'Strongly Agree' (or their inverse), attempts to derive even ordinal correlations tend to be misleading. Clustered, low-variance responses were found frequently in the analysis.

More critically still, generalized surveys of this sort do need to make claims towards quasi-universality, in order to ensure reliability in survey applications in different times and places. As opposed to the Grounded Theory approach adopted for the first version, here we have felt the need to articulate a positive theory of sustainability (hence Engaged Theory and Circles of Social Life) in order to know just of what the survey indicators are indicative. Because the survey measures a community member's *perceptions* of sustainability – leaving aside which objective measures, if any, these might conceivably correlate – this instrument may not be a useful predictive tool in and of itself, even if it certainly complements other instruments making use of global indicators.

To overcome these limitations, a series of workshops were held. A revised set of indicators/questions was drafted, with an associated set of reference questions and responses. These retained consonance with the existing survey yet sought to address the identified limitations. The revised questionnaire now measures sustainability explicitly against the four domains and their subdomains, which only formed the background to the original survey. More explicitly, community sustainability is assessed with reference to the following:

- Economic *prosperity* – the extent to which communities can engage in activities relevant to their economic well-being and be confident about the consequence of changing structures and pressures beyond their locale
- Ecological *resilience* – the extent to people's involvement with nature can enhance both their own physical well-being and the capacity of the environment to flourish in the face of external impact
- Political *engagement* – the extent to which members of communities can participate and collaborate meaningfully in structures and processes of power that affect them
- Cultural *vitality* – the extent to which communities are able to maintain and develop their beliefs, celebrate their practices and rituals and cultivate diverse systems of meaning

This basic taxonomy is elaborated through a series of subdomains or perspectives (seven per domain). It is also set against a matrix of cross-cutting social themes, which intersect with each of the domains, for example the social themes of authority – autonomy and needs – limits. In total, the revised structure of the indicator set proposes a total of seven of these cross-cutting categories, covering, in addition to the four domains, what we have termed *holistic* social variables. The holistic variables include those commonly incorporated into generalized surveys of well-being, happiness and satisfaction, such as the relation between inclusion and exclusion and between identity and difference. However, unlike the usual approaches, these dialectical themes have been mapped systematically across the questionnaire in a way that allows for an assessment of the nature of community *integration* in the locale being studied, not just the degree of community sustainability. When cross-correlated against the administrative variables in relation to community context and the demographic variables in relation to the characteristics of survey participants (gender, level of education, etc.), these holistic social variables are intended to give a nuanced sense of the ways in which respondents understand and live in social context.

In response to the survey results, we have further extended the indicator model to take account of spatial and social scope, as well as temporal tense or orientation. To capture the former, we have mapped the indicators by a threefold division into the following categories:

- Personal: sustainability as experienced by the self; mode is subjective.
- Communal: sustainability relating to the immediate communal group; mode is intersubjective.
- Global (regional, national): sustainability relating to the globe; mode is objective.

To capture temporal impressions of sustainability, we suggest a simple distinction between the following:

- Present (and immediate future): satisfaction with current state of affairs
- Future (medium and long term): confidence in eventual or anticipated state of affairs

Finally, we have also included two variables per domain in order to rank importance and significance of the domain itself, or potentially of specific issues within the domain (e.g. unemployment in the economic domain or pollution in the environmental domain). These variables can be used as initial points in a causal analysis, using the Driving Force, Pressure, State, Impact and Response (DPSIR) approach or some other causal model.

A sample of variables taken from the economic domain is presented in the following:

- Present economic prosperity of person
- Confidence in future economic prosperity of person
- Present economic prosperity of local community
- Confidence in future economic prosperity of local community
- Present economic prosperity of global community
- Confidence in future economic prosperity of global community
- Impact of global economy on economic prosperity of person
- Impact of global economy on economic prosperity of community
- Relative importance [DPSIR: IMPACT] of economic prosperity (relative to the other three domains)
- Relative significance [DPSIR: PRESSURE] of economic prosperity (relative to the other three domains)

In total, the revised structure of fifty questions presents seventy-four indicators of sustainability (see the Appendix to this chapter). In addition, in order to maintain the specificity of each project and place, we have continued the approach of allowing optional modules covering specific sociological aspects of a community, such as work, education, communication and so on. We have now also mapped the questions in the survey in relation to the Human Development or Capabilities approach, and this has indicated further areas for refinement. A series of approaches for generating composite, orderable indices from the indicators, based upon the composite factors presented above but using a mixture of weighted and unweighted averages, will also be trialled. We also note this instrument will sit alongside others piloted under the same project rubric, which will aim to complement the standardized subjective indicators of sustainability outlined here with locally developed, issue-based indicators.

APPENDIX: SOCIAL LIFE QUESTIONNAIRE

Circles of
Social Life

Research Location...

Interviewer's name....................................(if an interviewer conducts the process)

Date...

Social Life Questionnaire
Towards Sustainability, Liveability, Resilience and Vibrancy

Name of Locality, City, Country

This project is being conducted in . . . name of locality, as well as a number of other places around the world. Your contribution will help us to understand your locality and contribute to positive change.

Your input is vital. The results of this study will be shared with relevant organizations, including . . . name of organizations to generate policies and programs to improve the quality and sustainability of your life, your community, and your locality.

The results will be reported in a way that does not allow you to be identified. Your anonymity will be assured.

We know that it is sometimes difficult to give a simple answer in this kind of questionnaire. Many of the questions ask for subjective responses. Please answer each question as best you can. There are no right or wrong answers. If you do not wish to answer some questions or you do not have an opinion then please feel free to leave a box unmarked.

Your time today is greatly appreciated.

Thank you.

Throughout the entire questionnaire please mark one box only, unless indicated otherwise. If you make a mistake and mark more than one box, please indicate your final answer by crossing out the others.

If you do not know the answer to a question, or a question seems inappropriate, feel free not to respond.

1. What is the highest level of formal or school education that you have completed?
- 0☐ No school
- 1☐ Primary school
- 2☐ Some secondary school
- 3☐ Finished secondary school
- 4☐ Trade training
- 5☐ University (undergraduate)
- 6☐ University (postgraduate)

2. What is your age? ☐☐☐☐☐ (Please write how many years old you are.)

(Or if you are unsure or do not want to give your exact age, please fill in one of the age-range boxes.)

- 1☐ 16–19
- 2☐ 20–29
- 3☐ 30–39
- 4☐ 40–49
- 5☐ 50–59
- 6☐ 60–69
- 7☐ 70–79
- 8☐ 80–89
- 9☐ 90–
- 10☐ Don't know

3. What is your gender?
- 1 ☐ Female
- 2☐ Male

4. Financially speaking, how would you describe your household?
- 1☐ Well-off
- 2☐ Comfortable
- 3☐ Struggling
- 4☐ Poverty-stricken

5. Compared to other people of the same age, how would you describe your health?
- 1☐ Generally good
- 2☐ Sometimes good; sometimes poor
- 3☐ Generally poor
- 4☐ I don't know

6. Have there been times in the past twelve months when you did not have enough money for the health care that you or your family needed?
- 1 ☐ Yes
- 2☐ No

7. With whom do you live? (Choose the **best** way of describing your situation)
- 1☐ Alone
- 2☐ As a single person with children
- 3☐ With just your husband/wife or partner
- 4☐ With your husband/wife/partner and another person or persons—child or adult
- 5☐ With others (not your family) (For example, friends or housemates)
- 6☐ With one or both of your parents and/or brothers/sisters
- 7☐ With extended family (That is, including, but going beyond parents and/or siblings)

8. How many people live in your household presently?
☐1 ☐2 ☐3 ☐4 ☐5 ☐6 ☐7 ☐8 ☐9 ☐10 ☐ More than 10

9. For how many years have you lived in your current locality? (That is, in this local place or area)

☐☐☐☐ (Please write how many years.)

(Or if you are unsure please fill in one of the year-range boxes.)

- 1☐ less than 1 year
- 2☐ 1–5 yrs
- 3☐ 6–10 yrs
- 4☐ 11–20 yrs
- 5☐ 21–50 yrs
- 6☐ more than 51 yrs

10. What or whom do you identify as your main community?
- 1☐ The place in which you live (including village, town, neighbourhood, suburb, city, territory, etc.)
- 2☐ A particular group of people (including extended family, ethnicity, clan, tribe, nation, etc.)
- 3☐ Your place of work (including both formal and/or informal places)
- 4☐ Your place of education (including school, university, etc.)
- 5☐ A cultural or political institution (including sporting club, political party, etc.)
- 6☐ Your place of worship (including church, synagogue, mosque, temple, etc.)

Thinking about your own life and personal circumstances, how do you respond to the following questions?

	Very Satisfied	Satisfied	Neither Satisfied nor Unsatisfied	Dissatisfied	Very Dissatisfied
11. How satisfied are you with being part of your community?	5	4	3	2	1
12. How satisfied are you with the environment where you live?	5	4	3	2	1
13. How satisfied are you with your personal relationships?	5	4	3	2	1
14. How satisfied are you with the balance between your work and social life?	5	4	3	2	1
15. How satisfied are you with how safe you feel on a day-to-day basis?	5	4	3	2	1
16. How satisfied are you with your life as a whole these days?	5	4	3	2	1

To what extent do you agree or disagree with the following statements?

	Strongly agree	Agree	Neither Agree nor Disagree	Disagree	Strongly Disagree
17. I can influence people and institutions that have authority in relation to my life.	5	4	3	2	1
18. Political decisions made in relation to my community are generally made in the interests of the whole community.	5	4	3	2	1
19. Outside experts can be trusted when dealing with local issues.	5	4	3	2	1
20. Governments make decisions and laws that are good for the way I live locally.	5	4	3	2	1
21. I feel comfortable meeting and talking with people who are different from me.	5	4	3	2	1
22. Most people can be trusted most of the time.	5	4	3	2	1
23. Experts will always eventually find a way to solve environmental problems.	5	4	3	2	1
24. My identity is bound up with the local natural environment and landscape.	5	4	3	2	1
25. Conserving natural resources is unnecessary because alternatives will always be found.	5	4	3	2	1
26. Wealth is distributed widely enough to allow all people in our locality to enjoy a good standard of living.	5	4	3	2	1
27. Current levels of consumption in our locality are compatible with an environmentally sustainable future.	5	4	3	2	1
28. I feel that I can influence the generation of meanings and values in relation to our way of life.	5	4	3	2	1
29. Economic development should be excluded from wilderness areas to conserve natural diversity.	5	4	3	2	1
30. In our locality there is good access to places of nature.	5	4	3	2	1

To what extent are you concerned that the following issues might impact negatively on the people living in your locality?

	Not at All Concerned	A Little Concerned	Concerned	Very Concerned	Passionately Concerned
31. Global economic change	5	4	3	2	1
32. Global climate change	5	4	3	2	1
33. Globally fuelled political violence	5	4	3	2	1
34. Globally transmitted cultural values	5	4	3	2	1
35. A slump in the local economy	5	4	3	2	1
36. An incapacity to meet local needs for basic resources such as energy or water	5	4	3	2	1
37. A decline in the vitality of local cultural institutions	5	4	3	2	1
38. The corruption of local political institutions	5	4	3	2	1

To what extent do you agree or disagree with the following statements?

	Strongly Agree	Agree	Neither Agree nor Disagree	Disagree	Strongly Disagree
39. Technological innovation has served to liberate me in positive ways from limits that I have experienced in the past.	5	4	3	2	1
40. I am free to express my beliefs through meaningful creative activities.	5	4	3	2	1
41. My work allows me to fully express my identity.	5	4	3	2	1
42. Places of learning, health and recreation are distributed across our locality in a way that ensures good access by all.	5	4	3	2	1
43. Our governments should support economic growth as one of its highest priorities.	5	4	3	2	1
44. Continuing economic growth is compatible with environmental sustainability.	5	4	3	2	1
45. People can learn to live with others who are culturally different from themselves	5	4	3	2	1
46. People living in our locality are free to celebrate their own rituals and memories, even if those rituals are not part of the mainstream culture.	5	4	3	2	1
47. Outsiders are comfortable coming to live in our locality.	5	4	3	2	1
48. Keeping our economy sustainable requires that we place limits on the activities of foreign-owned businesses.	5	4	3	2	1
49. Keeping our economy sustainable requires that untrained migrants or refugees are excluded.	5	4	3	2	1
50. Keeping our economy sustainable requires that our needs for a wide range of consumer goods are fulfilled.	5	4	3	2	1

Background notes for researchers

This methodology behind this questionnaire is based on the *Circles of Sustainability* approach. It is intended as a means of measuring subjective responses to sustainability across four domains:

- economics
- ecology
- politics
- culture

Each of the domains is considered to be equally important for the human condition.

The questionnaire is intended for use in relation to communities, cities, regions or countries – in other words, a designated constituency of people living in a particular place or set of places, spatially bounded or otherwise. The three designations in the questionnaire are locality, community and way of life. Each of these has a different emphasis: spatial, affiliative and general, respectively. Locality is very specific and place bound. Community could range from the local to the global, and way of life moves from the particular to the general. It refers to generality of life in *this* place framed by practices and meanings from the local to the global. It has resonances with but is not the same as the concepts of *lifeworld* (Habermas 1987) or *habitus* (Bourdieu 1990).

Sensitive to the time taken to respond to any questionnaire and in order to keep the task manageable, this questionnaire has been limited to a set of around fifty questions. Questions can be deleted in order to make this questionnaire shorter and less time-consuming, but in doing so please be conscious of the need to maintain the basic demographic questions (Questions 1–10) and to keep a relative balance of questions across the four domains.

Please do not change any of the questions, except in the following ways:

- First, by adding to or deleting from the words marked in red inside the brackets. The words in red are intended to clarify the question for local meanings.
- Second, by adding words in brackets after any question to further clarify the local meaning of that question

More fundamental changes to the questionnaire might be done from time to time, but this will be done keeping in mind the need to maintain continuity and comparability. The current version of the questionnaire is Version 2 (2011–present).

If, in addition to this broad area of social sustainability, you want to focus on any particular issues please consider the additional thematic templates, and add any questions from any the templates as you wish, either imported as a whole template, as part, or as one or more additional questions. However, do not change the code numbers associated with those questions.

Sitting behind this organizing framework is a cross-cutting set of social themes:

- Accumulation–Distribution (the dominant theme today globally in the domain of economics)
- Risk–Security
- Needs–Limits (the dominant theme today globally in the domain of ecology)
- Well-Being–Adversity
- Authority–Autonomy (the dominant theme today globally in the domain of politics)
- Inclusion–Exclusion
- Identity–Difference (the dominant theme today globally in the domain of culture)

These dialectical braces – each of which has two thematic variables which stand together in tension – are treated as background themes to the questions. These social themes are treated in a matrix of relations that cross the four domains. Some of the questions are specific to one thematic variable in relation to one domain, some questions elucidate more than one social theme in relation to a domain, and some of the questions sit loosely across both terms within a social theme or themes. In other words, the relationships that underlie the questions run variably across the following variables:

- social domains
- social themes
- thematic variables within the social themes

The aim of the question selection is make sure that at least one question applies to each of the permutations of social domains and social themes.

In setting up the questionnaire we have aimed for the following balance:

Demographic questions (10 questions)
Domain-oriented questions
    Economics (10–20 questions)
    Ecology (10–20 questions)
    Politics (10–20 questions)
    Culture (10–20 questions)

Domain in relation to theme-oriented questions (at least one question relating to each permutation)
Domain in relation to the Capabilities approach (a broad spread across the different 'capabilities')
Domains in relation to beliefs – a threefold orientation around the following perspectives:

- beliefs in relation to one's self
- beliefs in relation to one's community or locality
- beliefs in relation to one's values (at least one question relating to each permutation)

Notes

1 The co-authors of this chapter were Liam Magee and Andy Scerri with Paul James. Numerous people contributed to developing the questionnaire, including, most important, Martin Mulligan. To give a sense of the reach of our indebtedness to others we list the researchers who were involved in the Papua New Guinea (PNG) project: Albert Age, Sama Arua, Kelly Donati, Jean Eparo, Beno Erepan, Julie Foster-Smith, Betty Gali-Malpo, Andrew Kedu, Max Kep, Leo Kulumbu, Karen Malone, Ronnie Mamia, Lita Mugugia, Martin Mulligan, Yaso Nadarajah, Gibson Oeka, Jalal Paraha, Peter Phipps, Leonie Rakanangu, Isabel Salatiel, Chris Scanlon, Victoria Stead, Pou Toivita, Kema Vegala, Naup Waup, Mollie Willie, and Joe Yomba. In addition, given the issue that the PNG project involved many languages across fifty villages in five provinces, we need to thank in particular, Gerard Arua, Vanapa, Central Province; Monica Arua, Yule Island, Central Province; Viki Avei, Boera, Central Province; Sunema Bagita, Provisional Community Development Advisor, Milne Bay Province; Mago Doelegu, Alotau, Milne Bay Province; Clement Dogale, Vanagi, Central Province; Jerry Gomuma, Alepa, Central Province; Alfred Kaket, Simbukanam/Tokain,

Madang Province; Yat Paol from the Bismark Ramu Group, Madang Province; Joseph Pulayasi, Omarakana, Milne Bay Province; Bing Sawanga, Yalu, Morobe Province; Alexia Tokau, Kananam, Madang Province; and Naup Waup, Wisini Village, Morobe Province. They became our formal research leaders in their respective locales and guides to language nuances.

2 This initial project was led by Martin Mulligan, Paul James, Kim Humphery, Chris Scanlon, Pia Smith, and Nicky Welch, culminating in the report, *Creating Community: Celebrations, Arts and Wellbeing within and across Local Communities* (2007).

References

Bourdieu, Pierre 1990, *The Logic of Practice*, Polity Press, Cambridge.

Habermas, Jurgen 1987, *The Theory of Communicative Action*, Polity Press, Cambridge.

Mulligan, Martin, James, Paul, Humphery, Kim, Scanlon, Chris, Smith, Pia & Welch, Niky 2007, *Creating Community: Celebrations, Arts and Wellbeing within and across Local Communities*, VicHealth, Melbourne, 2007.

9

CONDUCTING A PEER REVIEW[1]

Peer review is a method used in many fields. It happens as a matter of course when institutions seek external guidance about their own expertise from outside experts or consultants. In academia, peer review is the predominant process by which research is judged. Material is sent to relevant outside experts and is judged in relation to its contribution to the best current understandings in the field. It is a formalization of the basis by which the *modern* natural and social sciences have modified, built on and revolutionized knowledge. In this way, notwithstanding the hubris of modern epistemology, peer review can be positively revolutionary.

Peer review in the broad sense works best when it is complemented by peer exchange – that is by bringing field-related experts together in person to discuss basic developments in their field. The form of peer exchange that we all know best is the conference. In conjunction with circles of circulating written texts, actively discussed and debated, there is nothing more important for the development of knowledge than meaningful face-to-face exchange linked to extended dialogue. However, while peer exchange can be rich, it can also be empty. Conferences can be exciting and productive exchanges of knowledge. But often they can be empty rehearsals for banal information delivery. They can quickly descend into career-sensitive jostling or acts of going through the motion.

Similarly, peer review has enormous strengths, but it also has damning problems. It can be elitist. It can be a harsh process with final decisions made one way or another based on a small number of reviewers. It is often conducted confidentially for the wrong reasons. Bad non-transparency and political closure is regularly legitimized as giving objectivity to the process or upholding commercial integrity. Peer review can lead to new knowledge being jealously regarded while old fields of knowledge are zealously guarded. It can tend towards treating knowledge development as a competitive process akin to the capitalist market. Cultural capital accrues to those who are best at getting past the reviewers. It can end with its knowledge gatekeepers becoming powerful while locally applied ideas are dismissed. Through peer review, formal knowledge tends to be empowered at the expense of informal and implicit knowledge. Modern knowledge tends to be privileged over traditional or customary forms of understanding the world. It short, peer review can be deeply flawed. In practice it often does not meet the test of normative reflexivity discussed earlier (Chapter 5). However, for all of these limitations, when conducted well, peer review is the best method we have for assessing complex analytical or technical knowledge. This potential explains why peer review remains important in contemporary intellectual life.

Building on the strengths of peer review

Peer reviews are held regularly in a number of municipalities so that projects can be improved and suggestions can be made. For example, in the Philippines there is a programme known as *kaakbay* – which translates as 'arm in arm'. As part of this programme, cities regularly hold peer-to-peer coaching meetings; however, these are more training sessions than forums for problem-solving processes. In India, the National Institute of Urban Affairs has been conducting peer review forums called Peer Experience and Reflective Learning (PEARL; 2014). A series of workshops have been held since 2007. These have been marginally successful, but because of lack the intensity the National Institute is seeking to reform how they are run. In the European Union some cities or member states themselves often carry out reviews on specific topics: for example on issues such as responding to homelessness or reforming health care. The European Commission sees peer reviews as a key instrument of its Social Open Method of Coordination (2014). They are promoted as enabling open discussion in the different European member states and facilitating mutual learning. However, the reports tend to be carefully written set pieces showcasing existing national activities and policies rather than deeply exploratory and problem oriented.

Peer review is therefore not a new method for cities, nor is it unproblematic. However, with refinement it can work well. The test of practical usefulness (also discussed in Chapter 5) comes in here very strongly. In many cases, peer review is too expensive and too demanding. Important individuals are paid large sums of money, afforded business-class airfares and asked to attend multiple meetings. Consultants are enlisted at considerable expense to interview relevant participants and review processes, only to find that the final report tells you little more than what you and your colleagues imparted to the consultants in the first place. In effect, the consultancy legitimizes the decision that you already want to make. In a context of competitive judgement, multiple meetings, workshops lasting five or more days, extensive interviews with resource persons and comparative benchmarking are necessary but demanding. In any case, cities have such different starting points of framework conditions that establishing benchmarks is a very difficult process.

The peer review process developed here is a response to these strengths and weaknesses. The *Circles of Sustainability* peer-review process takes the robustness of peer reviewing and carefully qualifies its weaknesses. In this process developed by a Metropolis-Cities Programme team led by the City of Berlin the focus is on a major project in a city. Ideally this project should be in early development or at a critical juncture in its operation. This qualifies one of the common weaknesses of peer exchange events – empty rehearsals of information in gatherings where there is little immediately at stake beyond the cultural capital of the people in the room. This peer-review process is intended to have consequences.

With the Circles peer-review process, recommendations and ideas for the project under review are developed based on the peers' own experience. These are offered as reciprocal 'gifts' to the host city. The process builds on a very practical basis: the feedback given by the experts derives from their everyday working lives and from their long years of practical experience. Which of their recommendations will later be implemented and adapted to the city's needs depends on the host city. This means that the peers in this process are not scrutinizers. They are not critics on whose judgement good and bad news depends. Rather, they are something like critical friends involved in a circle of knowledge exchange. Peers know from experience how difficult it can sometimes be to avoid tripwires and hurdles when putting a project into practice. This knowledge is treated as reciprocal. In the process they also learn themselves by comparing their experience to the experience of others. By being 'given' a privileged insiders' warts-and-all introduction to a city's plans and project development, they learn in ways that are quite unique. Akin in some ways to Médecins sans Frontières, this process involves 'peers crossing borders'.

Phases in the peer-review process

The peer-review process follows the same seven-stage method as previously outlined (Chapter 6), but as with all our methods it is not a pathway to be followed mechanically. In the following description, the high-level definitions of the stages remain as previously expressed, but each is elaborated with specific recommendations for practice based on extensive field experience.

The simplified process presented here begins with written preliminary documentation of the project prepared by the host city and distributed to the peers before they come to see the project. The process then includes a concentrated period – optimally, two or three days – during which the peers are immersed in the on-the-ground reality of the project and then have time to work through what they have seen with local experts and practitioners in an extended round of discussion. A report on outcomes and recommendations is produced in the aftermath.

> *Commit* to responding creatively to a complex or seemingly intractable problem.

Because the peer-review process asks cities to open their work to a critical group of outsiders, taking on this process takes commitment – commitment of time and resources, commitment to openness and creatively and commitment to rethinking current plans rather than just showcasing best practices. Once a project or programme of activity has been identified that is suitable for a peer review, the host city spends considerable time preparing a written overview of that project to present to the peers. This has the virtue of giving project managers time to reflect: it is not the usual cut-and-paste process, taking stuff off the website that has been used to document success. Key figures involved in the project need to commit to the documentary preparation and to two or three days of hosting the peers.

Projects in a very early stage of implementation are most suitable for being reviewed. Such projects tend to be open to adjustment, reorientation and even reversals. They have not proceeded so far as to make reorientation or basic change counterproductive. Ideally, enough has been developed on the ground to see the future and to assess how locals are responding to the project. Alternatively, projects that face seemingly intractable forces or barriers are potentially given new efficacy by the process, as are projects that are a critical junctures, or projects that have become too complex to see possible gains.

> *Engage* local and global partners in the process of responding to the provisionally identified main issue.

A peer review at city level is a structured method aimed at extending *mutual* learning about a particular project or programme. Peers are invited on this basis. The process involves both review and exchange – possibly ongoing interchange. The success of the process turns substantially on appropriate peers being identified and then accepting the invitation in the collaborative spirit that it is extended. The invited team of around four to seven experts should include a range of people with skills oriented around two emphases: working with parallel projects and thinking broadly about the social whole. This means firstly engaging colleagues from other municipalities, technical experts, who know directly about the chosen general issue and its working intricacies. Secondly, and just as importantly, it means involving individuals with generalizing cross-domain knowledge that goes beyond the immediate project. One of these people, preferably a person with experience in peer reviewing should be named as the workshop facilitator. For example in the peer-review process conducted in Johannesburg in 2013, the subject was a Bus-Rapid-Transit system called Rea Vaya.[2] Three *comparable peers*, all involved in developing and running bus services came to Johannesburg from Ahmedabad, Lagos and Mexico City. Additionally, there were three *generalizing peers* with more generic knowledge about urban sustainability, planning and liveability who came from Berlin and Melbourne – one of whom served as the facilitator for the two-day workshop.

As a general rule, most comparable peers come from cities that are facing comparable problems, working in a similar environment. Each peer is familiar with the project topic and contributes his or her own viewpoint and experience. The host city thus has an opportunity to see its urban project or practice through the eyes of others in a way that can enhance the activities locally. The peers, on the other hand, are presented with a chance to reflect on their own practices as they give advice to the host city project and bring to bear examples from their own cities.

> *Assess* the nature of the problem, and analyse the current situation in relation to the general issue in contention across all social domains.

The assessment stage is conducted from two main perspectives: internal and external. The internal assessment begins with an initial report written by local practitioners and experts of the host city. This report is crucial for giving the external peers insight into the machinations of the project. It also allows them to think about the comparable examples from their own cities and about how lessons might be transferred. The report should give answers to the following questions:

- What is the project about? This means giving a short overview of the structure of the project or programme under review. It becomes a summary of the whole initial report.
- How does the project relate to the whole of the city?
- What are the main objectives of the project or programme? What is it trying to achieve?
- What are the main critical issues that it is confronting: ecologically, economically, politically and culturally?
- What are the corresponding planned and/or already implemented concrete actions to respond to those critical issues?
- What are the concrete objectives of these actions?
- What tools and instruments are used to meet these objectives?
- Which actors and stakeholders are included?
- What are the expected and already existing results?
- What pitfalls and problems, barriers and drivers were experienced during the process of implementing the project?
- What are and what were concrete solutions to overcome these barriers? How did people make use of the drivers?
- What questions still exist? What answers are expected from the peer review?

If a city has the capacity, it is a distinct advantage to also develop an urban profile of the whole city before the peer-review meeting (see Chapter 7). This enables the project to be seen figuratively and dramatically in the context of the strengths and weaknesses of the city.

The external perspective on the assessment, begins with the peers reading the initial report and then continues into the first period of the peer-review workshop (usually the first day of two) when the peers are afforded a detailed and comprehensive introduction to the project, including through presentations, site visits and the possibility of talking to people on the ground: workers, customers, users, locals – people who are affected by the project or programme. In the evening it is an advantage for the outside peers and those centrally involved in the project to socialize and share food together. During this first day in the city, working relationship are being initiated:

- An atmosphere of collegiality is being created that enables trust and open, problem-oriented discussions
- A milieu of knowledge exchange is developing, where peers get the chance to deepen their understanding of the project through formal presentations, informal discussion and site visits

> *Define* the terms of the problem, and identify the most important critical issues that will provide the focus of action in relation to the general issue.

The definition stage is done mutually with the internal and external experts working together in discussion. It has two main phases. The first is to interrogate the critical issues that are affecting the project and refine what the city hopes to do about them (as critical objectives). This can be done in the first couple of hours of the second day (if two days is the chosen length of the workshop). Refining the critical issues and objectives that affect the project and then testing the relationship between those critical objectives is often more revealing that is usually expected. In fact, while assessing the compatibility of critical objectives and resolving possible tensions between them is fundamental to the success of any project, it is usually handled tacitly rather than as a focused event. Such tensions always exist in some way, but they often they go unrecognized. In this phase it is worthwhile to test the range of critical issues and objectives against the four domains of the circle.

This stage in the peer-review process serves in particular to highlight patterns of strengths, consequence and tensions between different objectives. For example to take the usual elephant in the room, economic growth is often assumed as one of the objectives of urban development projects, but it is normally associated with increased use of non-renewable resources, which is incompatible with environmental sustainability, another common objective. Although this seems obvious when made explicit it is usually left unacknowledged. Explicitly recognizing the most salient of these tensions enhances the possibility that the city will be fully aware of countervailing forces and contradictory objectives, and thus policymakers, practitioners, and engaged locals can find ways to negotiate between these tensions or mitigate possible problems.

For example, in the peer-review process conducted in Johannesburg in 2013 in relation to its Bus-Rapid-Transit system, Rea Vaya, twenty main issues were identified. They are represented is summary form in Table 9.1 with each critical objective mapped against every other critical objective. The key points in tension are shown with a ' − ' sign, while the objectives that are mutually reinforcing are designated with a '+' and those which are neutral in relation to each other are marked with 'o'.

TABLE 9.1 Objectives Compatibility Matrix

Critical Objectives	1	2	3	4	5	6	7	8	9	10	11	12	13	14	15	16	17	18	19	20
1. Managing dispersal of urban settlement	o	+	+	+	−	o	o	o	o	+	+	o	o	o	o	o	o	o	o	o
2. Finding space for bus rapid transit corridors			+	+	o	+	o	o	o	+	+	o	o	o	o	o	o	o	o	o
3. Decreasing pollution, carbon emissions				−	o	o	o	o	o	+	+	o	o	o	o	o	o	o	o	o
4. Decreasing costs – overall service					+	+	+	−	o	−	+	−	+	−	o	o	o	o	o	o
5. Decreasing costs – maintenance						o	+	o	o	−	+	o	o	−	o	o	o	o	o	o
6. Increasing financial sustainability							o	o	o	+	+	o	+	o	o	o	o	o	o	o
7. Increasing patronage numbers								o	o	+	+	o	o	o	o	+	o	o	o	o
8. Decreasing social inequity									o	+	+	o	o	o	+	+	o	o	o	+
9. Decreasing turnover of staff										+	+	o	+	o	o	+	o	o	o	o
10. Increasing infrastructure quality										o	o	+	+	o	o	o	o	+	o	o
11. Achieving integrated planning											o	+	+	o	o	o	+	+	+	o
12. Decreasing conflict with minibus drivers													o	o	o	−	+	o	o	o
13. Facilitating good negotiation with bus companies														o	+	o	o	o	o	o
14. Facilitating good negotiation with bus drivers															o	o	o	o	o	o
15. Decreasing corruption																o	+	o	o	o
16. Enhancing training																	o	+	o	o
17. Overcoming mini-bus culture – drivers																		o	o	o
18. Overcoming mini-bus culture – passengers																			o	o
19. Redirecting car-driving culture																				o
20. Responding to cash-oriented culture																				

Not relevant (doubling up)
Neutral   o
Compatible (positive) +
In Tension −

Analysis of these critical-issue relationships can be extensive and worked through in detail in a full process report. However, here we have only the space to make some of the more stark points that are revealed by the mapping. In positive terms, the three most important issues concerning the Rea Vaya are decreasing inequality, maintaining infrastructure quality and improving integrated planning. These are closely followed by the importance of responding to urban sprawl and planning for space around urban corridors for transport-oriented development. This was not self-evident in the questions that the Rea Vaya project managers presented as the key issues in their preliminary report. Given the self-assessed strengths in the political area including organization and governance as shown in the urban profile process figure (see Figure 9.1 in this chapter's case study) building on that strength with a bold vision to respond to those five objectives in a manifold way becomes paramount. The most complicated issues are decreasing the cost of the overall service and decreasing carbon emissions. Again this requires considerable teasing out and further analysis, but it can be readily seen from Table 9.1 that there are nine points where objectives in obvious tension. These provide focus points for follow-up work after the workshop if the city so chooses.

The second phase in the definition stage is for the peers to present possible answers to questions formulated by the host city and raised during the process of refining the critical objectives. This is done based on their own project experience. Usually this review takes the second half of the second day. The workshop closes with a summary and votes of thanks.

> *Implement* measures to respond to the problem, and authorize the various aspects of the plan and its subprojects within project parameters.

This stage and the next are for the host city to decide based on their own judgement and the oral and written advice provided by the peer-review process.

> *Measure* and monitor activities, and assess progress towards achieving the normative goal and objectives of the project.

> *Communicate* progress and strategies in relation to the project through public documentation, publication and through engagement with stakeholders.

A key aspect of the communication stage is the writing and public dissemination of a final report on the recommendations. Ideally, a written report on the whole exercise should more broadly contextualize the recommendations and discuss the complexities of the project and its setting. However, what is really important for a peer review is that the host city informs the peers about which of their recommendations and suggestions are going to be implemented in the project. It would, of course, be positive for ideas to continue to be exchanged and further activities to be planned for after the review workshop, but in the busy working lives of such practitioners this is not always possible. Nevertheless, in a short period of the process, through intensive, open, trustful exchange of professional opinion, peer review can be the initial catalyst for fruitful cooperation among all those who were involved in the exercise – between the host and the peer cities and between individuals.

Conducted with reflexive care the peer-review process should have positive outcomes. Firstly, it offers an enriching learning experience by opening up opportunities to work both generally across the critical issues that pertain to a project and to delve deeply into the praxis-relevant experience of others in dealing with relevant problems confronted in the day-to-day work of a project. For example, it can extend a rounded understanding of the local steering regulations and organizational frameworks acquired through working through legal and administrative challenges in comparable contexts. Secondly, it provides a forum for intensive exchange between individual practitioners who examine and explore each other's practices and at the same time are called on to reflect on the situation in their own municipalities. This collegial relationship is ideally carried forward as the project progresses. Thirdly, it enables those people whose project is currently being reviewed to be able to react more freely to questioning and recommendations given by their peers than would be the case with directions from a consultant or from a government representative, both of whom are more remote from everyday realities of the project. Fourthly, it opens up new perspectives upon local debates. The fact that peers as external players can take a relatively neutral point of view in relation to local politics and local practices increases both the possibilities for creative learning and the credibility of the evaluation process. And fifthly, it validates local work by experts with regard to the local practices, while providing support in important areas of global protocol and process, for example in the form of suggesting new instruments or techniques.

Overall, the peer-review process can provide a simplified structure and cooperative ongoing relations for sound evaluation of a project that leads to a more integrated and holistic vision of what is possible. It is often simple expert assurances or realignments that make the difference. Often it is the emboldening of a vision that needs to be stronger. Technically brilliant city projects do not necessarily make for great cities.

CASE STUDY: JOHANNESBURG, SOUTH AFRICA

Johannesburg began its massive development under oppressive apartheid. In 1975, Ponte City, a cylindrical skyscraper of fifty-four storeys, was built in the white's-only area of Hillbrow, making it the highest residential tower in Africa. In the same year, the Western Bypass section of the N1 was completed as a route around the city centre to access Witwatersrand. Construction began in that year on the M1 De Villiers Graaff freeway connecting the south including Soweto to the city centre and extending to Sandton, the wealthy northern commercial centre of Johannesburg. All of these infrastructure developments became carriers of the post-apartheid spatial heritage of the city. In the south the poor continue to live in concrete shacks and have limited work, and in the north, the wealthy work in modern commercial buildings and go home to green leafy suburbs. Service jobs connected the two zones. These jobs are available to those in the south who can bear the heavy peak travelling times between the south and the north.

Johannesburg is now a much more positively inclusive and liveable city than under apartheid (see Figure 9.1), but there is much to be done. Today, long after the end of formal separate development, the prior configuration of stark spatial separation continues to confront the city. There are no walls dividing people, but the effect is no less confronting. The south-west freeway has just been massively upgraded, linking working-class Soweto and the downtown area of Johannesburg. But between them is a nether zone of continuing mining operations, slag heaps and undermined wastelands. These are bad lands where building will require considerable engineering care.

Urban development in Johannesburg now stretches along two axes. One projection focuses on the north and continues the spatial divide between the concrete shacks and commercial high-rises. Recently, a Hong Kong–based company, Shanghai Zendai Property Ltd, announced its intention to build an alternative financial centre to the Sandton business district (Crowley 2013). It will be 'on par with cities like New York and Hong Kong in the Far East', said Dai Zhikang, chairman of the company. What is intended is a gateway for Chinese firms investing in sub-Saharan Africa. This kind of development confirms the development of a dual city. The second axis pushes to the south-west into a vast zone of badly serviced suburbs for the poor.

This is the dual reality of the city. It is a metropolis with one of the highest levels of inequality in the world. Currently Johannesburg has 4.4 million inhabitants and a population growth rate of 3.4 per cent. A high proportion of those people are poor, with approximately 30 per cent unemployment and 67.4 per cent of households with an income of less than R3,200 per month. Consequently, and in line with national and provincial planning paradigms,

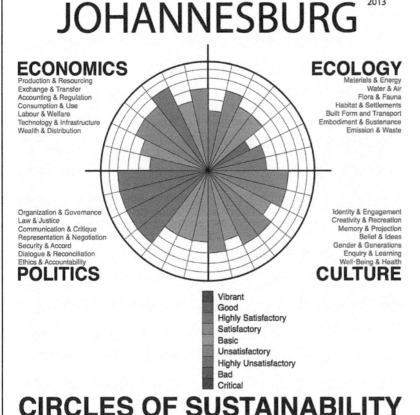

CIRCLES OF SUSTAINABILITY

FIGURE 9.1 Urban Sustainability Profile of Johannesburg, 2013

the city launched a 'Growth and Development Strategy' with a long-term vision to make 'Johannesburg as a world-class African city of the future – a vibrant, economically inclusive and multi-cultural African city; a city that provides real quality of life, for all its citizens' by 2040.

This led to the Department of Transport redefining its development goals:

- Building a leading, responsive and activist transportation sector in the city which works in partnership with stakeholders and residents
- Planning, policies and coordination for integrated and sustainable transport
- Promoting public transport, walking and cycling as modes of choice
- Building co-responsibility and a value-based culture to enable behavioural change towards transport issues

- Providing high-quality, safe, accessible, affordable and environmentally friendly public transport services
- Building, maintaining and managing the road infrastructure and systems to ensure safety, accessibility and mobility for all road users including pedestrians
- Transforming the construction, maintenance and management of storm water to respond to climate change and water scarcity and ensure the safety of residents and infrastructure
- Building, maintaining and managing public transport and non-motorized transport infrastructure to support walking, cycling and the use of public transport

The modal split between different modes of transport assessed in 2002 showed that, for non-car use, 47 per cent of the 35 million daily trips were made by public transport, whereas 72 per cent of them are made with privately operated vans. The vans had the advantage of flexibility, but they were often controlled by gangs, were polluting and were unsafe.

A fast bus system (a Bus-Rapid-Transit or BRT system) called the Rea Vaya was initiated in 2006, and three years later in August 2009 the first dedicated trunk route was operationalized from Soweto to the inner city of Johannesburg. Today this Phase 1A service carries 43,000 passengers per day and travels 6.5 million kilometres per annum on the trunk line, as well as linking to feeder routes and complementary slower buses. The decision on the selection of the route was influenced by the fact that it is a high-demand corridor linking Soweto to Sandton and thus the poor south with the rich north. Moreover, it linked the Soccer City and Ellis Park Stadiums to the 'accommodation hub' in Sandton during the FIFA World Cup in 2010.

Linking this back to the sustainability profile of Johannesburg (Figure 9.1), what the profile suggests is that there are *critical issues* that are less than satisfactory in Johannesburg pertaining to the areas of built form and transport; embodiment and sustenance, particularly relating to physical health of urban residents; emissions and waste; materials and energy, both connected to car and van dependency; and wealth and distribution. There is only space here to give the broadest response and explanation (leaving out much interpretive work that lies beneath the surface of this figure). However, in short, what the analysis tells us is that the Rea Vaya project could possibly have a central strategic position in relation to these critical issues.

More than a bus infrastructure project, the Rea Vaya needs to be considered in response to some fundamental ecological issues, and the basic economic issue of wealth distribution in the city supported by a skewed built form. If the Rea Vaya can change the spatial separation between the poorer south-west and the wealthier north, if the Rea Vaya can contribute to reducing carbon emissions and particulate emission and decrease dependency on heavy fossil-fuel use by cars, and if the Rea Vaya can be part of changing how people move around the city – then it could potentially make a substantial difference to improving the ecological and economic sustainability of the city. The heartening part of the analysis indicates that in the political domain there is the will, capacity and potential community engagement to develop the Rea Vaya in a way that could make a substantial difference.

Concretely the city has set up a strategy to identify and map the whole network of public transport, freight, walking and cycling corridors and nodes, and to identify the most appropriate mode, routes and services that will be contracted or licensed to operate in each corridor. Over time it will construct and develop already-identified public transport corridors and focus on the Rea Vaya system.

However, what the peer-review process conducted in 2013 suggested was that the vision needed to be even bigger. For all of its technical ecological innovations, it needed to give the bus service political edge and cultural identity. Patronage and cultural identification with the Rea Vaya continues to be limited. People in the south see it as just a fancy bus service. They are suspicious of the credit card system used to pay for the bus. The review confirmed that the integrated transport hubs and bus stations need to be associated with fully realized transport-oriented development. That is, it needed to develop a public vision projecting use of the stations as places around which to build carefully designed housing estates that will bring poor and well-off citizens into a living association. In 2013, in association with this kind of thinking, the main transit corridors for the Rea Vaya BRT were thus given the additional name of 'Corridors of Freedom' – with a vision to integrate disadvantaged people by providing affordable access to mobility.

Notes

1 The co-authors of this chapter are Han-Uve Schwedler, Michael Abraham and Barbara Berninger with Paul James as the main author.
2 The Johannesburg peer-review process was carried out within the context of the Berlin Metropolis Initiative 'Integrated Urban Governance—Successful Policy Transfer' in cooperation with the city of Johannesburg. The mayors of both cities, Mr Parks Tau from Johannesburg and Mr Michael Müller from Berlin, agreed at the Metropolis Board of Directors Meeting in Guangzhou in 2012 to organize this workshop conjointly in order to review the Johannesburg Bus-Rapid-Transit system and hold it concurrently with the Metropolis Annual Meeting in Johannesburg in 2013.

References

Crowley, Kevin 2013, 'Shanghai Zendai Plans $7.8 Billion "New of Africa"', *Bloomberg*, viewed 8 January 2014, <www.bloomberg.com/news/2013–11–05/shanghai-zendai-plans-7–8-billion-new-york-of-africa-.html>.
Employment, Social Affairs & Inclusion, Peer Reviews 2014, European Commission, viewed 28 February 2014, <http://ec.europa.eu/social/main.jsp?catId=1024&langId=en>.
PEARL (Peer Experience and Reflective Learning) 2014, National Institute of Urban Affairs, viewed 28 February 2014, <www.niua.org/pearl.asp>.

10

ADAPTING TO CLIMATE CHANGE[1]

The reduction of global greenhouse-gas emissions has since the early 1990s been on the agenda of decision-makers across all levels of government. The central debate has been over how to mitigate anthropogenic or human-made climate change and what targets for mitigation should be required. Much of the recent attention at the international level has focused on the task of the United Nations Framework Convention on Climate Change. Perhaps the key quandary has been how to facilitate a binding greenhouse-gas reduction agreement amongst national governments that could come into force after the Kyoto Protocol expired in 2012.

However, climate-change *adaptation* is just as important as mitigation. The Intergovernmental Panel on Climate Change has provided strong scientific evidence that climate change is already occurring and thus has presented a pressing case for simultaneously addressing the impacts of climate change through adaptation. In global negotiations on climate change, this paradigm shift has resulted in the Convention on Climate Change expanding its focus to include negotiations on governance regimes for responding to the impacts of climate change.

Thus, very recently, *both* climate-change mitigation and adaptation have become recognized in policy arenas and communities of practice as complementary strategies for responding to climate change. Mitigation and adaptation are inherently linked, but there are differences in how they should be approached. Adaptation to social and natural forces is a diffuse and difficult task. Originally a concept developed in evolutionary biology, its definition and goals are largely place based. They require an understanding not only of the impacts that are going to occur in a given place, but also, importantly, of the local fabric of economic, ecological, political and cultural life. The Intergovernmental Panel on Climate Change (IPCC) definition of adaptation is adjustment in natural or human systems in response to actual or expected climatic stimuli or their effects. It underlines the context-specific nature of adaptation. The definition does not, however, specify how 'adjustments' in systems should or will occur, or what these systems are. If the different social domains, or the combined socio-environmental 'systems', are considered the locus for climate-change adaptation, a clear understanding of the system under consideration is necessary for defining effective goals. It is crucial for devising actions that will work towards these goals within the limits and opportunities provided by that system.

Due to its highly contextual nature, adaptation also differs from mitigation in that it mainly results in localized benefits. Although the distribution of adaptation costs across beneficiaries is often contested, the local nature of adaptation benefits can be a significant incentive for individuals, local businesses and local authorities to invest in adaptation measures in their geographic area. For example, tree-planting programs in dense urban areas with limited green space can lead to a number of direct adaptation benefits, including improved shading on hot days, improved microclimate, and a reduction of the urban heat-island effect. Local adaptation approaches that draw on contextual knowledge of ecological, economic, political and cultural conditions can harness this potential, whereas local action on mitigation action is often impeded by concerns about the distribution of benefits and free-riding because localized investment can result in collective global benefits for those who have not invested.

Drawing on the terms of the *Circles of Sustainability* approach, our grounding premise in this chapter is that in adapting to climate change, cities should consider action across all domains of social life based on a *precautionary* version of the 'no regrets' approach. That is given the long-term uncertainty of climate change, and the possible irreversibility of some environmental outcomes of climate change, cities need to begin to respond now based on an active anticipation of compounding issues. This will entail public discussion and development an internally agreed series of principles of action. It will involve a strong duty of care. The core principles chosen here as orienting considerations are organized around the basic domains of sustainability:

> *Ecology*: Beyond choosing technical responses that enhance climate change adaptation, cities should seek to generate deeper and more integrated relationships with nature both inside the city and beyond the urban boundary.
>
> *Economics*: In adopting a 'no regrets' precautionary approach, urban development should be based on an economy organized around negotiated social needs rather than the conventional drive to economic growth.
>
> *Politics*: In adapting to climate change, cities should begin *now* to develop a clear vision and detailed adaptation plans through both expert deliberation and engaged civic involvement. These plans should be embedded across the board in all policymaking.
>
> *Culture*: In developing climate adaptation responses, cities should treat the process as one of deep cultural engagement involving broad cultural issues of social learning, symbolism, visualization, aesthetics and well-being.

None of these principles is given or simple to enact. Although significant progress on mitigation can be achieved by central regulation through binding inter-governmental and national agreements, positive adaptation requires deliberative

place-based approaches that integrate multiple levels of governance and link strategic top-down guidance with flexible, context-specific responses to local climate-
related hazards. This required flexibility exposes adaptation goals to the value-based
judgements of all the stakeholders and constituents involved. People's views will
differ substantially regarding what is to be protected from harm, which opportunities are to be exploited, and which vulnerabilities are worthwhile addressing, all
making for more complexity.

A primary criterion for success in climate-change adaptation therefore is to
develop a shared framing of what successful climate change adaptation means
in a given context. This will enable various actors to collaboratively design and
implement effective climate-change responses. Knowledge of, and agreement on
key conceptual and operational terms relevant to adaptation processes can help
establish such shared framing, but because of the complexity of the problem
it can be expected that actions will need to evolve creatively. It is for this reason that such complex challenges are often labelled as wicked problems and are
best addressed using collaborative approaches involving shared learning across
institutions. In this chapter, what it means to adapt to climate change and how
it might be done are described. Along the way the chapter clarifies commonly
used terminology and discusses how these different concepts are used in policy
development.

The framing considerations of adaptation often remain unacknowledged in
political discussions, in choices about planning approaches, and in the selection
of assessment methods. Making the terms of adaptation explicit is important for
establishing a collaborative process for action. Explicit consideration of a chosen
method's framing is also likely to influence the types of adaptation options and
pathways considered. The most commonly used methods of adaptation include the
following:

1. *A hazards approach.* Hazards are closely linked to disaster risk-management. This
    natural disasters frame has been a dominant consideration in policy discussion
    on climate change. Increasingly broader notions of climatic hazards are being
    adopted, linked with economic, cultural and ecological trends. For example, it
    is now recognized that unrestricted population expansion into coastal zones
    is likely to intensify the consequences of sea-level rise or storm surges. The
    strengths of a hazards approach is that it tends to draw heavily on quantitative
    data when available, leading to metrics-based conclusions that are often sought
    after by policy-developers and decision-makers in order to justify pursuing
    particular strategies. However, these apparently firm conclusions are actually
    beset by limits to certainty. It is not an intrinsic problem that climate models
    are not able to give completely accurate local and regional scenarios for the
    complex intersection of climatic variables. However, epistemological uncer-
    tainty can become a major problem in politically uncertain times. The perhaps
    necessary act of relocating the inhabitants of hazardous regions and locali-
    ties for example can be resource intensive and time-consuming, and keeping
    the uncertainty transparent (a positive process) does not make such actions

politically comfortable. This is an example of tensions between critical issues (see Chapter 6).

2. *A risk management approach.* This is the dominant organizational practice for dealing with many types of uncertainties in local government and the private sector. Central to the notion of risk is the fact of uncertainty and changing perceptions. Risk is defined as the combined product of hazards, exposure and vulnerability, and as such there is a close connection between hazards and risk management approaches. Risk-assessment and risk-management processes are suitable for organizations of various sizes, can fit well with existing organizational procedures and be readily integrated into existing risk management systems. However, the approach can lead government to be focused inwardly, often to the neglect of the interests of other departments, external stakeholders and local communities.

3. *A vulnerability approach.* This approach focuses on who or what will be affected and in what way. A wide range of possible policy responses to vulnerability is possible. For example outcome vulnerability relates to the residual impacts – for example on a habitat, an ecosystem or a municipality – after all feasible adaptation responses have been taken into account. A contextual framing of vulnerability considers different kinds of vulnerability in the broader context of interactions between climate and society. Good vulnerability assessments can add valuable bottom-up perspectives for adaptation and be used to build the case for adaptation based on local data and information, thus ensuring that adaptation options are designed in direct response to local needs, enhancing the potential for tangible local adaptation outcomes. Alternatively one weakness in this localizing strategy is that range of vulnerability assessment methods in use makes it difficult to compare the results from different assessments or to understand the spatial variability of vulnerability beyond the scope of the immediate analysis.

4. *A resilience approach.* The resilience concept originated in the field of ecology as the capacity of an environmental system to absorb disturbance but is now being translated and applied to human systems. These approaches have the virtue putting the social back into ecological systems analysis. Social resilience can be defined as the capacity of groups or communities to cope with external stresses and disturbances as a result of economic, political or ecological change. One lineage of this approach puts the emphasis on knowledge systems and adaptive learning as the basis for adapting to change or, better still, transforming for the better. The weakness of the approach derives from its own double sense of novelty and scientific precision – as if resilience is a more far-reaching concept than sustainability because of when and where it came from.

Each of these approaches has been influential in the development of climate-change assessment methods for good reasons. However understanding how these different assessment methods are framed is important given the role that assessments play in adaptation planning. Framing considerations can determine which government departments are involved and which minister is considered to have responsibility for addressing climate impacts. Clarity about the good qualities and limitations of different assessment approaches will inform the methods used to assess impacts and adaptation responses.

The choice of frame can lead to different types of climate-change assessments. Whichever approach is used, our argument is that adaptation needs to take into account all the domains of the human condition – ecology, economics, politics and culture. Moreover, it needs to develop a reflexive understanding of the intersecting driving forces and critical issues across these domains that complicate any response. The tendency in each of these approaches is to focus on a narrower range than is necessary for dealing with a phenomenon such as climate change that perforce has such social complexity. Hazards approaches for example tend to begin with the consequences of ecological forces (see Table 10.1). Risk-management approaches tend to focus on political responses to hazards that potentially could affect the economics of technology and infrastructure or the ecology of habitat, settlements, built form and transport. Vulnerability approaches tend to focus on local solutions. And resilience approaches tend to emphasize political-cultural responses to ecological change.

In summary, it is not choice of the method of action that matters most, but first, awareness of the strengths and weaknesses of that method. Secondly, whichever framework is chosen, climate change adaptation should be considered a process of continuous responsiveness across all the domains of social life. Thirdly, good adaptation requires good planning. Enacting a good adaption plan, like any plan, entails a comprehensive response: commitment, engagement, assessment, definition, implementation, measurement and communication (to use the seven-stage process path discussed earlier in Chapter 6). All of these steps are accompanied by ongoing dialogue and learning. In a situation of constrained time and financial resources, the choice of a particular adaptation approach or a combination of approaches will be highly influential in establishing a particular dominant framing for an adaptation process. Ideally, policy developers and decision-makers should pause and query why a type of approach or method will be applied to any particular adaptation project and should ascertain the relevance of the underlying concepts for the purposes of the activity. They should not allow the ideological assumptions of a particular approach to blind them to the need for treating climate change as a holistic issue across all the domains of social life.

Setting objectives for adaptation

Setting high-level goals and associated critical objectives for climate-change adaptation needs to be an iterative process so that emerging information on climate-change impacts, the policy context and the activities of stakeholders and constituents can be incorporated at regular intervals. Like all goal statements, the named adaptation objectives need to be achievable and time bound to be able to effectively drive adaptation processes. However, the definition of time-bound objectives needs to be revisited iteratively in order to accommodate changing climatic or local-context parameters. Although a broad vision is needed at the adaptation policy level (e.g., at the level of state government), more detailed and involved sectoral planning

TABLE 10.1 Examples of Ecological Forces, Events and Critical Issues through the Lens of a Hazards Approach[2]

Ecological forces		Events in the ecological domain	Critical issues in the ecological domain	Onset	Duration
Temperature	Average temperature increase • Increase in atmospheric circulation • Increased melting of polar ice • Thermal expansion of sea-water • Reduction in frost periods and snow-cover	Wind storms	Coastal storm damage	Sudden	Short
			Storm damage to built environment and habitats	Sudden	Short
		Sea-level rise	Coastal inundation	Slow	Continuous
			Coastal erosion	Sudden or slow	Continuous
		Heat waves	Heat stress	Sudden	Short
	Increase in extreme temperatures	Bushfires	Fire damage to built environment and habitats	Sudden	Short
Precipitation	Average precipitation decrease/increase	Droughts	Drinking water scarcity	Slow	Short to extended
			Irrigation water scarcity	Slow	Short to extended
			Reduced water flows having an impact on river systems	Slow	Short to extended
	Increase in extreme precipitation	Torrential rain or extended periods of precipitation	Flood damage to built environment	Sudden	Short
		Hailstorms	Impact damage to built environment	Sudden	Short
		Thunderstorms	Water damage and fire damage	Sudden	Short

Source: Adapted from Smit *et al.* (2000).

is needed to specify different sector-by-sector objectives, to define concrete targets, and to generate set of appropriate indicators. Setting adaptation objectives also needs to strike a delicate balance between providing clear guidance on the one hand and allowing for a certain degree of flexibility on the other.

How does adaptation occur?

Developing a shared understanding of current and future climatic forces and their potential impact – including which forces are critical to a particular location, and what elements of a chosen system are at risk – are essential starting points for adaptation processes that are workable at local and regional scale. This needs to be done in the *assessment stage* while continually re-engaging people through dialogue and learning. Even though it may be impossible to achieve a truly shared public framework for understanding adaptation, making different views explicit paves the way for properly defining the objectives of adaptation and for choosing the processes and tools to be used to achieve these objectives. It makes it more likely that a suite of adaptation measures will be chosen that align with local needs and capacities.

Even after it is agreed that something needs to be done, the evidence suggests that the question of how adaptation is going to occur, the terms of which should primarily developed during a publicly projected *definition stage*, remains an ongoing contentious issue for local and regional-scale adaptation. The 'how' question connects reflections on the purpose of adaptation with basic political decisions on the task to be done. Adaptation planning can take place through various activities leading to different types of *outcomes*, and therefore, clarity is needed about the intended outcomes as well as the methods, tools and *processes* used for achieving them. It is useful to briefly examine these two orientations in more detail: adaptation as outcome driven, and adaption as process driven.

Adaptation as outcome driven

At the level of international climate negotiations, adaptation is often referred to as being necessary as a direct result of having to deal with the relatively known anticipated negative impacts of climate change. This view follows the argument that adaptation is a way of responding to climate change only because a certain degree of social change can no longer be avoided. When, in these terms, adaptation is framed predominantly as an outcome-driven top-down process, it emphasizes questions of what the desired state of 'being adapted' would look like, what degree of adaptation is technologically possible, and who should be held legally responsible for its associated costs. This outcome-oriented frame also relates well to a gently modified 'business as usual' approach. This approach is described though the metaphor of 'fitting in'; fitting into existing dominant structures. Fitting in, or thin adaptation, tends to occur when the act of adapting is considered to be a comfortably understood and relatively predetermined addition to a given dominant set of existing ways of doing things. Incorporating a few climate-change adaptation considerations into existing land-use practices without fundamentally changing those practices is an example of fitting in.

Although a framework that emphasizes outcomes is useful for arguing the case for mitigation, and can provide an impetus for agreeing on adaptation goals, its usefulness is limited when it comes to working towards sets of changing adaptation options, dealing with complex community responses and devising multidimensional adaptation measures. Within such a framework, questions concerning 'how to' act are addressed by turning to conventional planning methods and by using readily applied technologies. Typically in circumstances of outcome-focused adaptation, technological options feature prominently in measures to reduce or compensate against hazards and risks (thus invoking only one perspective of just one domain – the technology and infrastructure perspective). This focus on achieving relatively predictable outcomes is one of the reasons why technology and infrastructure responses, such as building sea walls and flood barriers, are often treated as the first option and favoured over alternative 'soft' adaptation options. The validity of an outcome-oriented top-down framing of adaptation lies in developing a better understanding of what different futures may look like for example as part of scenario-planning exercises (see Chapter 11), but its weakness lies in not being adequately handle complexity.

Adaptation as process driven

Adaptation framing which focuses on process tends to place greater emphasis on adapting to climate-change impacts by adopting a systems perspective. Such framing recognizes that adaptation is a continuous process of interaction between human social 'systems' and the environment. Adaptation is thus characterized more by ongoing social learning than outcomes. Process-oriented framing of adaptation inevitably emphasizes the role of people and institutions, their evolving capacity of effectively dealing with climate change impacts, commonly referred to as 'adaptive capacity'. It tends to work across the range of non-technological and technological adaptation measures.

While bringing global protocols for climate-change adaption down to local, urban and regional levels can certainly prove useful for decision-making, they need to be complemented by more reflexive bottom-up approaches to adaptation planning. This approach acknowledges that effective adaptation needs to be deeply embedded in local knowledge. Framing climate-change adaptation as a learning process is useful in providing answers to the question of how adaptation is going to occur at local level and, therefore, should be considered a vital and self-conscious component of any operational adaptation framework. In embracing a process of institutional and individual learning for climate-change adaptation, local decision-makers are enabled to explore a broad range of adaptation options that will become more sophisticated as their adaptive capacity increases. It is strongest when coupled with a qualified version of outcome-driven adaptation.

Cross-domain options for adaptation

Decision-makers and local communities can come up with an infinite number of adaptation measures to achieve stated objectives, and the broad range of options available can often be overwhelming to practitioners. Table 10.2 provides a typology of possible climate-change adaptation measures, which can help understand broad options available to policy developers, both formal and informal. In keeping with the *Circles of Sustainability* approach, four interrelated categories of adaptation measures are proposed: namely ecological measures such as re-establishing self-generating natural protection zones; economic measures, ranging from technological responses to financial schemes; political measures, for example institutional capacity-building and regulatory frameworks; and cultural measures, for example learning and communication tools. All of these measures can be implemented at different levels of government using a combination of policies and regulations, market-based and non-market-based incentives, and different projections or cultural visions that go beyond self-interest and the need for material incentives.

TABLE 10.2 Types of Adaptation Measures across the Different Domains of Social Life

Domains	Perspectives	Examples of Local and Citywide Responses
Ecology	Materials and Energy	• Setting up distributed renewable energy systems less prone to extreme weather problems.
	Water and Air	• Reclaiming natural verges and flood plains along waterways to mitigate the inundation of unsuitably located buildings.
	Flora and Fauna	• Planting native trees and plants to increase the resilience of urban parks and gardens in the face of climate extremes.
	Habitat and Settlements	• Building sea walls, albeit back from the present immediate shoreline, in anticipation of potential sea-level rise and storm surges
	Built Form and Transport	• Retrofitting buildings to better protect people from extreme heat
	Embodiment and Sustenance	• Establishing robust, seasonal, local food production, including through urban agriculture and aquaponics
	Emission and Waste	• Improving the capacity of urban drainage systems
Economics	Production and Resourcing	• Securing supply lines of basic commodities
	Exchange and Transfer	• Providing funds for conducting local climate-impact assessments
	Accounting and Regulation	• Spreading climate risks equitably across insurance providers
	Consumption and Use	• Setting up bulk-buying schemes for domestic rainwater tanks
	Labour and Welfare	• Recognizing that in the aftermath of extreme weather events people might need time off work for home renewal
	Technology and Infrastructure	• Installing water metres to monitor and help address wasteful water use
	Wealth and Distribution	• Providing compensation for those who are required to move their places of abode away from hazard zones
Politics	Organization and Governance	• Changing the organizational structure of municipalities and governments to increase the ability to respond to climate change

(Continued)

TABLE 10.2 (*Continued*)

Domains	Perspectives	Examples of Local and Citywide Responses
	Law and Justice	• Setting restrictive development controls in coastal hazard zones
	Communication and Critique	• Disseminating up-to-date information on extreme weather events via social media
	Representation and Negotiation	• Inviting community groups and local leaders to decide priorities and participate in adaptation planning processes
	Security and Accord	• Anticipating and planning for security problems due to complex emergencies
	Dialogue and Reconciliation	• Conducting scenario-planning exercises that explicitly attempt to reconcile needs and limits
	Ethics and Accountability	• Acting on support for climate-change refugees
Culture	Identity and Engagement	• Reorienting identity away from high mass-consumption products
	Creativity and Recreation	• Engaging artists to symbolically represent the consequences of climate change
	Memory and Projection	• Projecting scenarios of possible adaptation futures
	Beliefs and Ideas	• Generating public discussions and debates about different adaptation measures and their variable impact
	Gender and Generations	• Responding to the potential of the elderly and the vulnerable to be affected by extreme heat and cold periods
	Enquiry and Learning	• Training local government staff on climate-change methodologies
	Well-Being and Health	• Anticipating measures needed to respond to increased water-borne and insect-transmitted diseases

Decision-making on local adaptation measures requires some form of qualitative or quantitative evaluation of the various adaptation options available. For each identified climate-change impact, a range of options exist that could potentially be equally effective in combating negative climate-change impacts or, alternatively, harnessing new opportunities. For example, to decrease the urban heat-island effect in densely built up areas a combination of the following options may be found appropriate:

• Increasing shading of buildings and sealed surfaces, for example by planting trees
• Increasing evapotranspiration in the area, for example by converting sealed areas into green spaces and constructing water features

- Ensuring better ventilation of the area, for example by creating building corridors that enable cooler airflow into the area
- Rendering buildings in reflective colour to decrease heat absorption into thermal mass

Each of these measures comes with an associated financial cost, a specific minimum timeline for implementation and a series of secondary environmental and social effects that will inform public opinion and decision-making. In the example of the heat-island effect, adaptation metrics can be employed to assess cost–benefit ratios of the various options available *ex ante*, under current and projected climate change. In the context of midterm to long-term adaptation and whenever nontechnological adaptation is included in the equation, it is, however, far less straightforward to establish which adaptation options are most suitable, because many of the potential benefits may be unknown and lie in the future. Although cost–benefit analysis can be a suitable tool for many technological adaptations (e.g. building or upgrading of infrastructure to protect from flooding), it has significant methodological limitations when it comes to measuring the expected costs and benefits of non-financial factors.

Ex post evaluation of adaptation measures is similarly difficult, in particular in terms of providing guidance for adaptation to future extreme events, which occur infrequently, at irregular intervals, but with potentially devastating impacts. Current extreme events may provide a significant trigger and incentive for adaptive action, which are likely to also reduce future vulnerabilities. It may prove politically difficult, however, to justify and agree on large-scale investment into costly adaptation measures for preventing future catastrophic impacts, in particular when an empirical evaluation of the suitability and effectiveness of measures already implemented cannot be ascertained within standard planning and political cycles.

This conundrum points to the limited suitability of cost–benefit analyses for guiding effective climate change adaptation at the local and regional levels. Cost–benefit analyses and similar economic tools need to be supplemented and informed by additional qualitative studies, for example exploratory research investigating past and present local practice of dealing with climate change. Such climate analogues can provide important contextual information on how socio-ecological systems are likely to respond to particular adaptation measures.

Furthermore, the limitations of applying a cost–benefit approach towards evaluating different adaptation options highlight the need for applying alternative metrics to the costing of climate change impacts that are able to accommodate non-financial costs and take into account contextual economic parameters. The shortcoming of economic assessment tools also reiterate that a focus on the process aspects of adaptation may provide a more flexible way forward in adaptation planning, rather than relying mainly on substantive adaptation outcomes that have been determined using conventional economically rational decision-making.

Different measures need also to have different *temporal* scopes, laying out steps between short-term and long-term implementation. They need to be developed with a specification of different *spatial* scopes, for example, local, municipal, regional or national). And they require awareness of the status of the *epistemological* scope whether they are being devised in reaction (1) to a documented and known existing climate impact, (2) during the occurrence of a changing impact or (3) in anticipation of an (expected) impact in the distant future.

Avoiding maladaptation

In the absence of a large evidence base on what constitutes good adaptation, adaptation efforts should therefore at a minimum endeavour to avoid any 'bad' adaptations, including the following:

- Measures that increase greenhouse gas emissions or other adverse ecological consequences
- Measures that disproportionately burden the most vulnerable social groups
- Measures that come with high opportunity costs – that is high economic, ecological, political or cultural costs in comparison with sound alternatives
- Measures that reduce the incentive for actors to adapt – for example by increasing the reliance of actors on others' actions or the activities or different levels of government
- Measures that create a path dependency – that is measures that adopt trajectories that are difficult to change in the future due to high costs involved in such change (Barnett & O'Neill 2010)

Such maladaptations not only pose a risk of significant ecological, economic, political and cultural costs, they can also undermine the support of key adaptation actors.

Risk assessment methods

In the previous section we have provided an overview of what we consider to be key issues in the context of adaptation framing. In this section we elaborate upon two common approaches used in adaptation processes and unpack the conceptual frames inherent in these approaches. The first, risk assessment, as part of a risk-management approach, provides a process for dealing with uncertainty. Although risk can be quantified using various formulas, qualitative or perception-based approaches often inform risk assessments. This occurs in particular when political or cultural systems are the subject of risk assessments. Standard risk-assessment matrices are used to assess the likelihood and expected consequences of a climate change impact under different scenarios, resulting in ratings of 'low', 'medium', 'high' or 'extreme' risk, which indicate the level of priority with which a risk should be treated (Table 10.3).

The Australian government's Climate Change Impacts and Risk Management guide suggests a sequential process for climate risk assessment and management is suggested, consisting of five major steps (Figure 10.1 below). This relies on the active

TABLE 10.3 Priority Risk-Rating Matrix[3]

Likelihood	Consequences				
	Insignificant	Minor	Moderate	Major	Catastrophic
Almost certain	Medium	Medium	High	Extreme	Extreme
Likely	Low	Medium	High	High	Extreme
Possible	Low	Medium	Medium	High	High
Unlikely	Low	Low	Medium	Medium	Medium
Rare	Low	Low	Low	Low	Medium

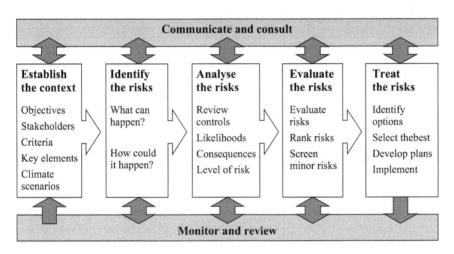

FIGURE 10.1 Steps in the Risk-Management Process
Source: Australian Government (2006).

participation of stakeholders: establishing the context, identifying, analysing and evaluating climate change risks and treating the risks by identifying adaptation options. The process, although sequential, relies on ongoing monitoring and evaluation. In many ways it is a simpler version of the Circles of Social Life process pathway laid out earlier in Chapter 6.

As part of establishing the context for climate risk-management, the guide recommends carrying out a scoping exercise, which includes setting clear objectives, identifying key stakeholders, setting success criteria to be used for evaluating the outcomes of the risk-management process, as well as identifying key elements at risk and choosing one or several climate scenarios that will inform the process. To ensure the validity of the process and its outcomes, it is critical that a diverse group of key stakeholders participates in the process. Part of the initial scoping process is also developing context-specific scales that define different levels of risk likelihood and consequence. These likelihood and consequence scales are to be developed based on strategic organizational objectives (referring back to the understanding that risk means a threat to an organization achieving its objectives). They usually build on both qualitative and quantitative elements.

The second step in the process involves identifying climate-change risks that various key elements (or exposure units, in the language of impact assessment) will be exposed to under different climate-change scenarios, using participatory brainstorming and data-gathering techniques. Qualitative cause–effect statements can help clarify why a particular issue is considered a risk. Risk analysis is conducted mainly qualitatively, by assigning each risk a level of priority based on the likelihood of the risk eventuating under different climate change scenarios and its expected consequences. The likelihood and consequence scales developed during the first step are applied here. When possible, a qualitative risk analysis and priority rating should be supported by quantitative studies that explain why a particular likelihood or consequence rating is appropriate.

During the third step, assigned priority risk ratings are evaluated by ensuring they are consistent with one another and match the stakeholders' interpretation of the local context in which they are operating. This assessment process, consisting of risk identification, analysis and evaluation, then forms the basis for exploring options for 'risk treatment' – that is, the development, selection and implementation of adaptation measures that reduce the levels of risk.

Climate risk-management processes are suitable for organizations of various sizes, from community organizations to government departments. Because of these processes' reliance on qualitative data and expert knowledge, engaging a suitable group of stakeholders from different backgrounds is essential to the effectiveness of the adaptation options developed in the final stage of the process. One of the strengths of risk-assessment approaches to climate change is that they can fit with existing organizational procedures and can readily be integrated into existing risk-management systems and structures. A risk-based approach to climate-change assessments enables stakeholders to establish likely cause–effect type links between projected climatic changes and the operational context in their department, their community or their organization. By getting stakeholders to engage with projected changes in climatic parameters through understanding how these relate back to organizational objectives and services, ownership for adaptation processes can be created. This is critical for ensuring that adaptation measures derived from risk assessments are meaningful, feasible and effective. Again the process outline here is very similar to the broader sustainability assessment process in the *Circles of Sustainability* approach discussed earlier.

One limitation, and difference from the *Circles* approach is that in the context of governmental organizations the implementation of risk-assessment processes tends to be focused inwardly, often to the neglect of external stakeholders, services and activities that are considered peripheral to an organization. For example in the local government sector, a risk-management approach to climate change typically focuses on corporate risk – that is, risks that threaten the key objectives of the organization. Such assessment processes, to be conducted properly, need to broaden to consider climate risks to the community (e.g., via organizational objectives that relate to service delivery, community satisfaction and well-being). Organization assessments can thus be a suitable entry point to a more holistic approach to adaptation.

Another limitation of using simple risk-management process templates, such as the one outlined, is that it relies to a significant extent on the views of individual stakeholders. In this context, it is important to acknowledge that an ideal-world scenario of equal representation and engagement of key constituents from different disciplinary backgrounds is rarely achieved in adaptation processes. It is more likely that some individuals will be more involved in the process than others, some will be able to dominate the discussions more than others, and that some constituents may choose not to participate or express their views. Therefore, careful and professional facilitation is required for any climate-change assessment, including climate risk-assessment processes, and transparency about who is involved in what role needs to be achieved early in the process.

Vulnerability assessment methods

Vulnerability assessment has emerged as a common practice in climate change adaptation processes, and, due to a lack of standardization and the multifaceted nature of the concept of vulnerability, it is implemented in many different ways, using a range of definitions of vulnerability and various assessment methods. The following sections are an attempt to provide an overview, acknowledging that it is difficult to do full justice to this diversity.

Objectives and methods

Conducting a vulnerability assessment is seen by many as a critical component of climate change adaptation processes at the local level, because it can elicit knowledge about the expected distribution of impacts across a system. Vulnerability assessments typically consist of assessing the characteristics of a vulnerable system, the type and number of stressors affecting that system, and the effects these have on the system. The widely used IPCC definition of vulnerability suggests that assessing vulnerability becomes meaningful and practicable only if it is conducted only in relation to a specified hazard, a range of hazards or a specific system. As opposed to climate-impact assessment and risk assessment, vulnerability assessment is less rigidly defined, and processes labelled as vulnerability assessments reveal a great diversity in approach and methodologies used.

Over the past decade, vulnerability assessment methodologies have moved from an exclusive focus on the biophysical environment and questions of physical vulnerability towards the inclusion of, and a greater focus on, an assessment of the social vulnerability of segments of the local population. Different types of vulnerability assessment continue to co-exist, however, reflecting the broad applicability of the vulnerability concept across different social and environmental phenomena.

A biophysical vulnerability assessment may, for example, focus on evaluating the impact of increasing average night-time temperatures on the evapotranspiration of trees in an urban park. A social vulnerability assessment of heat stress will identify groups within the population that are particularly under threat of suffering health and well-being impacts during a heat wave. A combined biophysical and social assessment may analyse, among other factors, the combined effects of changing evapotranspiration patterns of urban trees and the effect of heat fatigue due to warmer night-time temperatures. In many vulnerability assessment methodologies, four elements stand out as particular relevant:

1. Focus on a *vulnerable system*, which forms the scope for analysis and assessment. Depending on the disciplinary perspective and the scoping process, these typically comprise a coupled socio-ecological system, a social system or subsystems (such as a social group) or a particular geographic region or area.
2. Consideration of the *elements at risk* within the system. Examples of typical elements at risk to climate change impacts are human lives, flora and fauna species, habitats, cultural and religious values, buildings and infrastructure.
3. Identification of a particular *hazard*, which denotes a potentially damaging influence on the system of analysis. Hazards are sometimes differentiated into discrete hazards, or perturbations, and continuous hazards, or stress/stressors.
4. A *temporal reference*, which scopes out the time-frame used for vulnerability assessment. Applying an explicit time-frame is particularly relevant in the context of climate-change adaptation, where impacts, to a large extent, lie in the future (Füssel 2007).

A technical paper informing the UN Development Programme's Adaptation Policy Framework serves as an example of how these elements are translated into a method for assessing social vulnerability, consisting of five discrete steps (Lim & Spanger-Siegried 2005; see Table 10.4). Similar to other types of assessment approaches discussed earlier, a definition phase is outlined, focusing predominantly on specifying a conceptual framework and a workable definition for vulnerability. The identification of vulnerable groups (step 2) focuses on the scoping of system boundaries, including which groups are exposed to hazards.

This is followed by an assessment of sensitivity of the system and identified vulnerable groups, that is gaining an understanding of how climate hazards translate into climate impacts, risks and disasters. Importantly, the approach uses the identification of the drivers of current vulnerability to assess how future vulnerability is likely to be determined and what role processes of autonomous adaptation can play in the reduction of vulnerability (step 4). In a final step, assessment outcomes inform adaptation policy and decision-making.

Strengths and limitations

Vulnerability assessments can add a valuable, bottom-up perspective to climate change adaptation processes. Their strength is that they build the case for adaptation

TABLE 10.4 Five-Step Approach to Vulnerability Assessment[4]

No.	Objective of activity	Description
1	Structuring the vulnerability assessment: definitions, frameworks and objectives	Clarifying the conceptual framework and analytical definitions of vulnerability being used for the assessment
2	Identifying vulnerable groups: exposure and assessment boundaries	Defining the system chosen for the assessment, including who is vulnerable, to what, in what way and where. System characteristics to be defined include sectors, stakeholders and institutions, geographical regions and scales and periods
3	Assessing sensitivity: current vulnerability of the selected system and vulnerable group	Developing an understanding of the process by which climate outcomes (e.g., hydrological and meteorological variables) translate into risks and disasters. This includes identifying points of intervention and options for response to vulnerability.
4	Assessing future vulnerability	Developing a qualitative understanding of current drivers of vulnerability in order to better understand possible future vulnerability, including ways in which planned or autonomous adaptation may modify climate risks.
5	Linking vulnerability assessment outputs with adaptation policy	Relating vulnerability assessment outputs (2–4 above) to stakeholder decision-making, public awareness and further assessments.

Source: Downing and Patwardhan (2005).

based on local data and information, thus helping ensure that adaptation options developed during planning processes can be designed in a way that they directly respond to local needs. If implemented in a participatory way, drawing on the knowledge and views of various local stakeholders, vulnerability assessments have the potential to pave the way for tangible local adaptation outcomes. Also, through the analysis carried out as part of vulnerability assessments, future climate impacts become directly linked to current contextual drivers of vulnerability (e.g., broader socio-economic processes affecting a particular place), hence enabling the identification of 'starting points' for adaptation by focusing on current vulnerability.

Vulnerability assessment is most useful for analysing how current climate variability and projected climate change impacts may affect different populations (or other system components), in different ways. Depending on the approach used the can add a quantitative or qualitative layer of local knowledge and information to decision-making processes, focused on the needs of vulnerable groups or system components. When vulnerability assessments mainly produce qualitative data on the expected consequences of climate change, their outputs often don't meet current needs for an evidence-base to decision-making, for example in relation to costly infrastructure investments. This limitation, however, applies to other types of assessments as well, and purely quantitative assessment outputs, on the other hand, can suggest a degree of certainty that doesn't reflect the complex and variable nature of climate change.

The heterogeneity of the various vulnerability assessment methods used also means that it is difficult to compare the results from different assessments, for example in order to understand the spatial variability of vulnerability. Maps of relative vulnerability, which are popular with planners and decision-makers in outcome-orientated organizations, suggest that vulnerability is quantifiable. Although such maps can be a useful visualization tool for communicating projected climate change impacts at local level, they contain a range of assumptions inherent in the methodology, including significant degrees of uncertainty, which need to be discussed with stakeholders, constituents and end users.

Our alternative extended approach, to adaptation planning brings both risk and vulnerability assessment together with stronger community engagement in assessing their own capacities for resilience and adaptation. It puts greater emphasis on qualitative aspects and the need for embedding vulnerability assessment as a bottom-up process in local knowledge and 'wisdom'. Stage 3 in the seven-step model outlined in Figure 10.2 therefore emphasizes the need for getting to know

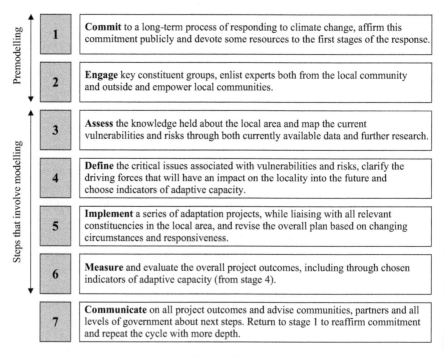

FIGURE 10.2 Seven-Stage Model for Global Climate Change Response Assessment

the study location but without assuming an external researcher is conducting the assessment as the only involved party. Also, this approach explicitly mentions the use of adaptive-capacity indicators, which constitute a model of vulnerability and risk response used for implementing the adaptation projects (stage 5).

Using various approaches to vulnerability and risk assessment, numerous studies have tried to develop composite local vulnerability indices, to assist communicating assessment outcomes, with mixed results. For example overlaying vulnerability indicator data collected during an assessment with demographic information can produce maps of relative vulnerability and its variation across space. For all of this pointed focus, the only way of managing a process of climate change adaptation adequately is treating the general of climate change like any other complex problem, and treating a planned response as part of holistic, community-engaged approach which takes research and analysis seriously, seeks to measure outcomes, and returns constantly to basic questions of local social commitment rather than leaving it just in the hands of experts.

Notes

1 Darryn McEvoy and Hartmut Fünfgeld were main co-authors of this chapter with Paul James.
2 Adapted from Smit *et al.* (2000).
3 The Australian government developed this matrix over the 2000s.
4 Downing and Patwardhan (2005).

References

Australian Government, 2006 *Climate Change Impacts and Risk Management*, Commonwealth of Australia, Canberra.
Barnett, J. & O'Neill, S. 2010, 'Maladaptation', *Global Environmental Change*, vol. 20, pp. 211–13.
Downing, T.E. & Patwardhan, A. in Lim, B. & Spanger-Siegried, E. (eds) 2005, *Adaptation Policy Frameworks for Climate Change: Developing Strategies, Policies and Measures*, Cambridge University Press, Cambridge.
Füssel, H. M. 2007, 'Vulnerability: A Generally Applicable Conceptual Framework for Climate Change Research', *Global Environmental Change*, vol. 17, pp. 155–67.
Lim, B. & Spanger-Siegried, E. (eds) 2005, *Adaptation Policy Frameworks for Climate Change: Developing Strategies, Policies and Measures*, Cambridge University Press, Cambridge.
Smit, B., Burton, I., Klein, R.J.T., & Wandel, J. 2000, 'An Anatomy of Adaptation to Climate Change and Variability', *Climatic Change*, vol. 45, pp. 223–51.

11

PROJECTING ALTERNATIVE FUTURES[1]

The future is uncertain and exploring uncertainties is one of the most difficult of all the planning processes. Planners and forecasters have become so bound up in a modern sense of linear time that the future is too often described as stretching from the present in a relatively consistent line of upward progress or downward failure. That is, the future is described as a line from the present based on trends that stretch directly from the past. This belief, partly a self-confirming one, is true enough (and therefore wrong enough) to be completely misleading. Metrics-based trajectories from the past to the present are only one indication of possible futures.

It is indicative of how difficult this area of understanding is that futurologists are not very good at predicting the future. Those lines on graphs that seem to prom- ise relative clarity when it comes to predicting what the world will look like in a generation's time do not take into account all the many possibilities that unfold as complex determinants intersect. Technological developments and reversals, disasters and accidents, revolutions in thought and practice, contingencies and exceptions, faraway butterflies flapping their wings and close-up things that people have cast from their minds as irrelevant to the future all contribute to what will happen in the future.

As we have described earlier, ideologies, however much they appear as simply true now, tend to change much faster than do imaginaries and ontologies. It is thus these ideologically informed common-sense understandings about the pres- ent and the future that this method is attempting in the first instance to defami- larize. However, more than that, it attempts to challenge the taken-for-granted dominance of modern time and the idea of progress. Development does not nec- essarily have to mean moving ever *upward*. Prosperity does not have to mean ever- increasing *growth*. Sustainable development depends upon projecting how we want to live, projecting a transitional practice for getting there, and beginning to live that vision now. Sometimes that means slowing down and relating to nature and others differently.

The *Circles of Sustainability* approach is concerned to build a sense of complexity and temporal awareness into any understanding of what is to be done in response to perceived issues of sustainability in the present. The method of scenario projection attempts to bring these issues to the fore. In particular, it acknowledges that different futures are possible, and that the future in part depends upon what we decide to do now. The method involves a process for exploring different scenarios and how a city or community might embrace or avoid certain projected possibilities. It is not an attempt to predict the future. It is a process for uncovering different uncertainties and negotiating what can be done about them. The process thus involves telling stories about the future rather than just tracing linear trajectories.

In this chapter, we set out the various steps of a basic but still sufficiently complex scenario projection process to open up real divergences. Rather than focusing upon the development of singular normative scenarios of some aspired future, the variation developed here encourages the development of multiple scenarios that explore some of the limits of possibility for the future. The process aligns with processes discussed in earlier chapters such as in relation to critical issue selection and sustainability assessment.

In the first stage of any scenario process, it is important to explore limits and uncertainties in order to ascertain the range of possibilities with which policy needs to deal. This requires the involvement of people from very different walks of life, including urban experts, coming together to argue about their perceptions of the city, the region or the organization and its possible futures. The second stage of the approach involves setting up a session (again supported by, rather than simply conducted by, urban experts) to explore an aspirational future working backwards within the range of possibilities elucidated. Here we concentrate on the first stage, but both stages have the common feature of enabling individuals and groups to explore the limits of possibility for the unfolding of the issue under consideration over a specified time-scale, within the confines of what is currently known, knowable and plausible.

Actual implementation of the method may take place across a range of time scales, from one day to several iterations over months. Whichever approach you adopt to conduct a scenario projection process, we provide a set of basic ground rules that should be helpful to making the process work well. These set the context for challenging business-as-usual thinking, for supporting negotiated inclusiveness and for facilitating the expression of multiple viewpoints on the matter at hand. The ground rules are also intended to minimize the risk of interpersonal challenge and conflict between participants. If these rules are not followed, there is a risk of breakdown of the process, with some individuals becoming alienated and excluded and powerful actors dominating and closing down the discussion.

Developing a scenario projection process

The following is a list of the seven main steps into which we subdivide the first stage of a workable scenario process:

Step 1.   Invite individuals to be involved in the process and distribute relevant background materials.

Step 2.   Collaborate with the working group to refine the definition of the general issue (usually expressed as a question) and to set the spatial focus and the scenario time scale.

Step 3.   Determine the critical issues – working first individually, then as a group – and then clustering the critical issues through further group discussion to develop, test and name the clusters.

Step 4.   Define the cluster outcomes – defining two extreme, but yet highly plausible, and hence possible, outcomes for each of the clusters over the scenario time scale.

Step 5.   Set up an impact/uncertainty matrix – determining the key scenario clusters.

Step 6.   Frame the scenarios – defining the extreme outcomes of the key clusters – and scope the scenarios by building the set of broad descriptors for four scenarios.

Step 7.   Develop the scenarios – working in sub-groups to develop scenario storylines, including key events, their chronological structure, and the who and why of what happens. This step is important to communicating the outcomes to the broader public. Although *the process* is important to the working group as much as the scenario outcomes are, communication of these outcomes of the process is a key to making them significant beyond the experience of the immediate working group.

This scenario method offers *one* approach to understanding and analysing seemingly intractable problems where there are critical uncertainties that span a range of subject areas or disciplinary boundaries. This approach is inclusive rather than selective. As such, it can be used in conjunction with, can incorporate information and data from, and can provide input to other methods in our toolshed. Groups make sense of the chosen general issue by using all available sources, including quantitative and qualitative research data, published reports and media outputs – any material that is relevant and informs thinking. The scenario method is a democratic process where all viewpoints are considered equal and all ideas can be aired and discussed using an open and non-confrontational approach. The degree of probability of whether or not any event *will* happen is left to one side. The process is concerned only its plausibility and the possibility that it *could* happen.

Guiding principles

Whatever the scale or context of the project, these principles should be known and held to by all participants:

1.   The scenario process is one of creative thinking where the aim is to open up consideration of all possibilities in a complex and ambiguous world, not to close down thinking through selectivity and exclusion.
2.   Whilst the process is one of innovative and creative thinking, we prescribe a very structured approach set out in clear steps. This structure is designed to

avoid either a decline into messiness or domination by powerful individuals, with the result that some members may be marginalized or drop out.

3. The scenario process lays out its projections into the future on modern time-lines, but at the same time it seeks to qualify or at least be aware of the power of modern notions of progress, growth and forward motion.

4. The scenario stories themselves are *not* linear predictions of the future. Rather, the method offers a range of future possibilities against which to test current plans, develop and appraise new options and, hopefully, make better-informed and more robust decisions on how a transitional practice that can be developed now.

5. The structure provides guidelines rather than being inflexibly prescriptive. Guidelines can be flexibly adapted to suit specific needs, but this needs to be done systematically and preferably before the process begins rather than on an *ad hoc* basis.

6. At any step in the process new ideas can be added. This is particularly relevant at the later steps when it might be thought that only those ideas that have emerged at the earlier steps can be allowed to enter the scenario stories.

7. The scenario method does not provide the answer to a problem. Rather, scenarios provide a means of better understanding the complexity and ambiguity of the present.

Ground rules

The following ground rules should be agreed on by team members and adhered to as carefully as possible:

1. Allocate the roles of facilitator, timekeeper and scribe at the outset. The facilitator guides the discussion, a timekeeper keeps the process flowing in accordance with the agreed timetable, and a scribe takes notes, keeps control of the paperwork and develops the story-lines on paper;

2. Keep an open mind to all possibilities and be willing to challenge your own business-as-usual thinking.

3. Avoid debates over opinions and encourage only questions of clarification in response to opinions – questions such as 'Why do you think that . . .', 'What would happen if . . .'

4. Include a round-robin approach to discussion within each session, with each member getting to express his or her opinion in turn by working around the whole group. Ideally, start with a different person in relation to each new issue.

5. Take note of all generated viewpoints and build them into your consideration of the broadest range of possibilities.

6. Do not allow any idea to be excluded on the basis that it is 'wrong' or 'nonsense' unless it can be proved so without doubt and with *everyone's* agreement.

7. Accept that the outcome of the round robin may be consensus, majority/minority viewpoints, or complete fragmentation. Positive tensions between ideas are to be encouraged.

Experience has shown that the best learning approach to the scenario method is through active participation. The participants are always the focus of content generation and context-specific expertise – so, it is *the participants'* thinking and analysis that is crucial in determining the end result, not that of the facilitators. However, in keeping with the dialectic of *participation/authority* (see Chapter 4) the scenario process is one of deliberative democracy, not rule by those participants whose prejudgements remain implacably certain throughout the process. The role of the facilitators is to continue to bring relevant material and evidence to the table, gently and carefully questioning existing common sense.

The scenario process in action

Step 1: Involving a group of diverse participants in the process

The first step in the process is to invite a group of key constituents to be involved in the process. The invitation should come from the group we called the management group and include members of the critical reference group and others (see Chapter 6). The invitation should be based firstly on a named organizational setting or geographical focus, a specified setting from the local to the regional. In theory this process could be conducted on a national or global scale, but the larger the scale, the task becomes increasingly unwieldy. Second, the invitations should be based on the chosen general issue. Here the all-affected principle provides a guiding framework. Invitees should be given a preliminary sense of the general issue to be explored, for example adaptation to climate change in the city, the future of work in the locale or the consequences of current teenage aspirations on the life of the town.

Because the most productive scenario projects are participatory and engaging, we suggest that every participant should be sent reference documentation that enables him or her to follow the process. In many projects, we have constructed, printed and distributed a 'Scenario Process Workbook' which is issued to every participant in advance of the event, and which they are required to bring to the workshop. Not only does this enable them to follow the process, step by step; it also allows them to be aware in advance of what the full process is and what each step involves and hopefully to understand why though early steps may appear to be restrictive and directive the process will open up into the type of creative thinking that is necessary for the outcome to be useful.

The initial role of the invited participants is to refine the *general issue* for discussion. This provides a basis for later brainstorming the *key critical uncertainties* about the future faced by a city, region, organization or community, and developing the alternative storylines about the different futures that may come to pass. Therefore, the participants need to be invited with a view to their relevant knowledge or interest in the general issue, their relation to the entity under discussion, and their place in a socially diverse local–global world. Everyone invited should have a stake in the future of the named entity, but not necessarily as an insider. Outside persons with a deep knowledge of a given area can be an important inclusion. (For conceptual guidance in thinking about who should be included see the discussion of the themes of difference/identity and inclusion/exclusion in Chapter 4).

The most important thing here is to make sure that different views are represented and that the people involved have a relevant standing in relation to the larger diversity of the locale or the issue under discussion. It should not be a group of like-minded individuals, especially not at the ideological level. One of our scenarios workshops held in Vietnam turned out to be of very limited value because we failed to invite a sufficiently diverse range of participants. Good liberal-thinking experts from Vietnam, Australian, Indonesia, Korea, Japan and the United States took part in a two-day forum on the future of Ho Chi Minh City given the risk of climate change, and ironically everybody ended up agreeing that there was no choice about what needed to be done. The people of Ho Chi Minh City all had to be evacuated to the hills of Vietnam. There were no dissenting voices asking what will happen to the people who currently live in the hills or how might this massive upheaval be effected. There was nobody asking what would happen when the sons and daughters of catfish farmers on the Mekong Delta rejected the injunction to leave their homes.

Step 2: Working with the invited group to frame the agenda

Although the general issue should be already broadly in place as a starting point for inviting participants, their role is to refine the terms of the general issue and turn it into a question that has some precision. This includes deciding upon an appropriate future timeframe with which to work. This frame should not extend so far into the future as to require 'science fiction' thinking or be so close that the future is fairly predictable. It should represent a reasonable long-term planning horizon in relation to the general issue. The timeframe varies in relation to the general issue. For the computer software industry, the time horizon is best done fairly close to the present, but beyond obvious current trajectories. By comparison when considering the future care needs for the elderly the timeframe is likely to be stretched further ahead, at least a generation.

Example
What are the most important climate change risks for our city across the next generation, and how can we best respond to those risks? Or, 'How sustainable will our city be over the next thirty years – will it survive and thrive, or decay and decline?'

Preparation

Before coming to any scenario workshop, participants should be asked to undertake some initial reading on the general issue that will form the focus of the event. How this is structured and directed will vary considerably, depending upon the type of scenario project and its time scale. At a basic level, if you are running a one-day scenario project in order to explore the limits of possibility for a set of predetermined uncertainties, you can ask participants to do homework on it, or you can direct them to specific readings. If, however, you are setting up a complex project that involves a wide range of stakeholders who are not yet aware of what the critical uncertainties are, you will need to set up some more in-depth prior investigation.

One way of doing this – albeit a way that entails significant research resources – is to identify the broadest range of key decision-making, power holding and directly affected constituents and arrange to conduct a series of semi-structured interviews or strategic conversations with them (see Chapter 4). Interviews or conversations allow interviewees to express their own views about what is important and how they feel about these matters, and offer some direction towards what is necessary to inform a scenario project. The use of a set of interviews also allows consideration of the degree of convergence and divergence that exists amongst key people in relation to specific issues. The degree of such agreement or diversity can provide early indication as to whether such issues are largely predetermined in terms of outcomes, or represent critical uncertainties. Because scenarios are concerned with exploring the future in order to inform the present, questions might include the following:

- What do you think have been the main factors over the past five years in bringing us to where we are now?
- What are the social forces and critical issues that will have an impact on . . . over the next thirty years' time?
- What are the most important driving forces that sit behind these critical issues?
- How would you describe an ideal future for the . . . across the next thirty years?
- What do you think will be the key factors and events that will be necessary to make this happen?
- What factors at the present time do you see as forming foundations for the ideal future?
- What obstacles do you see in the present that might prevent this future happening?

From these interviews we undertake the content analysis process, to identify the common themes and issues in order to compile a project briefing report. In presenting the content of different interviews under the headings of common themes and issues, the report will also show up differences in opinion about how these issues are perceived by different stakeholders. The interview report forms the agenda for the third step of the process, when the group identifies the key issue around which the scenarios are developed. The report also sensitizes participants to consider the full range of 'critical issues' that might impact the general issue. It asks them to think beyond their own immediate context of operation and to consider whether the identified driving forces point towards predetermined outcomes or towards uncertainties for further consideration.

Having collated and transcribed the individual interviews, we undertake content analysis. This involves reading and rereading the interviews in order to identify relevant *critical issues* being raised and discussed. With dozens of statements and a wide range of issues identified, we group the issues to identify a smaller range of higher-level *themes* that encapsulate sets of critical issues. For example, within a theme of 'teenage aspirations' there may well be a range of more specific issues that emerge in relation to matters such as authority/participation, inclusion/exclusion, needs/limits and so on. The range of overarching themes might for example relate to political structures, to economic conditions, to cultural relationships, to geographic or climatic conditions. The key element of content analysis is that the issues and themes emerge from the interview content and from what the interviewees have found important, not from the reader's mind and what he or she thinks *should* be important. From this content analysis, a report is compiled in which all statements are included under these emergent theme/issue titles and none are attributed to individuals.

Once the process of content analysis is completed, which may involve several iterations of reading and coding (that is identifying themes and issues), with changes of themes and refinement of their content, the interview content can be restructured into a project report. This report presents all of the interview statements, set out under the theme and issue headings and without attribution to the individual who originally said each (*note*: editing *may* be required to remove names within a quotation or text that links a contentious statement back to an identifiable source. Any such editing should be minimal and must not change the meaning). This may appear a lengthy and resource-intensive process. However, it is invaluable in setting the scene for a scenario project involving diverse and possibly conflicting constituent concerns. The report provides background reading that enables project participants to gain an overview and understanding of the broad range of views and opinions held about the context of the project. Frequently, it raises awareness in individuals of viewpoints to which they were previously oblivious.

Whether you are leading a simple or a complex scenario project, we advise that you should direct participants' initial thinking about the issue as follows. You should ask them to consider what *they* see as the *critical issues* – economic, ecological, political and cultural factors – that will have an impact on it over the coming years. (Consider using the Circles of Social Life figure at the start of the book as a prompt to frame peoples' thinking about the kind of aspects to cover.) Identifying the greatest possible range of critical issues forms the starting point for our exploration. Participant should be asked to bring with them any notes they prepare, key documents that they have read, press cuttings they consider of interest and so on for use and reference during the workshop.

Step 3: Determining the critical issues

Scenario method is used to analyse and make sense of the broad context in which the issue is situated – the economic, ecological, political and cultural context. It explores the range of possible and plausible futures that might unfold and in which the key issue will evolve in response to both the external environment and the different strategies and actions by stakeholders. Therefore, one of the key steps in the process is determining the critical issues that will possibly affect the future.

The process of identifying critical issues is conducted first on an individual basis, to elicit multiple perspectives on the focal issue and to ensure that they are recorded and presented as such. In order to do this, it helps to encourage thinking in terms of the broad *Circles of Sustainability* approach (ecological, economic, political and cultural). The Circles domains and subdomains are, however, mere topics, and as such, they do not constitute critical issues by themselves.

Critical issues should be defined in as few words as necessary, but sufficient to make them understandable to everyone without further explanation. Critical issues are distinguished from subjects, topics or events by pointing to an outcome. The terminology might usefully include phrases such as 'outcome of . . .', 'extent of . . .', 'changing attitudes to . . .', 'number of . . .' and so on. The terminology used should not assume a particular outcome (e.g. 'increase in . . .'). You are encouraged to think broadly to identify the range of critical issues, whilst thinking very specifically and with focus to define individual critical issues.

Every critical issue must be recorded on an individual Post-it® Note (*note*: once the group has collated all its notes, the members should be coded numerically, 1, 2, 3, . . .). In large, complex projects the step of individual noting of critical issues should not be time constrained. In addition, if the lead in to a project enables it to happen, it is useful to encourage participants to think of critical issues in advance of the event, and to bring notes on these with them. In shorter projects, however, it may be necessary to set a time limit. In either case, participants should be asked to define the issues, as above, in fairly simple terms, focused on individual issues and indicating a point of impact relevant to the general issue.

After individuals have completed their issue identification, use a round-robin approach to go through them all as a group, to clarify any of those where the wording and meaning is unclear. At this stage, it is only required that there should be agreement on the meaning of the terminology used, not on the nature and the impact of the force defined. However, because according to psychologists we can comfortably make sense of a maximum of about a dozen concepts at one time in relation to each other, we need to cluster the ideas that have been thrown up. In large scenario projects, hundreds of critical issues may be generated. How do we make sense of this mass of ideas? One option is to jump to making decisions about 'what is important'. In scenario thinking this is seen as risking that a key issue which may have a major impact is excluded from discussion. The approach taken here is that of *clustering* – holding a group conversation about how the critical issues relate to one another in one of two ways:

- By *cause/effect* – that the emergence of the outcome of one critical issue will have a direct impact on the outcome of another

> **Example**
>   It might be reasonably assumed that the outcome of a critical issue of 'effectiveness of Internet security for online banking' will have some impact on one which posits 'extent of cyber-fraud in retail banking', which might in turn impact one on 'degree of customer confidence in Internet banking'.

- By *chronology* – that the outcome of one critical issue is dependent on the prior reconciliation of another

> **Example**
>   The outcome of a critical issue on 'changing focus of US carbon-pricing policy' will likely be influenced over, say, a ten-year time horizon by ones relating to the outcome of presidential elections that *will* take place in November 2016.

The aim of the clustering exercise is to find one set out of an indefinite number of possibilities of linkages to identify a smaller number (around ten to twenty maximum) of higher-level factors that directly affect the general issue. Figure 11.1 indicates what a completed cluster diagram might typically look like from a scenario project on futures of urban transport networks. This cluster addresses possible levels

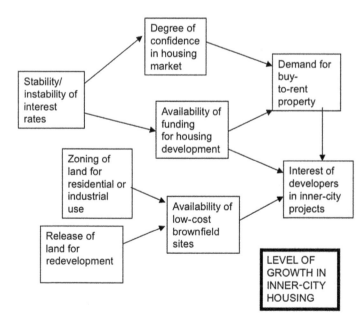

FIGURE 11.1 Representative Cluster

of growth in inner-city housing, which relates to intensification of land-use and will compare with suburban development and increasing urban sprawl.

Once the critical issues are clustered, the logic of the clusters is tested in two ways:

1. by drawing linkages of cause/effect and chronology between the elements within each cluster so that every component driving force is linked in some way to every other one *and*
2. by 'naming' the cluster in terms of the higher-level factor, then checking that every driving force is relevant to this factor. If any driving force is not encapsulated by the selected name, either revisit the name or check what other cluster the driving force to which does relate. There may be a single critical issue that does not fit within any of the named clusters. It is perfectly justifiable to have a 'cluster' of one.)

Step 4: Defining the cluster outcomes

For each issue cluster, the group debates and discusses the range of possible *extreme outcomes* that might arise from it over the scenario time-scale. These can be described as the two extreme, but very plausible – and hence very possible – outcomes. However, as with individual critical issues, they may be very complex in their make-up and not capable of being defined along a single continuum. It may be helpful to think of the extreme outcomes like two of many lines of dominoes, stacked to run out from the 'epicentre' of the cluster. They may not run straight, possibly not in opposite directions to each other, but when – not if – the dominoes fall, these two sets will create the greatest impact on their surroundings.

The group should brainstorm short descriptions of how they envisage the extreme outcomes of each issue cluster, again thinking of extremes that are both possible and plausible – scenario method in the form used here does not engage with implausible extremes beyond what is relatively possible within the scenario time-frame. In considering the extreme outcomes of each factor, do not confine thinking only to descriptors that are directly related to that issue cluster – for example, the outcomes of the individual critical issues within it. Rather, develop thinking here on impacts across other fields to start to explore and understand the inherent cause-and-effect linkages that exist between them. The set of outcomes for each issue cluster should be recorded on flip-chart sheets or large sheets of paper.

Example

Consider how structural failure in the US sub-prime mortgage market had rolling impacts, first, on banks across the United States, Europe and other areas; then on broader financial markets, affecting investment fund availability and investor confidence; and, ultimately, on country economies and the entire global financial system.

Step 5: Impact/uncertainty matrix

Having determined the higher-level issue clusters we now move towards a frame-work for construction of the scenario stories. This framework is structured around *two key factors* (labelled factor A and factor B). In order to identify these key factors, we first draw a matrix with two axes, with which we work sequentially, as follows:

- Horizontal Axis: Low to High Impact – First, we consider the *relative degree of impact* of each of the issue clusters *on the general issue* over the project time scale. This is done through a critically discursive debate on the range of possible events and impacts that each cluster might generate and the relative significance of these in determining the overall general issue outcome. We place the issue cluster Post-its® along the full length of this axis by a process of negotiation and debate.
- Vertical Axis: Low to High Uncertainty – Once we have completed the hori-zontal axis, and *not before*, we consider the *relative degree of uncertainty* about impact of each issue cluster *on the general issue* over the project time scale. Here, we must be absolutely clear that we are *not* discussing certainty/uncertainty about *whether* there will be an impact but about *what* that impact may be.

Example

We may be considering a factor that we are absolutely certain will occur, such as 'impact of climate change', based on there seeming to be consensus that the Earth's climate *is* changing. However, we may remain very uncertain about the actual outcomes. At present, there remains a wide discrepancy in the views of dif-ferent scientific and political bodies as to both the cause of change and the possible extent of its impacts. In this example, the factor 'impact of climate change' would likely be rated as a 'high uncertainty' factor because the differences in opinion on the possible *outcomes* of change, despite any consensus on the *existence* of change.

Factors A and B are the two highest-level issue clusters which are considered to combine the highest impact on the general issue with the greatest uncertainty about what that impact may be. A crucial step is to test whether the two factors that have been selected are independent of one another. To do this, consider the resolu-tion of the contents of factor A as the outcome A1. Consider also the resolution of the contents of factor B as the outcome B1. If A1 and not B1 could plausibly coexist in the same future, they have some independence. If so, consider A1 and B2 and ask the same question. Next, consider A2 and B1 and then A2 and B2. If all four positive–negative combinations are plausible, then factor A and factor B can be viewed as independent of one another, and it will be possible to develop four scenarios. If one or more of the four positive–negative combinations is viewed by the scenario team as implausible, then factors A and B are not independent of one another. At this point, factors A and B could be combined as one factor and another possible factor, factor C, should be selected as a potential second factor from the previously developed impact/predictability matrix.

Example

In the example of the scenario project on urban transport networks, it is likely that outcomes of a cluster on 'policy decisions on road versus rail networks' will be intrinsically linked to those for one on 'level of investment in suburban rail network'. On the other hand, the outcomes of a cluster on 'public demand for suburban rail travel' will not necessarily be closely linked to levels of investment and therefore are relatively independent even if they influence each other.

It should be noted here, that whilst other decision-analysis tools might draw on probability analysis or similar analyses in order to make choices about what is *most likely* to happen, the scenario method moves forward without such probability assessments. Rather, it maintains consideration only of everything that might feasibly happen and prepares us for any eventuality. Any use of probability analysis should follow completion of the scenario program, as a separate exercise.

Step 6: Framing the scenarios

Whilst each of the higher-level clusters from step 4 is seen as having an impact on the general issue and as having an influence on its possible futures, the nature of its outcome is likely to vary across different future scenarios. At this point, we return to consideration of the extreme outcomes of the various factors that we outlined in step 4. We discuss the range of outcomes from all the issue clusters, but specifically in relation to those of factors A and B. Do they make sense as an overall set? Can we identify gaps in logic, scale, and information, among other areas? Do we need to bring in other factors and outcomes in order to complete our understanding? As we outlined previously, the process structure set out here should not become a straitjacket. It is designed to enable and support creative and lateral thinking, not exclude it. However, whatever confirmation, augmentation, amendment or addition to the extreme outcomes in step is developed here, the recording should again be methodical, on a flip chart or large sheets of paper, for future reference as necessary.

On longer scenario projects that are not tightly time constrained, particularly when they involve multiple iterations of scenario generation with research undertaken between, this step is expanded by consideration of a much wider set of extreme outcomes, derived from consideration of individual critical issues rather than just the clusters. In longer projects, this step can lead to much more focused analytic thinking and can provide reality checks on cause/effect relationships. In short projects with limited time and shallow prior research, it can become an exercise in 'holding a finger to the wind' for a more basic check.

Having reflected on and refined the various sets of extreme outcomes in terms of general logic, we now move to build them into four internally consistent, separate-but-related scenario outlines.

Step 7: Scoping the scenarios

Drawing first on the extreme outcomes of factors A and B, we consider how the sets of conditions defined by the two extreme outcomes of each interact with each other in the four possible combinations (A1/B1, A1/B2, A2/B1 and A2/B2) in order to produce what – in simplistic terms – might be described as best/best, best/worst, worst/best and worst/worst 'worlds' in which the future will unfold. Again, we brainstorm a very broad range of descriptors of each of these future worlds. For each, we consider what would be the state of the economy, politics, culture and ecology evidenced by such things as technology, national politics, local government, local business, employment, climate, migration, education, crime, transport, cost of living, optimism, pessimism and so on.

Arriving at these sets of descriptors involves critical discussion and debate, engaging with questions of who, what, why, where and when. This is done in order to build a logical structure to each future that can be shown to have some justifiable foundation for its possibility and plausibility in terms of what is currently either known or knowable. Adoption of a 'devil's advocate' approach is highly valuable at this stage, and the group sceptic should be allowed free reign to probe and challenge (but without breaking the ground rules set out previously).

At this stage, the group should draw on all of the extreme outcomes for all the factors in order to give substance to the emerging scenarios. This again involves critical discussion and debate on relationships of cause and effect, action and outcome and chronology because the aim is to place every significant outcome into the scenario (or scenarios) where it logically sits. Here, it should be clear that there are relationships between factors that will make some linkages immediately credible and others nonsensical. Also, there may be factors that were identified earlier as having a great impact but as being highly predictable in terms of what that impact will be. Such factors will need to be incorporated into every scenario, with the actual impact fine-tuned as necessary in order to take account to any mediating impact from other factors.

Example

If we have a set of extreme outcomes that outline a world in which economic uncertainty and instability have led to governments adopting policies of protectionism through the application of non-tariff barriers, it would be unrealistic to match these to another set of extreme outcomes that describe a world of free trade that is blossoming because of the removal of tariff barriers.

Whilst not all linkages will be so obvious the strategic conversation around the full range of issues will generally point to them fitting into one or two scenarios. Any item which falls into more than one scenario can be duplicated if it is an important issue, or it can be placed where it has maximum impact.

These combination descriptors form the basis of our four scenario storylines. The four scenarios that will be developed are *not* stand-alone stories or individual 'predictions' of a possible future. Rather, they must be read as a group of possible futures, framing the limits of possibility for what might reasonably be expected to happen over time. Together, they act as a set of tools for making sense of complexity and ambiguity and for understanding the linkages across different areas of interest. Since history has never so far unfolded with a combination of all factors being at their best or worst, it is often in the mediation of some 'good' outcomes by the impact of other 'bad' ones (the A1/B2 and A2/B1 scenarios) that broader and more challenging possibilities for the future start to unfold.

Step 8: Developing the scenarios

At this stage, the scenario outlines consist of a set of descriptors of four possible futures framed by the interaction of factors A and B, defined in terms of their extreme outcomes at the scenario horizon date. Now, we move to building the storylines that will show, logically and consistently, how we might get from where we are today to each of these future states. As the storylines are developed some elements may be omitted from the stories when they add little or no impact and detract from the core story. Remember that the focus of scenario analysis is on understanding the complexity and ambiguity of the world outside the organization.

In a full scenario project the aim of the group is to outline a set of scenario stories which start in some coherent and plausible explanation of the present, then move through a series of further plausible and possible events in order to outline a set of futures which are internally consistent and coherent and follow on from the logic of the events outlined. Remember that there are events in the future which, barring the unknowable (which scenarios do not deal with), *will* happen, often with known key actors.

Example

We know at the time of writing that there *will* be presidential elections in the United States in November 2016 and every four years thereafter. At this time, we know that, barring the unknowable – a coup for example – that Barack Obama *will not* be his party's candidate in 2016, because he will be ineligible to stand for re-election given that, unlike the United Kingdom and Australia, there is no history of incumbent leaders being extended beyond the limit of a maximum of two terms.

Whilst the dates of elections in other countries are not set in stone as in the United States, there are often maximum terms between elections, so dates can be reasonably assumed in scenario development. Whilst we state here that scenarios do not deal with unknowable events, you may say that it is often these very occurrences that have the greatest impact on what follows. For example events of 9/11 had an impact on air travel globally. In addition, there are also trends that we may see as likely to continue – for example that IT will continue to get faster and more powerful but will continue to fail to deliver the results that its designers' claim for it. These, like known events, can be incorporated, when relevant, into all scenarios.

In working as a group to develop the scenario storylines, it can be very helpful to set up a whiteboard or some other appropriate surface and to draw a timeline for the scenario period. The various events that are considered and discussed can then be set out and discussed in relation to links of cause and effect and chronology. This is particularly helpful in enabling discussion of the cross-linkages between factors and events that have previously been located in different cluster groupings.

The key aim in writing scenarios is to grab the attention of the intended audience in order to convey clear and plausible stories about what types of futures might unfold as a direct outcome of decisions made in the present and over time in relation to the chosen general issue. The ways in which this can be done are many. Scenarios can be presented as fairly simple texts that recount what might happen in future. They can be delivered as mock newspaper or magazine articles that recount what has already happened at the scenario end date. Scenarios can be presented as live performances to the target audience, or can take the form of a telecast debate. Whatever approach is used, the focus is on the deep impact of the content, not the superficiality of the presentation media.

Beyond the first stage of scenario development

Scenario stories in isolation serve no purpose *per se*. Whilst some approaches to scenario work place an emphasis on the scenario stories themselves as narratives of some 'real world' futures, we see them as providing primarily a better understanding of, and a broader range of perspectives on the present. Their function within the strategic planning process is threefold: first, to open up a wider set of perspectives on the present than currently exists; second, to provide a set of 'wind tunnel' conditions under which to test existing strategies in order to check their robustness under the different conditions of the full range of plausible and possible futures that they outline; and, third, to provide feedback from the future to the present in order to support development of new strategies and plans in response to perceived alternative future contexts. Having done the first stage of scenario development emphasizing critical issues, uncertainties and risks, a second stage can now be usefully entered of setting up alternative normative scenarios, that is projecting an optimal future, a bleak future and a future based on business as usual. These can now be done successfully by taking into account the limits of the first-stage scenarios.

Note

1 George Cairns and George Wright are the main co-authors of this chapter with Paul James. The chapter is based on work done by George Wright and George Cairns for their recent book *Scenario Thinking: Practical Approaches to the Future* (2011). For elaboration we suggest reading the book, but be aware that a lot has changed in the translation of the original scenario thinking into the present method.

Reference

Wright, George & Cairns, George 2011, *Scenario Thinking: Practical Approaches to the Future*, Palgrave Macmillan, Basingstoke.

12

SIMULATING FUTURE TRENDS[1]

Cities face immense pressures. In the context of intensifying global trends, cities are presented with manifold and cross-cutting issues to which they must respond. Among the most pressing is the immediate need to accommodate surging populations while maintaining environmental sustainability, economic prosperity, political engagement and cultural diversity into the future. In this process of planning the future, harnessing technological innovation and initiating programmes for positive development hold out much promise. However, all too often such programmes succumb to the common pitfalls of lack of integration, a reductive emphasis on technological fixes and a lack of attention to anticipating unintended consequences.

Simulating change in cities has become an industry. Different versions of software are constantly being created that simulate growth in cities, map sustainability in cities and track infrastructure issues in cities. They range from readily available Sim City–like software to proprietary software that is only available as part of an expensive consultancy arrangement. The tendency is for designers to build a software package that is big on the front end – designed to enthral with beautiful 'flash' graphics – and small on back-end analytic capability. In the context of the crisis-level environmental and social issues facing cities today, there is a pressing need for a simulation package that is relatively easy to use, can be tailored for different city configurations, does not require a consultant to interpret the data, and is based on sound analytically derived algorithms that track both linear and non-linear change.

Innovation needs to be balanced against multiple ongoing imperatives, from governing equitably in a world that is becoming more unequal to enhancing liveability in urban settings where resources are becoming more strained. Simulation tools present opportunities for those faced with future planning to experiment and explore different scenarios. It allows a city to 'fail' softly across many trials. With the growing diversity and complexity of such tools, however, some of the basic affordances and flexibilities of good modelling have tended to get lost. This chapter presents a city simulator which incorporates an innovative blend of elements intended to overcome these problems: an integrated approach to sustainability, a 'whole of city' focus on interrelated programmes, a modelling approach built on empirical research, and an easy-to-use wizard-driven user interface. In this chapter the philosophical background to the simulator is outlined, initial findings presented and future directions projected.

Are cities actually like elephants?

This complexity of the task is further compounded when the effects of intervention are no longer linear with respect to an apparently simple dimension such as city size. As an attempt to simplify these complications, Luis Bettencourt and Geoffrey West (2010) have argued that many characteristics of cities – levels of innovation, crime, economic activity and density – can be tolerably well estimated based on population statistics alone. They describe how cities, like organisms, hold properties that grow at low exponential rather than linear rates with respect to size. Hence, larger cities are said to be like elephants. They are not only more susceptible to environmental change but also more capable to adapting to such change. At one level, recognition of exponential change of key variables with respect to size allows planners to better anticipate the consequences of urban programs – intended and otherwise. On the other hand, this analogy ignores the capacities of cities, at any scale, to exhibit agency or otherwise in response to these characteristics. Failure to invest in necessary infrastructure, for example, will mean negative variables such as congestion and pollution may continue to grow while the city's economy does not.

Closely associated with the notion of biological size is that of intelligence. If the organic analogy holds, larger cities should be smarter. This can be reflected in indirect measures of 'intelligent' activities – Bettencourt and West highlight higher levels of patent development for example. However, a more tantalizing prospect for measuring intelligence would be through the capacities of the city itself – to monitor, regulate, adapt and even heal itself in response to sustainability threats. Facilitating this kind of urban intelligence therefore becomes an important desideratum for urban planners, designers and technology providers. Cities that can reflexively monitor and regulate their infrastructure can be justified against multiple dimensions of sustainability: lower economic costs and greater vibrancy, lower environmental impacts and greater resilience and improved social equity and quality-of-life outcomes. To give urban intelligence meaning, however, 'infrastructure' here needs a suitably broad definition. Technological hardware – smart grids and buildings, roll-out of electric vehicles, meters, and sensors, equipment replacement programs, upgrade of waste and water management systems – are a necessary but insufficient condition for its emergence.

Urban futurists offer tantalizing visions of smart cities based around the excitement of technological innovations in transport, communications and infrastructure. However, we argue these are a mixed blessing. Cities also need to develop corresponding capabilities at the level of institutional and individual actors, a far less tangible goal. 'Intelligence', at any scale, needs to be considered not only in the narrow sense of technological capability and adaptation, but also in the broader sense of the integrated whole of the city. This includes community engagement, ongoing reflexive learning about the social impact of technological systems, and the integration of technologies into the urban economic, political and cultural fabric.

The world of city simulators

In the past two decades, considerable academic and commercial attention has been directed towards various kinds of simulation of urban environments. Simulators have been further classified by methodological approaches, scope, subject and user interface. An example of the first distinction is whether a simulator uses equation-based or agent-based models. The latter class has become increasingly popular as a means of handling processes with high degrees of unknown or stochastic variables. Equation-based models meanwhile continue to be widely applied to problem domains with greater degrees of determinacy (either in the real situations being modelled or in the level of confidence in the information contained in the model).

- Equation based (rather than agent based)
- Holistic citywide rather than particular, problem-specific focus
- Employing a wizard-style interface for user input and navigation
- Using statistics and equations derived from empirical research
- Hosted online (but with no collaboration features currently)

With regard to city simulators, no other simulator presently combines this series of characteristics. The use of existing city data and equations means the simulator can quickly show effects of programmes of activity to audiences familiar with traditional forms of modelling. The citywide focus means that the modelling activity can however be extended to a broad range of relevant urban indicators. Hosting the application online provides opportunity for users to discuss and share simulator results. The simulator can therefore suit a range of scenarios for which other approaches require either too much configuration (agent-based, gaming approaches) or expertise (problem-specific, equation-based approaches). Consensus in the simulation community seems to have settled on agreement that no 'one size fits all' – different problem domains and contexts warrant different approaches. The Intelligent City Simulator exhibits a useful set of features not currently employed by existing city simulator tools surveyed.

The key dimension that any simulator needs to be able to handle is the paradoxical and even contradictory outcomes of contemporary cities, the complex knot of sustainability. As we outlined in the introductory chapter, responses to complex problems cannot be posed as one-dimensional solutions. One apparently simple example should suffice. Electric vehicles are being touted as the answer to the double crisis of automobile pollution and peak oil. Across the world it would seem to be obvious that establishing electric vehicles in major metropolitan centres should be an imperative. However, simulating a series of trajectory lines in Melbourne shows that the city would actually become less sustainable with the introduction of electric vehicles. The supposed technological saviour would increase the greenhouse gas emissions of the city. How? Because of the sprawl of the city, the kilometre average that people drive to work and the fact that the city's major source of electrical power is generated using brown coal. It would mean that, all else being equal, in terms of greenhouse emissions Melbourne would be better off subsidizing small efficient petroleum-based cars. Of course, this is not an appropriate response either, but the point is clear. Solutionism – reliance on single-dimensional 'smart' solutions – is problematic. In Amsterdam, where Melbourne's knotted ecological problem does not pertain, electric vehicles still may not be the best way to proceed, all else being equal. Why? This time the knot crosses into the cultural domain: the culture of identity and engagement. Because the highest take up on electrical vehicle use is by self-identified environmentally conscious consumers who often would otherwise be bicycle users, more sustainable machines – bicycles – are being replaced by less sustainable ones.

Foundations of the approach

Let us go back to basics. The Intelligent City Simulator, version 2.0, represents a collaborative partnership between Accenture and the United Nations Cities Programme. Its development took place in Australia, France and India across 2010. Version 1.0 of the software already represented an innovative approach to modelling particular programme effects on urban environments. Many of these programmes were dedicated to technological infrastructure, reflecting Accenture's expertise in this domain. Results could be seen in large-scale variables such as emissions, as well as particular indicators such as electrical vehicle (EV) uptake. The new version of the software pursues three additional goals:

- The incorporation of a robust and comprehensive social theoretic framework (in this case, the *Circles of Sustainability* approach)
- The inclusion of a range of additional socially oriented programmes and associated indicators to broaden the perspective and context of the simulated urban environment, such as crime rate and housing density
- The extension of modelling research methods to incorporate statistical, computational and theoretical findings from relevant academic, government and industry literature

Although these goals were pursued with a view towards realistically capturing both business-as-usual and programme-intervention scenarios, the ultimate aim has not been simply to predict programme effects, albeit within given margins of error. Rather, our efforts are directed towards describing the anticipated impacts of radically diverse activities as they intersect with each other in a field of other possible programmed activities and measured against their effects on well-know indicator sets. In other words, each programme is placed within a range of other broadly commensurable possibilities and these are related to each algorithmically based on best-case current social science research.

This integrated field of programmes and indicators is then presented for the user in a readily understandable fashion through a software interface. As the findings suggest, even this more limited aim met with partial rather than comprehensive success. That said, given the complexity of the social world and the difficulty of representing it algorithmically, the outcomes were encouraging. They suggest that the general paradigm and specific research inputs to the simulator warrant further discussion and pursuit. In particular, we conclude that those involved in city planning have much to gain from thinking through, in a strategic planning context, the relative costs and benefits of various social and technological initiatives in a holistic, whole-of-city fashion, prior to subjecting candidate programmes to more exacting analysis.

One of the key considerations of the current iteration of the simulator – the foundational consideration – was to found the approach upon a robust philosophical framework that systematically describes the dimensions of a city's sustainability. This meant, in our view, treating urban sustainability as field that crossed the human condition of social sustainability in general. Attempts to develop such a holistic approach to sustainability are not novel. However, two contemporary tendencies have militated against this sense of integrated investigation. The first, ironically, came out of an attempt to sensitize practitioners to the importance of thinking holistically and beyond market-oriented determinations. Mainstream approaches project the concept of 'the environmental' as the master adjective in relation to 'sustainability', thus attempting to naturalize the phrase 'environmental sustainability' as part of a taken-for-granted discourse on sustainability.

The second tendency, still dominant in relation to the first, is to treat economics as the master domain against which the environment is accounted for as an externality. In this tendency, the concept of sustainability becomes a second order concern in relation to a taken-for-granted privileging of the economic bottom line – hence all the limitations of the Triple Bottom Line approach that we have previously raised. Arguably the voluminous literature on sustainability thus departs from the insight that one-sided or partial views of survival, directed by specific disciplines such as the biosciences or economics, cast aside many of the features that broadly socialized beings regard as most worthy of sustaining: the reservoirs of meaning in the arts and sciences; the accomplishments of historical consequence enshrined in legal, justice and economic institutions; the findings of scholarly and scientific enquiry which suggest that uninhibited commodity production cycles affect natural and social environments; and so on.

The task of developing taxonomic structures which reflect the inherent complications in any holistic notion of social relations is however immensely difficult. Such structures need, on one hand, to reflect certain social generalities – relations of power, representations of culture, practices of economic production – and, on the other hand, be applicable to the extraordinary diversity of societies, urban and otherwise, modern and otherwise. These twin imperatives may be analytically possible to meet, but in practice they remain essentially contested. In practice, any claim to taxonomic generality struggles to gain consensus across the broad disciplinary gamut of the social and natural sciences. Nevertheless, we contend, a taxonomy which states its categories circumspectly and with awareness of their historical and contextual contingency can lay claim to being useful as a mechanism for orienting and organizing 'downstream' concerns, such as human interventions into an urban environment context. Here the turnkeys are usefulness, applicability and generality.

The *Circles of Sustainability* approach is one such effort. It represents an alternative to prevailing Triple Bottom Line models, adopting a broad Engaged Theory perspective. The social is not some partial, delimitable segment of human action; instead, it defines the very landscape in which that activity takes place. Within that frame, human agents organize around what can be understood in modern terms as four intersecting spheres or domains of activity: ecology, economics, politics and culture. These are not readily partitioned, as per the Triple Bottom Line model, but rather reflect different dimensions of any given social experience or activity. Nevertheless, some activities belong conspicuously more to one domain than another. As discussed in the following, the domains, and a series of analytically derived but more specific subdomains, become the instrument for navigating through the programmes modelled by the simulator. In addition to being an orientation tool, however, the four domains also serve to remind users of the broader balance required of a sustainable future, prompting a number of questions:

- Are all domains and subdomains of a city sufficiently satisfied by the series of proposed initiatives?
- What domains and subdomains are potentially in tension, based on some proposed programme – most obviously, perhaps, the economic and the ecological?
- What kinds of causal dependencies, linear and non-linear, directional and cyclic, exist between specific actions, programmes and interventions across different domains and subdomains?

As might be expected when trying to weld a framework of such apparent abstraction to a concrete set of programmes, a number of difficulties were encountered early on during the design process. These were partially navigated by the introduction of several methodological working principles, which translated or bridged the respective worlds of theoretical constructs and empirical indicators. These principles informed the designing of programme models in particular. The principles include the following:

- Social scientific literature is a key input into understanding effects, but it requires considerable interpolation for a number of variables: size, range and rigour of documented empirical studies; estimation of centrality, variance and outlier status of city cases studied; and consistency with other available studies. Although documented effects were therefore used typically as bases for programme models, they were often adjusted – with documented rationales – to correct for perceived distortions in the cases used.

- Not all affected variables change in a linear fashion in themselves or with respect to each other. City size in particular is a vital determinant of programme effect, although not an overdetermining one. Different variables are therefore programmed to increase sub-linearly, linearly, or super-linearly with respect to the city's size (measured either as population or as density).

- Similarly, programmes themselves are understood to have complex non-linear effects, with various forms of reinforcing and undermining feedback loops at work between them. Simulation design needs to be sensitive to compounding or undercutting effects in underlying variables, as well as to the more straightforward case of programme dependencies. As mentioned later, this design desideratum could not, because of practical constraints, be easily accommodated in practice – at least for the present version.

- The business-as-usual case is not static. With or without particular interventions, cities continually change and evolve. The simulator must reflect these changes, even at the expense of ease of interpretation of programme effects.

- Effects on standardized indexes such as the Human Development Index and the Liveability Index are logarithmic. The higher a city's existing ranking, the more difficult it is for that city to raise its ranking still further – especially because other highly ranked cities are, in practice, likely to be undertaking just the same programmes themselves.

- In contrast to all of the previously mentioned items, there is a requirement for useability to 'Keep It Simple, Stupid'. Where possible, simplifications were made to programme models, in order to keep algorithms relatively transparent and, more critically, to keep programme effects comprehensible to people who are not domain experts.

As suggested in the language used, systems theory proved a key instrument for galvanizing many of these principles with the *Circles of Sustainability* framework. Moreover, systems theory provided useful points of translation across social and natural scientific boundaries, as well as between the academic and corporate research groups.

Putting theory into practice

In May 2010, teams from the Royal Melbourne Institute of Technology and Accenture began work revising existing and developing new programmes for the simulator. Starting with an initial pool of twenty-three programmes in version 1.0, thirty-six programmes were to be included in version 2.0. Initially this work was due to be completed in mid-June, in order to brush up the simulator for an early July launch. However, in practice this took much longer. Despite a large dedicated team, a soft launch of the tool did not take place until late October, and the programmes were refined continually throughout the intervening period. A team in

France developed the software, supported by programmers in India, using a combination of Java, Flex and Flash technologies. Each programme followed more or less the same development trajectory:

- If a programme existed, its input and output parameters were examined. If no programme existed, a brief description was written, and some initial parameters developed.
- For each programme we conducted an extensive literature review, to refine parameters, to understand what relationships exist between inputs and outputs and to establish some degree of variance in the results of available studies. For some of the more obscure programmes, this proved exceedingly difficult; programmes had been documented in either too much or too little in available literature, and quantitative relationships documented in either too fine strokes, or not at all.
- Assumptions, calculations, discussion points and references were then included in programme design documents.
- The research group met regularly to review and debate the effects described in the documents.
- Refined, baseline versions of the design documents were sent to the simulator development team, for further review and implementation.
- An extensive period of testing and review of the simulator, followed by further refinements to the design documents, was then undertaken.
- Prior to launch, the simulator was demonstrated in both university and corporate contexts, to elicit further feedback and commentary. Where warranted and practical, this feedback was also incorporated (hastily) in the weeks leading up to the launch.

The following section describes one of the thirty-six models developed, the roll-out of EVs in a city.

Scenario: Rolling out EVs

Consider a city attempting to reduce its transport emissions. EVs seem to be an obvious answer – they would take inefficient internal combustion engine vehicles off the road and replace them with cleaner EVs. They also have the potential to smooth out energy demand peakiness and hence allow the city to make more efficient use of generating capacity. However, on closer investigation, some major questions arise:

Penetration rates

1. What penetration of electric vehicles is possible for a given investment for a particular city?
2. What are the different ways in which that city could promote EV take-up?
3. How does their effectiveness vary depending on the city characteristics?

Timing of Investment

4. What is the 'natural' uptake of electric vehicles in the absence of any city action?
5. What is the best time to begin investment?

Effectiveness of EVs in Reducing Carbon Emissions

6. Are electric vehicles in fact cleaner?
7. What city factors influence whether electric vehicles are better for the environment?

The simulator enables the exploration of these questions through the modelling of different scenarios to see what effects different timings, programmes and city parameters have on results. Let's explore one of these.

What factors influence EV penetration in a city?

A model for EV uptake was developed based on our work in the city of Amsterdam. This model was based on research which shows that EV uptake is based on the following considerations:

*   Total cost of ownership of an electric vehicle
*   Availability of charging stations
*   The degree of technological capability and knowledge held by city inhabitants

The two graphics below (Figures 12.1 and 12.2) displays the EV infrastructure programme being enacted for two fictional cities from 2010 onwards. EV1 has a *low* population density and a low HDI ranking, and EV2 has a high-population density and a high HDI ranking.

Comparing the two figures, we can see that EV2 has a higher penetration of EVs than EV1 for a lower cost. The lower cost comes from the reduced need to roll out infrastructure due to city area being smaller. The higher penetration comes from the higher propensity of city inhabitants to adopt new technology. This higher penetration leads to an increase in city liveability through lower noise and exhaust-pipe emissions. We can also see, by looking at both cities, that the penetration of EVs increases dramatically over time. What might cause this? The answer is the total cost of ownership. Built into the modelling calculations of the simulator (see Figure 12.1) are increasing petrol prices as oil extraction becomes ever-more expensive, and lower costs of electric vehicle manufacture as manufacturers reach economies of scale. So EV penetration will increase on its own, without any intervention, as the total cost of ownership ratio between EVs and ICEs tilts in favour of EVs.

Does this mean that governments should not intervene and we should allow only the cost of ownership factors to influence individuals? Not necessarily. Figure 12.3

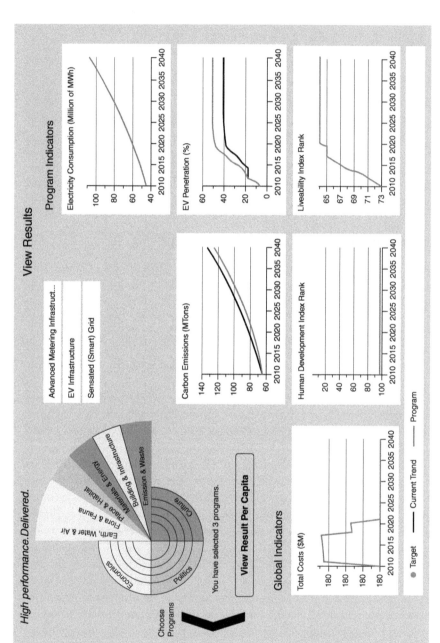

FIGURE 12.1 Electric Vehicles 1

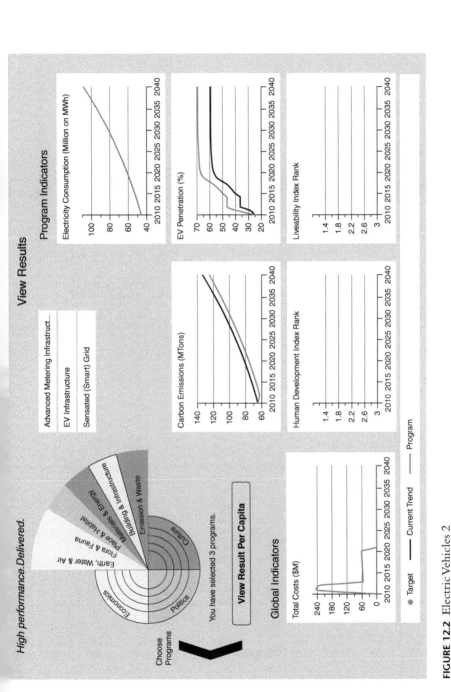

FIGURE 12.2 Electric Vehicles 2

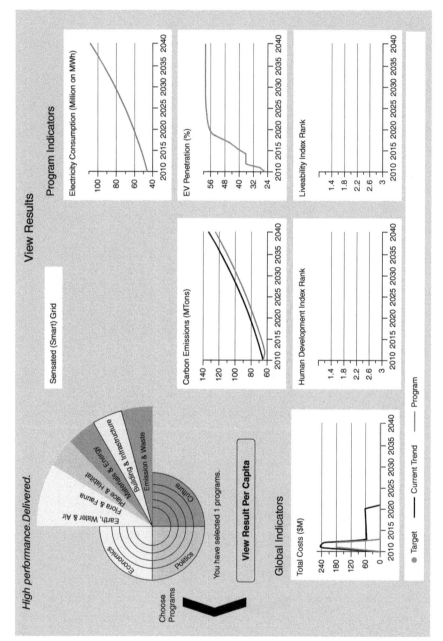

FIGURE 12.3 Electric Vehicles 3

shows the EV penetration without any EV infrastructure in place. It is immediately obvious that the EV penetration is not nearly as much as with EV infrastructure in place, and that in fact it plateaus at a certain point. This arises from the requirement of many individuals to have charging infrastructure before buying an electric vehicle, even if the total cost of ownership was favourable to EVs. So could charging infrastructure be put in place once the EV penetration reached a critical mass? Yes – but it would need to accommodate the time lag for infrastructure projects.

Figure 12.4 below depicts the same EV infrastructure project implemented as from before beginning in 2025. There is a period from X to Y where the EV infrastructure is not yet sufficiently in place and EV penetration plateaus, before ramping up again once infrastructure is rolled out.

Simulating the future?

Version 2.0 of the Intelligent City Simulator provided a series of useful demonstrations of how given programmes and interventions would have an impact on a city. However, a number of limitations of the simulator have become apparent during the design and testing of the tool. First and foremost – and in spite of the self-reflexive understanding of the design team that even a holistic approach cannot model everything about the world and needs to be indicative – the simulator needs greater sensitivity both to the effects of given programmes and to the conditions of given cities. Invariably this requires a more extensive knowledge base, modelling a larger number of variables and data points. Related to this, the tool also needs capture relationships between programmes in a quantitative fashion. Presently relationships are expressed as fairly simple dependencies, which do not reflect how the relative change in an independent programme affects variables in dependent ones.

More generally, it would also be useful to allow users to compare the effects of different programmes side by side, according to different general parameters: cost, CO_2 emissions and Human Development Index and livability indexes, for example. Similarly, we would like to display how different cities fare given the same programme. The metrics for both sets of comparisons are currently available. The task here is largely one of user-interface design. Yet a further extension would permit users to see optimized programme plans, given the particularities of the city and desired cost, emissions and other targets. The web-based nature of the tool would also make possible simultaneous collaboration and discussion between different users, opening new possibilities for simulation and optimization.

More generally still, a tool like this is still a long way from delivering planners, decision-makers and other stakeholders in urban contexts what it takes to build a smart city. There is a large set of epistemological considerations involved in such an ambitious undertaking. Simulation tools and the like are at best robust approximations rather than precise predictive instruments. However, exhibiting 'intelligence' remains an approximating undertaking. Tools such as the simulator presented here can go a long way towards providing concrete cases for human planning and action. Certainly we feel one feature of this intelligence is an orientation towards holism – the view

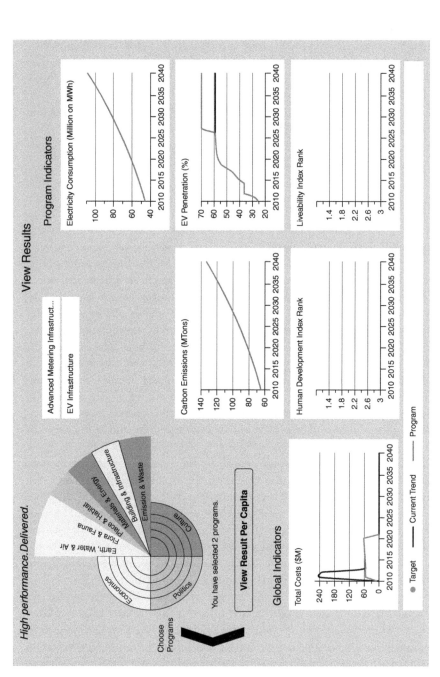

FIGURE 12.4 Electric Vehicles 4

that a city's future is not determined by a series of discrete but unrelated activities, but is rather woven together from a series of interconnected strands, which spread across a multitude of areas including technological infrastructure, economic activity, political security and stability, cultural diversity, and environmental sustainability. Here the simulator is at least on the right path, building upon the theoretical rubric of the *Circles of Sustainability* approach. However, considerable more work needs to be done to understand quantitatively how diverse sets of programmes and variables interrelate and to work on how to convey the potential richness of these data to end users.

Another feature is resilience: the capacity for planning with margins for error, recovery strategies, flexibility and adaptability to changing circumstances. This feature is captured algorithmically by introducing stochastic variables that show some degree of randomness. Because our best views of the future are tainted both by chance and by its sometimes non-linear effects, a simulation tool needs to show, in addition to a calculated effect, bands of confidence, degrees of probability and respond to 'what-if' scenario modelling.

Yet another feature of intelligence can be described in the concept of reflexivity. Participants in an intelligent city are continuously and everywhere engaged in the creative planning of its future, through processes of taking stock, reviewing, forecasting, deliberating and debating. These in turn lead to the virtuous cycle of vibrant communities, where different 'flows' within the economic, cultural, political and ecological domains are optimally self-reinforcing rather than constantly in tension. Such pragmatic utopias are at least partially realizable through critical and reflexive analysis, in conjunction with the right kinds of civic structures and tools for facilitating action.

Although the Intelligent City Simulator is a small step towards the realization of intelligent cities, and will always form part of a much greater assemblage, its promise is one of translating the intellectual density and rigour of various disciplinary literature into a series of visual motifs. These in turn can be readily demonstrated and explained to a variety of audiences without much sacrifice of rigour. It therefore can help stakeholders in urban environments learn, plan and build our future cities.

Note

1 The main co-authors of this chapter are Liam Magee and Paul James with Dominic Mendonca and Simon Vardy. Along with software and design consultants in France, India and Australia, they were also primary participants in developing the Intelligent City Simulator system that underlies the software.

Reference

Bettencourt, Luis & West, Geoffrey 2010, 'A Unified Theory of Urban Living', *Nature*, no. 467, pp. 912–13.

CONCLUSION

Read almost any piece of writing on urban development and you'll see how much narrowly conceived thinking informs urban practice. An emphasis on economic growth, smart technologies and environmental externalities currently rules mainstream thinking. As important as economic vitality, information management, and carbon reduction are, staying in this tight triangle is self-defeating. There is so much more. Curtailing expanding resource use and reducing carbon emissions, for example, is not just an economic or ecological question. It entails also connecting these issues to considerations of political governance and cultural meaning. The culture of consumption is particularly relevant. By using the *Circles of Sustainability* method or some similar variation as an orienting guide, it is possible to explore such key considerations in each of the domains of social life, knowing that these relate to a systematic understanding of the social whole.

This book, in contradistinction to most treatments caught up with faddish catch-cries – smarter, faster, cleaner, safer – is intended as a contribution to understanding how a city works in all its complexity. It provides a deep transitional practice for understanding complexity without demanding an immediate and complete revolution. It supports communities, organizations and businesses to choose, plan and manage local–global principles and priorities across a holistic sense of the human condition. On one hand, it is intended to offer globally relevant ways of approaching urban sustainability that provides gentle guidance on best practice. On the other hand, this guidance qualifies the usual certainty about master plans so that locally generated engagement, critical energy and lively serendipity can be enhanced. This could include such considerations as localized playful messiness, if using careful deliberative processes that is what locals decide that they want. Deliberative dialogue should bring together local people, local experts and outside experts into a mutual and collaborative learning process that comes up with outcomes based on both evidence and passion.

Grounded in this way through a series of forums across the world in 2013 and 2014, we came up with a systematic set of proposals for a positive urban future. Arguably if some of the following were achieved it would contribute to making our urban planet more sustainable.

Ecological propositions

Urban settlements should develop a deeper and more integrated relationship with nature:

1. With urban settlements organized around locally distributed renewable energy, planned on a precinct-wide basis, and with all existing buildings retrofitted for resource-use efficiency
2. With waterways returned to their pre-settlement condition, flanked, where possible, by indigenous natural green spaces
3. With green parklands – including areas which provide habitat for indigenous animals and birds – increased or consolidated within the urban area, connected by further linear green ribbons
4. With urban settlements organized into regional clusters around natural limits and fixed urban-growth boundaries to contain sprawl and renew an urban–rural divide; and with growth zones of increased urban density within those urban settlements focused on public transport nodes
5. With paths for walking, lanes for non-motorized vehicles, and corridors for sustainable public transport, given spatial priority over roads for cars; and with those dedicated paths networked throughout the city
6. With food production invigorated in the urban precinct, including through setting aside dedicated spaces for commercial and community food gardens
7. With waste management directed fundamentally towards green composting, hard-waste recycling and hard-waste mining

Economic propositions

Urban settlements should be based on an economy organized around social needs rather than growth:

1. With production and exchange shifted from an emphasis on production for export and global consumption to an economics that is oriented towards local production consumption
2. With urban financial governance moved towards 'participatory budgeting' on a significant proportion of the city's annual infrastructure and services spending
3. With regulation negotiated publicly through extensive consultation and deliberative programs – including an emphasis on regulation for resource-use reduction
4. With consumption substantially reduced and shifted away from those goods that are not produced regionally or for the reproduction of basic living – food, housing, clothing, music and so on

5.   With workplaces brought back into closer spatial relation to residential areas, while taking into account dangers and noise hazards through sustainable and appropriate building
6.   With technology used primarily as a tool for good living rather than a means of transcending the limits of nature and embodiment
7.   With the institution of redistributive processes that break radically with current cycles of interclass and intergenerational inequality

Political propositions

Urban settlements should have an enhanced emphasis on engaged and negotiated civic involvement:

1.   With governance conducted through a deep deliberative democratic process that brings together comprehensive community engagement, expert knowledge and extended public debate about all aspects of development
2.   With legislation enacted for socially just land tenure, including, when necessary, municipal and state acquisition of ecologically, economically and culturally sensitive areas
3.   With public non-profit communication services and media outlets materially supported and subsidized where necessary
4.   With political participation and representation going deeper than electoral engagement
5.   With basic security afforded to all people through a shift to human security considerations
6.   With reconciliation with Indigenous peoples becoming an active and ongoing focus of all urban politics
7.   With ethical debates concerning how we are to live becoming a mainstream requirement at all levels of education and in all disciplines from the humanities to medicine and engineering

Cultural propositions

Urban settlements should come to terms with the uncomfortable intersections of identity and difference:

1.   With recognition and celebration of the complex layers of community-based identity that have made the urban region, including cross-cutting customary, traditional, modern and postmodern identities
2.   With the development of consolidated cultural activity zones, emphasizing active street-frontage and public spaces for face-to-face engagement, festivals and events – for example all new commercial and residential apartment buildings should have an active ground floor, with part of that space zoned for rent-subsidized cultural use such as studios, theatres and workshops
3.   With museums, cultural centres and other public spaces dedicated to the urban region's own cross-cutting cultural histories – public spaces which at the same

time actively seek to represent visually alternative trajectories of urban development from the present into the future

4. With locally relevant fundamental beliefs from across the globe – except those that vilify and degrade – woven into the fabric of the built environment: symbolically, artistically and practically

5. With conditions for gender equality pursued in all aspects of social life, while negotiating relations of cultural inclusion and exclusion that allow for gendered differences

6. With the possibilities for facilitated enquiry and learning available to all from birth to old age across people's lives, not just through formal education structures but also through well-supported libraries and community learning centres

7. With public spaces and buildings aesthetically designed and curated to enhance the emotional well-being of people, including by involving local people in that curation

These propositions are organized around a four-domain model of social life, integrating ecology, economics, politics and culture as equally important in considering positive sustainability. It is the descriptive basis for the book as a whole. These propositions might be our preferences, but they are only indicative. They are not ethical principles as such, and they are not given as pronouncements. In Chapter 4 questions of ethics were raised, but even then the argument is that ethics involves a process of negotiation, including across ontologically different ways of understanding what is 'good'.

To put forward these propositions as universal guidelines would go against the spirit of what we are arguing. That is, the whole thrust of this book has advocated social engagement and debate at a city level across the various domains of social life. Using the *Circles of Sustainability* method is intended to lead to each city or town or village developing a comprehensive sense of its own critical issues and enacting its own priorities and actions.

All we are suggesting in conclusion is that the range of activities that any city or town takes up needs to be equally broad and well considered in order to make good urban places. Although the current mainstream propensity is to focus on making cities smarter, more liveable, or more competitive, so far this has not worked to improve substantially the lives of more than a minority. And, despite the hype, it is unlikely to do so. Most approaches treat those aspirations as single-dimensional activities. For example, being smarter tends to be reduced to rolling out more data management. Our concern is that such one-dimensionality threatens to kill positive urban life. Other ways are possible. There are many other pathways to enhancing the vibrancy of social life. The method presented here is only illustrative of what is possible when committed people put their minds and bodies to a collaborative transitional practice. In the words of Leonard Cohen, first we need to take Manhattan, then Berlin, then Shanghai, . . .

Over the modern period, cities have evolved substantially, along with many other social changes. Ancient, medieval and even early modern cities served primarily as places of economic exchange, political consolidation of power and cultural expression of connection to the gods and the heavens. Today, modern cities are layered in abstraction. They can be described as massively complex networks of networks, layered interconnected spaces, within which communities, families and individuals search for places to live.

These networks include vertical as well as horizontal arrangements of people, mixtures of the exotic and the mundane, concatenations of modern and heritage architectures, overlapping public and private transport grids, reservoirs and pipelines of both clean and dirty water, funnels and incubators of public and private enterprise, multiple wired and wireless communication networks, centres of regional and international power and meeting points for the ever-increasing diaspora of intermingling global cultures. Against this complexity, our tools for measuring properties such as sustainability, resilience, vulnerability and adaptability can seem hopelessly inept.

However, as we have argued, the highly networked and relational character of cities makes them paradoxical more complex and distressingly fragile. They are highly dependent on – or let's say interdependent with – both the larger natural and social environments in which they reside. And these environments, which embrace the diversity of contemporary hazards from climate change and financial crises through to the commodification of cultural artefacts and mounting political instability, seem more fragile day by day. In one sense, the *Circles of Sustainability* approach offers 'yet another' conceptualization and toolset through which to understand, assess and act on the challenges that face the city. However, we would argue, it does so in ways that avoid some of the pitfalls of more established methods.

Far more importantly, it opens – rather than closes – new pathways for exploring, through everyday acts of dialogue, observation and engagement. It allows people to argue about what constitutes 'the good' in these spaces of our collective living. In that way our approach does not postulate a fixed set of conceptual categories, filled in with today's particular fashions about 'the good life'. Instead, the metaphor of the circle is used to suggest that it is this an ongoing social process of communication, between and among ourselves about what warrants sustaining, especially at a time when the overflow of forms of communication seem to threaten our ability to listen to difference. This work, then, offers another way, one we hope resonates with those who study, develop policies for and participate in the marvellous diversity of contemporary urban life.

INDEX